T0244357

THE
BEACON
BIKE

THE
BEACON
BIKE

AROUND ENGLAND AND WALES
IN 327 LIGHTHOUSES

EDWARD PEPPITT

ICON

Published in the UK and USA in 2024 by
Icon Books Ltd, Omnibus Business Centre,
39–41 North Road, London N7 9DP
email: info@iconbooks.com
www.iconbooks.com

ISBN: 978-1-83773-168-8
ebook: 978-1-83773-169-5

Typesetting by SJmagic DESIGN SERVICES, India

Printed and bound in the UK

CONTENTS

— ACKNOWLEDGEMENTS —

I should really start by thanking Derrick Jackson, the author of *Lighthouses of England and Wales*, who is entirely responsible for my interest and love of everything lighthouse-related.

My cycling adventure would not have been possible without the help of George Pepper and the wonderfully supportive team at Shift.ms that he has established. Thank you all. If you or anyone you know is diagnosed with MS, then Shift.ms should be your first call.

I'm also indebted to the Association of Lighthouse Keepers for their help in planning my route, supporting me along the way, and hooking me up with members to meet, former keepers to talk to, and beds to sleep in. The Association has become my second family, and I am grateful to you all.

I am very grateful to Robert Gwyn Palmer, who helped me to secure so many valuable connections, including that feature in the weekend *Telegraph*.

I owe heartfelt thanks to anyone who followed my progress, sent messages of support or donated to Shift.ms. So many times I would have given up without your encouragement.

I was extraordinarily lucky to meet Phil Sorrell, a fellow MSer, who set me up with a brilliant application that plotted my live location on my website map every step of the way. Thank you, Phil. You helped my followers feel so much more connected to my daily progress.

I would like to thank all my followers on social media, but James Sharp in particular, my most prolific and loyal Twitter follower by a distance. I am also indebted to my friend Paul Uttley, whose generosity ensured I could complete the expedition.

With the cycling behind me, so many others helped me in the making of this book:

Thank you, Karena, for convincing me that it was worth writing, as well as for helping me get started. Thank you, Jo, for the ongoing encouragement and for improving my writing in every chapter.

My friend Adrian deserves eternal praise and glory for the time and patience he took to illustrate every one of the 327 lighthouses I saw.

Thank you to my agent, Tom Cull, for agreeing to represent me and finding the perfect home for *The Beacon Bike*. You are the real deal.

And thank you to Connor Stait and the team at Icon Books, for making the magic happen.

That only leaves arguably the two most influential people who have helped turn a childhood dream into reality ...

Allan, my wingman, who was there at the start and again at the finish line, who was ready to travel to Ilfracombe, Lundy, Clevedon, Carlisle, Berwick and Dungeness to make sure I stayed on course.

Lastly, and most of all, my thanks to my long-suffering wife, Emily, for encouraging me to make the journey, tolerating my sabbatical from parental duties, and for her patience, support and kindness throughout.

─── PROLOGUE ───

Somewhere in the space between wakefulness and sleep, I become aware of the regular blink of light. It permeates the inky blue darkness and momentarily brightens the plain white walls. I begin to count the interval between flickers – always ten seconds – each flash illuminating the room, punctuating the dark reassuringly. I climb out of bed and make my way to the window, looking out to find the source. And then it comes to me. The light is travelling through the night from Dungeness, from the beacon that keeps ships from running aground and sailors safe, that marks the end of the land and the beginning of the sea. The lighthouse.

Seeing the light

When I was a child, a part of each school holiday was spent at my grandmother's house on Romney Marsh in Kent, about half a mile from the sea. It was a house divided into two – she had bought a large town house after the war, then set about splitting it down the middle and selling one half to an old friend. The hallway had two unlocked doors, one to each side of the original house, where my grandmother and her friend met each morning to allocate the morning post. They even shared a party phone line between them, and you could often listen to Mrs Kemp's tittle-tattle just by picking up the receiver. I had a bedroom in the eaves, and from the mullioned window I could see for miles around.

It was July 1974 when I made the discovery that it was the lighthouse that projected its flash onto my bedroom wall. I was just six years old. It felt comforting, reassuring somehow. Each day of our holidays on Romney Marsh, I climbed the stairs to my room at dusk to check that the light was still flashing. And I remember the sense of relief and wonder each time I saw it.

We had a routine for every holiday. There would be a trip to Dymchurch, dubbed 'the children's paradise' and home to fish and chip shops, a funfair and the Romney, Hythe and Dymchurch railway that ran along the coast from Hythe. We'd schedule a stop at Dungeness, and my dad would buy fish from the seafront shack run by Mrs Thomas. She's still there today, although it is her son rather than her husband who brings in the catch, most of which is supplied direct to local restaurateurs. You have to be on the shore early and meet the boat to compete for the pick of the freshest fish.

Then we'd walk our Labrador, Sam, along the shingle beach, towards the pair of lighthouses. I discovered that the earlier 1904 lighthouse had been made redundant once the nuclear power station was built in the sixties, which obstructed its beam of light across the distinctive shingle spit. A new lighthouse had to be built in 1961, unmanned and automated, and one of the last new lighthouses that Trinity House, the body that governs lighthouses in England and Wales, ever built.

On some trips, when the weather allowed, Dad would go night fishing with long lines, setting up his fishing paraphernalia, his flask and his lamp on the shingle at dusk. I sometimes joined him, but only in the hope that I might meet the lighthouse keeper arriving for his night duty. I imagined him with a large bunch of keys, immaculately dressed in smart Trinity House uniform and distinctive white-trimmed cap. With hindsight, he must have looked a lot like Captain Birdseye. But he never did arrive, a fact that mystified me, as come what may, the light would unfailingly start to flash as dusk approached.

That's when my obsession with lighthouses began. My parents noticed, and presented me with a copy of *Lighthouses of England and Wales* by Derrick Jackson, a book that became my favourite companion for many years. I learned how, when and where they were built, and that every lighthouse has a unique character, with no two sharing the same light, colour and flashing pattern, so that mariners could distinguish one light from another.

I suppose I could have become just as obsessed with steam engines, toy cars, football, sticker albums or any other pastime that tended to attract boys of my age. But for me it was only ever lighthouses.

When I was ten or eleven, and enjoying some independence with the help of my bicycle, I formulated a plan for an adventure that one day I would undertake. I would cycle around the coast, clockwise from my grandmother's house, ticking off each lighthouse that I'd read about obsessively in my book. I recently discovered five rusty-stapled pieces of paper in the back of a filing cabinet that outlined my proposed journey, how far I would cycle each day, which lights I would see and where I might stay.

It was an expedition I was confident that I would undertake one day, but, like many dreams or ambitions formed in childhood, life got in the way. It was always a trip that I planned to make one day soon. Nevertheless, lighthouses remained a constant feature of my life. I remember every family holiday not by the cottages we rented or the food we ate, but by the lighthouses that were nearby. Summers in the West Country meant Start Point, the Lizard or Tater Du on the south coast, and Hartland Point, Lynmouth Foreland or Trevose Head on the north coast. The August weather had been so poor over the summers of 1974 and 1975 that my parents decided to holiday inland in 1976. We rented a cottage in Kettlewell in the Yorkshire Dales and promptly sweated out the hottest, driest fortnight for 100 years. My mum assumed that my quietness during that holiday was because I was missing the beach and a bucket and spade. But I knew it was because there wasn't a single lighthouse within 40 miles.

The summer holidays that followed Kettlewell were almost perfect for me. My aunt had bought a small cottage in Llanmadoc, on the Gower Peninsula in Wales, and we stayed there for three consecutive summers. From the cottage, I could walk to the ruined wrought-iron lighthouse at Whiteford Point, and rainy days meant Swansea Market followed by a glimpse of the lighthouse at Mumbles.

After university, I joined up with a number of other slightly rudderless would-be travellers by getting a job at Stanfords, the map and travel bookshop in Covent Garden in London. Here the staff were incredibly knowledgeable, but held a shared belief that they should be, and deserved to be, travelling somewhere. As a result the retail part of the job was never taken very seriously, and serving customers was always regarded as an unwelcome and somewhat disagreeable aspect of saving up for the next big trip.

Retail staff came, saved up their funds, went travelling and then returned to start the process all over again. I quickly learned the hierarchy: seasoned, global travellers worked upstairs on the international desk, sharing their stories of travelling through unmapped and politically unstable parts of the globe. Those with fewer expeditions under their belt worked at the European desk on the ground floor. From here, they were as likely to be called upon to help with the choice of gallery, restaurant or hotel on a romantic city break, as with possible places to camp on a long-distance trek across the Alps. That left me in the basement – a windowless, dark and rather damp space – selling local walking maps and guides to British towns and cities.

There were three of us in the basement. At one end of the floor sat John, a 30-something amateur sailor who ran the maritime department. His passion was for boats rather than retail, and he despised most of the customers he was called upon to serve. He reserved the strongest disdain for customers who asked questions, and also for those who took books or maps off his shelves, even if they subsequently purchased them. But he had one unrivalled skill that became his party piece. Describe a sailing or boat trip anywhere in British waters, and John could tell you which British Admiralty chart or charts you would need. From a catalogue extending to hundreds of pages, this was an impressive feat to witness.

At the other end of the floor was Jon without an h, in charge of all maps and books published by Ordnance Survey. Now, Jon had already clocked up twenty years of service at Stanfords, almost all of which had been served in the basement. He had exceptionally blond hair and pale skin, and I wondered if it was natural or had resulted from a lack of sunlight. He had an extraordinary memory, as well as a trick up his sleeve of his own. Name any village, town or city in the UK and Jon would know, instantly, which of the 250 or so large-scale Ordnance Survey walking maps it appeared on.

I took the central sales area of the basement, and my role covered general UK tour guides, street maps and road atlases. But I spent a lot of my day trying to appease or apologise to customers who'd had dramatic fallings out with John. On one occasion a customer approached my friend David at the international desk and asked for help with selecting an Admiralty chart. When David suggested that he needed to head down to the basement, the customer begged him to come with him, explaining that he 'daren't ask that ghastly man for help again!'.

I may have had some natural talent for retail, but I realised that I needed my own party trick if I was to hold my own in the basement. It came very quickly and easily to me. Name any point on the UK coast, and I could reel off the ten nearest lighthouses heading either clockwise or anti-clockwise. Admittedly, mine was the least valuable skill from a retail perspective and it was seldom called upon. But it was always something of which I was immensely proud.

Stanfords was also where I met my wife, Emily. It's fair to say that she has endured, rather than embraced, my passion for lighthouses, but she has always been supportive of my slightly quirky interest, nonetheless. She once arranged a surprise holiday on Lundy Island, where we stayed in the old lighthouse, converted by the Landmark Trust into fabulous holiday accommodation. And so when we were planning our wedding Lundy had seemed the obvious location, if only we could pull it off.

We made it work, but at quite a cost. From a financial perspective, it was only possible if we married out of season. We persuaded the local rector at Appledore, on the North Devon coast, to officiate at the marriage ceremony, and a team of bell ringers to bring the St Helen's Church to life on the morning of the service. We chartered the MS *Oldenburg* to bring our guests across from Ilfracombe on the last weekend of February in 1998. And from there it all went wrong. There was a force 9 gale that day, and a crossing that should take two hours took nearly four. Our 60 guests made use of more than 100 sick bags between them, and on reaching land several of them kissed the ground. It was a tough start to our wedding weekend, but the vast majority of the guests took it well. Certainly, the conversation in the pub on the first night was not about how they each knew the bride or groom, but how sick they had been on the boat. I got to spend my honeymoon in the old lighthouse, and it is still a wedding that friends talk about with great fondness, more than 25 years later.

So, 45 years after my first encounter with the flashing light in the attic bedroom, my love for lighthouses endures. I have my own family now, and British holidays invariably involve the coast – and making a beeline to the nearest lighthouse, much to my children's irritation. But my cycle touring dream remained unfulfilled. As with so many romantic notions, stuff got in the way. You get a job, you buy a house, you get married and have a family. Before you know it, taking twelve weeks off work to cycle around the coast isn't practical, and just seems a bit indulgent. And in my case, it wasn't only work and family stuff that got in the way.

Into the dark

Fast forward to March 2008. I am lying flat out on the kitchen floor, dizzy with fear, coming round from having fainted. We have just returned from a week-long family holiday in Belgium. At the start of the week I was absolutely fine, but as the week progressed I felt increasingly exhausted, experienced constant nerve pains in my legs, and every step I took was an ordeal.

The first thing I did when I'd recovered sufficiently was to phone my aunt, the one with the cottage on the Gower Peninsula, who was then a doctor in general practice. Now, I have always adored my aunt Shirley, but if ever there was a time for her to drop her trademark 'tell it like it is' approach, this was it.

I described my symptoms over the phone, and she started a response that began, 'Well, I don't think it's multiple sclerosis because if it was, then you'd also have ...' And then she listed a series of symptoms and sensations that I knew I had been ignoring for much of my adult life. And that's when I fainted.

Over the four years that followed, I was put through an endless array of medical tests and interventions, all of which were inconclusive. Multiple Sclerosis (MS) is an imprecise condition to diagnose formally, and one that the NHS is loath to get wrong. MRI scans, eye co-ordination and balance tests became routine. The results showed that my myelin sheath (the coating that protects the spinal column) was eroding, but not at a rate that required invasive or immediate intervention.

What was frustrating for me, and is for most other MS patients, is that until the myelin deterioration reaches a certain level, no formal diagnosis of MS can be made. I knew very well that I had MS. The consultant neurologist discussed with me how best to cope with the condition, but felt able only to make ambiguous statements such as: 'You are presenting with symptoms that are consistent with a diagnosis of MS, but could be an unrelated neurological condition or disorder.'

Despite the lack of conclusions from the various tests, my health gradually deteriorated. I had worked for myself for more than a decade, and maintaining any sort of schedule or routine was becoming increasingly challenging. I started to feel a constant fatigue, which meant that I couldn't get through a day without having a rest, or sleep, for a couple of hours. My legs felt like lead, and buzzed with what felt like an electric current, coupled with near-permanent pins and needles. And then things really took a turn for the worse.

I remember waiting on the platform at Appledore, my local unstaffed railway station, having arranged to meet a friend for a drink further down the line in Hastings. I waited on the platform, conscious that the train was running late. I tried to read the scrolling information sign, but for some reason I couldn't make sense of the words on the screen, even when I got up close. Instinctively, I covered my right eye, thinking that I might see better with just the left. Instead of helping, everything went dark. I realised that I couldn't read the display because only one eye was functioning, and the resulting imbalance was disorienting and very frightening. This partial blindness lasted nearly three months, and my sight was only restored with steroids.

The partial blindness prompted a new round of tests and scans, and this time the diagnosis was clear. I had relapsing and remitting multiple sclerosis, and it was time to talk about 'disease-modifying treatments'. It might seem strange, but the diagnosis came as a relief. Finally, I knew for certain that I had been right about my condition all the time. There would be no more limbo, no more indecision, no more 'come back in six months'.

For someone who only has to look at a needle and faint, a treatment involving daily self-administered injections was never going to be easy. Yet of all the treatments offered, it was the option that promised the fewest side effects. Currently there is no cure for MS, and so the principle behind many of the treatments available is to stop or slow down what are referred to as 'MS episodes', giving patients more time while waiting for a permanent solution to be developed.

After my diagnosis, people who knew me well thought I was taking everything in my stride. I knew that I didn't want to be defined by my illness and I was determined never to be the person who says, 'I can't do that because I've got MS.' But beneath the façade I was in a permanent state of anxiety. I had stopped dreaming of the future, of what I would and could do – and particularly of my lighthouse-to-lighthouse cycle trip.

With the tiredness, the loss of my sight and the heaviness in my legs, I had resigned myself to the fact that my dream was over. Friends and family rallied round and offered their support, as well as suggestions they imagined might help. Perhaps I could make the trip shorter, by including only the coastal lighthouses and not the offshore ones? Or how about driving rather than cycling? Or visiting a handful of lighthouses each summer, until I had completed them all? All sensible suggestions, but they held no appeal.

It wasn't just visiting every lighthouse that was important to me. It was the idea of a journey that had no formal end point or time limit. I craved the independence of doing it all under my own steam. I decided I'd rather leave the cycle tour behind than compromise in any way. In fact, I gave up on lighthouses altogether.

It was a bleak time, but salvation was to come.

Just a glimmer

It was Jason, a former client who had become a friend, who managed to rekindle my belief that the trip was still possible.

Around ten years earlier, he had realised his own dream by visiting every UK pleasure pier using only public buses. He had always fancied a new challenge and on the surface seemed determined not only to help me, but to join me on the way as well.

Just talking about it with him over a pint one evening brought back some of the old excitement. However well-intentioned, he is also a savvy businessman as well as a great fixer of problems. It didn't take him very long to come up with a solution for how the trip could still go ahead in spite of my health.

He suggested that my condition meant a bike would be out of the question, and that an Aston Martin DB9 on loan from his local dealer would provide more appropriate transport. He was confident that he could pull it off.

It wouldn't be possible to visit every lighthouse, he continued, so we should handpick 30 or 40 of the lights most accessible from the principal motorway network. We wouldn't need much luggage. And there would be no need to wash clothes en route because his PA would simply courier us a bag of clean ones every few days.

Over the course of an hour, what began as a free-range bicycle tour around our coast had become a two-week, high-speed rally sponsored by Aston Martin.

The evening had a profound effect. My passion for lighthouses had returned, the excitement about the trip was palpable, but I knew that compromise on its length or scope was out of the question. So was the Aston Martin. For a while I wondered if this was the effect that he had intended all along. I'm too proud to ask him and, in any case, we are no longer in touch.

Nevertheless, my desire to fulfil the mission had returned. After my initial diagnosis, I had joined several of the MS charities, but it was Shift.ms, a social network for people connected by the condition, where I felt I really belonged. Its founder, George Pepper, was diagnosed with MS when he was just 22, and his response was extraordinary. Deciding to travel the world while he still could, he set off on a six-month adventure to visit India, Japan, Indonesia, Argentina, Brazil and Australia. On his return, he set up the charity to motivate, encourage and bring together other people with MS.

George's inspiring story resonated with me, and provided confirmation that I had given up on my dream too soon. But it was the Shift.ms motto that really attracted my attention:

MS doesn't mean giving up on your ambitions. It just means rethinking how to achieve them.

Since starting my daily disease-modifying injections, my health had apparently stabilised. However, there were still two significant hurdles to overcome if I was to re-engage with my dream of visiting every lighthouse around our coast. The first was money. The trip would take more than 100 days, and even if I camped or stayed in budget B&Bs, the cost would escalate out of control very quickly. George Pepper offered to email the Shift.ms membership database, and the desire to support me was overwhelming. The offers of accommodation started to land.

I joined a fabulous charity called the Association of Lighthouse Keepers (ALK), whose remit is to keep lighthouse heritage alive. Their support was also humbling, and by publicising my adventure to their membership, several more offers of overnight stays resulted.

The other hurdle related to my health. My injection routine was helping me feel well, but was it artificial? Could I seriously ride a bike every day, for more than 100 days, covering upwards of 3,500 miles?

I concluded that it was worth trying, recognising that I could switch from a regular touring bike to an electric bike if my health deteriorated. And if I did need or want to swap my mode of transport, it would give my friend Allan his perfect role.

Allan knew only too well of my lighthouse obsession. He was one of the 60 wedding guests who had survived the force 9 gale in the Bristol Channel back in March 1998. He had stayed in the old lighthouse the night before the ceremony, and I think just a little of the magic had rubbed off on him. He had always wanted to play a part in my adventure, and quickly volunteered to keep an electric bike safely in his garage in Oxford and drive out with it to meet me on the coast if the need arose.

The only bike I actually owned was rusting away in the shed, with buckled wheels and a couple of flat tyres. It wouldn't get me to the first lighthouse on the list, Dungeness, let alone all of them. It's a shame, really, because it was a very fine bike in its day, an electric-blue Dawes Street Sharp that I bought in 1990, when I lived in London and commuted from Whitechapel to Shepherd's Bush each day. It must have been one of the last hand-built, British-made Dawes models, before the brand was sold and the factory closed.

My plan, then, was to look for a new touring bike, preferably a British one, that could accommodate my ample frame. At six-foot-five and weighing a shade (ahem) more than sixteen stone, it was unlikely that I could buy something off the peg. My research suggested that just as microbreweries have offered an antidote to the giant multi-brand beer brewers, so dozens of smaller, specialist and highly regarded cycle builders have begun to crop up all over the British Isles. While this meant that I had plenty of choice, I am no cycling expert and had no idea at all about which way to turn.

Allan introduced me to Simon Hood, a keen cyclist and York City FC supporter who had cycled to every game, home and away, over the course of the 2010/11 season. I had read Simon's book about this mad and ultimately futile venture, *Bicycle Kicks*, and had enjoyed it immensely.

It was Simon who initially suggested that Thorn Cycles would be a good match for me. I drove down to Bridgewater to meet the company's founder, Robin Thorn, and their longstanding touring-bike designer, Andy Blance. I had been a little apprehensive about my visit, not least because a Google search had revealed slightly disingenuous descriptions of the two men, such as 'maverick', 'cantankerous' and 'abrasive'. I feared that my lack of cycling knowledge and jargon would leave me open to ridicule, but I needn't have worried.

Andy met me in Thorn's foyer and gave me a tour of the factory and warehouse. Spread across several outbuildings behind a side street in Bridgewater, it gladdened me that British companies like this still exist. Thorn is the cycling equivalent of Morgan cars. Every bike is hand built from the ground up, and matched and fitted precisely to its rider. With an options list running to dozens of pages, no two Thorn bikes are the same. And like a Morgan, you have to be prepared to wait for it.

Andy talked me through the three principal frame designs from which all Thorn bikes are built, and the advantages and disadvantages of each for an expedition like mine. In all honesty I would have been happy with any of the three, but I opted for the one he described as 'bulletproof like a Land Rover'. It was a 'Tonka' yellow Nomad tourer, with front and back racks and a dynamo hub that powered the lights. The only drawback was that it came with an eight-week wait.

It was now the end of March, and the only major decision left was when, exactly, to set off. I wanted to cover as much ground as I could during school term time, partly because I thought accommodation might be a bit cheaper, but also so that I could perform my parental duties and be with the family during the holidays. I settled for the first Monday in May.

While waiting for Thorn to build my transport, I turned my attention to money. I spent a few days in the garden shed, listing redundant garden machinery on eBay. Simon managed to secure me a complete set of Carradice panniers, a Brooks saddle and a decent Lazer helmet in a series of sponsorship deals. Money would be tight, but it was starting to look as though I would be okay.

I collected the bike from Thorn on the Wednesday before setting off. That left me four days to train and practise, which turned into just two after the delivery of my saddle was delayed until the Friday. I decided to ignore a note that accompanied it, suggesting that it would take up to 100 hours of riding before the seat leather would feel supple and comfortable.

My friend Sue introduced me to her publicity agent, who had managed to secure a handful of press and media interviews. Everyone I spoke to wanted to know about my preparation and training routine over recent months. I lied for the first few, and described tough timed trials along the seafront, filling my panniers with increasingly heavy weights from the gym. But when a charming freelance writer for the *Sunday Telegraph* asked me the same question, I admitted that I had done absolutely nothing.

Despite the lack of preparation, I was committed. I cycled the five miles from my home to Dungeness and back three times over the May Bank Holiday weekend. It seemed to go okay. I fashioned a bag lined with ice packs to keep my Copaxone injections (my MS medication) as cool as possible during each day's ride. I practised taking the panniers off and putting them back on again, something that would become a daily ritual.

These were just distractions, however, designed to make me feel prepared, and to muffle the doubt that was increasing by the hour. In May 2015, 45 years after that small boy lay awake in the attic bedroom dreaming of a great adventure, it was time to seek out the lights. All of them.

WEEK 1

Day 1

The plan was to set off at 10am and cycle the five miles from home to the lighthouse and cafe at Dungeness, where my family and a few friends would raise a toast and send me on my way. Inevitably, I was still at my desk, tying off loose ends. I was working as a copywriter, and when Allan asked whether I was excited, the only emotion I felt was anxiety about the work that was still to be done and the email inbox that needed to be emptied.

It wasn't until 9:45 that I started to pack. In fact, I had no idea whether what I proposed to pack would even fit into my panniers. I remembered watching a YouTube video that illustrated how to pack panniers evenly, and which items to pack where. So I did a quick search and watched it again.

Allan and I worked in tandem. I filled a rear pannier with clothes and shoes, then passed it to Allan for weighing. Then I filled the other rear pannier with technology – my camera, camcorder, tablet, Kindle – together with a handful of books, notepads and pens. Allan duly weighed it, only to highlight the massive imbalance. With a fair amount of swapping around, we got the weight roughly balanced between the two. So now it was the turn of the front panniers. In one went my first aid box and a bicycle toolkit. In the other, a month's worth of pre-filled syringes for treating my MS and the handheld injector gun that delivers the daily dose. Once again, the weight was imbalanced. I halved the contents of the first aid kit. I also took a good look at the cycle tool kit and removed a couple of heavy-looking items whose function I could not determine.

I drank three mugs of coffee, skim read the instructions for my lights, mileage counter, camera and the GPS app on my phone. Like everything else in my life, this was all very last minute. I had the right kit but had not invested the time to get to know how it worked or what it could do. When someone came up with the phrase 'all the gear and no idea', they were referring to me.

I have never been able to travel light, and looking down at the four heavily laden panniers in front of me, this expedition was clearly to be no exception. Reluctantly, I compromised a little, rejecting a second casual sweater and a third pair of jeans.

When I finally set off, I took the flat, straight road to Dungeness very gently indeed. This was not a race, I kept reminding myself, and I wanted to arrive at the cafe looking calm and full of energy. I had expected half a dozen to be waiting by the Old Lighthouse at Dungeness, but it turned out to be more like 40. I arrived to cheers, bunting, posters wishing me well and a huge homemade cake. My eldest daughter took on the role of chief photographer, while my youngest proudly held up one end of a 'Good Luck' banner. My son Tom seemed bemused by all the fuss. Typically, my parents held back, reluctant to be in the spotlight.

I stayed chatting too long, and it was past lunchtime before I finally set off. I got my camera out to take a picture of the first lighthouse of the journey, and as I did so I heard my friend Dinny say: 'It's got to be a selfie, surely?'

It hadn't crossed my mind, but I realised immediately that he was right. A series of selfies, however indulgent, was the perfect way to record my journey. I took the first one in front of the Old Lighthouse, then cycled the few-hundred yards to the current lighthouse to take my second.

The moment I posted the two photographs online, there was no going back. The expedition had begun.

Dungeness is one of the largest expanses of shingle in Europe and is officially classified as a desert by the Met Office. There have been several lighthouses here, the first built nearly 500 years ago.

The current and old lighthouses at Dungeness.

The receding shoreline left the original 1635 light stranded by the sea, and it was eventually replaced with a 1792 tower designed by the architect Samuel Wyatt. The shifting tides left this tower more than 500 metres from the sea, and a new lighthouse (now known as the old one!) was built in 1904.

Following the construction of the nuclear power station in the sixties, another new lighthouse was needed. Built in 1961, this is the lighthouse that operates today. It has a tall concrete tower, with lantern and gallery above. It flashes a white light, once every ten seconds, which is visible for 21 miles.

My journey proper began along the main road to Lydd, the most southerly village in Kent, and then joined a dedicated cycle path towards Camber. A few miles outside Lydd I passed a caravan and camping site, directly opposite an army firing range and next to a vast industrial cement works. The fixed caravans and mobile homes were neatly arranged around the base of a huge electricity pylon, which was humming loudly. At the entrance was a somewhat optimistic sign that read: 'Do you want the quiet life?'

My first stop was the medieval town of Rye, one of the Cinque Ports, just over the county border into East Sussex. There were once several navigation lights in and around Rye, but after storms changed the course of the River Rother and cut the town off from the sea, the town's importance as a port began to decline and now no traces of these lights remain.

I was making for Rye Harbour, a popular village and nature reserve about two miles beyond the medieval town centre. As I approached the harbour office, I thought it odd that I couldn't picture the harbour lighthouse, given that I had lived locally for many years. It was only after opening my guidebook that I discovered that the hexagonal tower had been demolished more than 40 years earlier, and replaced with a pair of cheerless, forgettable wood and metal lattice structures.

I wasn't expecting my lack of preparation to be apparent so soon. If I had known that these lights were just a pair of beacons, I probably wouldn't have stopped here. Should I even count harbour lights as lighthouses? This and many other questions ran through my mind, barely three hours after setting off.

I photographed the two lights, before retiring to the excellent Bosun's Bite cafe. A lean, weathered man in his sixties pointed at my bike and told me that I had made the right choice. He had been riding Thorn bikes for thirty years, and he and his wife toured regularly on a Thorn tandem. Looking at my four heavily laden panniers, he asked me where I was heading, so I told him about my adventure.

'Wow!' he replied. 'You look exhausted! How much further have you got to go?'

I stammered a hasty, non-committal reply, and decided it was time to get going towards Hastings.

The steep climb through Fairlight village was torture, and before long I was off the bike and pushing. Progress was painfully slow, and at one point I suffered the indignity of being overtaken by an elderly lady walking her dog. She told me that I was nearly halfway up, which only served to dampen my mood further.

After Fairlight the going got much easier, and I dropped down into Hastings at speed. There are two lights in Hastings, both operated and maintained by the council, guiding the local fishing fleet back to the shingle beach from which they launch. I made my way to the higher light (known as the rear light), positioned on the cliffs above the shore at West Hill. Normally a sleepy, genteel part of town, today the crowds had descended to enjoy the May Day parade. The freshly mown parkland was strewn with thousands of beer cans and bottles, and hundreds of revellers, many drunk, were singing, shouting, arguing and fighting. When I approached two female police officers to ask where I might find the local lighthouse, they seemed genuinely pleased that I was sober and unlikely to cause trouble. They weren't locals themselves, however, so couldn't help.

In one corner of the park I saw what I was looking for: a pentagonal, wooden weather-boarded structure, looking more like a beehive than a lighthouse. This is the rear of a pair of range lights which, when aligned, mark the safe passage for shipping. With its elevated position, it emits a fixed red light with a range of four miles. It wasn't what you'd call a lighthouse, but it seemed a lot closer than what I had found at Rye Harbour. The front range light at the water's edge, however, was no one's idea of a lighthouse – just a fixed red light mounted on a short metal pole.

With photographic evidence secured, I set off along the coast towards Eastbourne, where I was due to stay with Adrian, my go-to graphic designer and illustrator from my days in publishing, who swapped London for a quieter life on the Sussex coast nearly a decade ago. Having driven between Hastings and Eastbourne many times, I remembered it as a fast, busy and dangerous stretch of road. But the National Cycle Network (NCN) Route 2 stayed off-road, hugging the seafront, all the way from St Leonards to beyond Pevensey.

After Pevensey Bay the route returned to the main A259, but by now the road was much quieter and there was a dedicated cycle lane along much of its length.

At Sovereign Harbour I stopped to locate a beacon mounted on top of the Martello tower, one of a number of small defensive forts built along this section of coast to protect against possible invasion from France in Napoleonic times. For the third time that day, I stood in front of a structure that bore little resemblance to a lighthouse, and was conscious of the need to establish a meaningful definition of what counted as one, and what should not.

From Sovereign Harbour I could make out the Royal Sovereign Lighthouse, built by Trinity House in 1971 to replace the lightvessel which had marked the shoal since 1875. It is an extraordinary structure, closely resembling an oil rig, with a rectangular platform containing living accommodation perched

Royal Sovereign.

on top of a concrete pillar, with a short red-and-white banded light tower and helipad above. It may not be the archetypal lighthouse of children's drawings, but there is something special about Royal Sovereign. It is one of the last lighthouses Trinity House built, and it plays an important role in guiding shipping away from the many shoals and sandbanks so prevalent off this stretch of coast. Until 2022, it displayed a flashing white light, visible for twelve miles, but has since been decommissioned and dismantled.

By the time I reached Eastbourne's elegant Victorian seafront and was less than a mile from Adrian's house, it was getting dark. Despite arriving two hours later than expected, Adrian and his partner Samina were enormously welcoming and great company. Adrian and I reminisced about the characters we had worked with during our publishing days over a wonderful homemade goulash, a couple of pints of bitter brewed in the Lake District and an excellent bottle of Rioja. Unsurprisingly, I slept very well indeed.

Day 2

I was up early to hear that gales were forecast across the country. Adrian is a keen cyclist himself, and he advised me to get up onto Beachy Head via Duke's Hill, rather than the route along the main road that I had planned. He warned me that it was quite steep, but that it should only take around fifteen minutes if I took it steadily.

'Oh! And another thing,' he said. 'As you turn the final bend it sometimes gets a bit choppy on the top.'

An understatement, if ever there was one. As I made the final turn, the wind was so strong that it blew me into the bushes with my bike wedged firmly on top of me. I saw a large, empty car park about half a mile ahead of me, which I took to be where tourists parked to walk onto the South Downs. But no matter how hard I pushed, I made no progress towards it whatsoever. Twice more the winds pushed me into the side of the road. I tried getting off the road altogether and onto the slightly more sheltered South Downs Way footpath. For a while it seemed like a good call. But as I emerged from the shelter of a group of gorse bushes, I struggled to stay upright, so for an hour or so I just stayed where I was.

With strength renewed, I pushed back from the footpath to the road, and this time made it to the car park, where by now a solitary ice-cream van was its only occupant. I lay my bike flat on the ground, tapped on the van's window and shouted my order for a large cornet. The man sealed inside the van made my ice cream, but as soon as it was ready, we both realised we had a problem. The moment he passed my cornet through his window, the ice cream would surely blow away. On the other hand, I wasn't prepared to hand over my money until the ice cream was safely delivered. There was only one solution, and it was not a dignified one. He opened his sliding window just wide enough for me to poke my head through into his van. For as long as my head remained inside his van, I could eat the ice cream safely. It was only a small van, and I dislike invading people's space at the best of times. But this really was the only solution. I ate quickly, paid up, locked my bike to a bench, and strode off towards the cliff edge to search for Beachy Head Lighthouse.

For a lighthouse enthusiast it's unfortunate that I don't like heights. The closer I got to what I knew to be a sheer cliff edge, the more frightened I became. And with the wind unrelenting, I was simply unable to get too close from fear. Eventually, I found a single spot where I could remain on safe, solid ground and take a very quick photo of the lighthouse hundreds of feet below me.

The current lighthouse at Beachy Head was commissioned in 1899 after the former Belle Tout Lighthouse was abandoned, as it was regularly shrouded in mist and fog. The current tower was brought into service some three years later, in 1902, and is sited at sea level, about 165 metres from the base of the cliffs. It has a tapering granite tower, with lantern and gallery above. It flashes a white light, twice every twenty seconds, which is visible for sixteen miles. The lighthouse was electrified in 1920 and automated in June 1983.

The ride from Beachy Head to the car park below Belle Tout Lighthouse should have been a joyous, five-minute freewheel downhill. Cycling into a fierce headwind, however, it felt at times as though I was actually going backwards. I was grateful there was so little traffic, because the wind would periodically blow me forwards, backwards, out into the middle of the road, or off it altogether.

Belle Tout Lighthouse is currently a luxury B&B, and its location alone makes it a wild and romantic place to stay. Its proximity to the South Downs Way, however, evidently encourages unwanted visitors, and as I circled the perimeter of the tower I noticed signs everywhere discouraging the riff-raff: *Private. No entry. Keep out. No access. No parking. Residents only.* They gave the place an austere and inhospitable feeling, and although this was a lighthouse I had long wanted to visit, I wasn't sorry to leave.

Beachy Head.

Belle Tout was built on the cliff top above Beachy Head in 1832, with its location meticulously planned so that the light would be visible for twenty miles out to sea but would be obscured by the edge of the cliff if ships sailed too close to the shore. However, its position so high above the shore was flawed, and the light was frequently obscured by sea mists, significantly reducing its range. More importantly, the chalk cliff face suffered intense coastal erosion, and the light was decommissioned in 1899, replaced by the more familiar Beachy Head Lighthouse at the base of the cliffs in 1902.

The lighthouse has had a varied and chequered history ever since. After the war the building changed hands several times, and was at various times a tea shop, a private dwelling and even a film location, before continuing erosion left it perilously close to the cliff edge. The lighthouse came to public prominence in 1999, when its owners undertook to move the entire structure seventeen metres back from the cliff edge. This extraordinary feat of engineering was filmed and turned into a television documentary.

After refuelling at the National Trust cafe at Birling Gap, I pushed on to Seaford. I had wanted to dislike the place, because I once rented a flat in London from an appalling woman who lived there. She had insisted on leaving most of her belongings in the flat's cupboards and drawers, spent every day for a month painting a single window frame, disappeared whenever there was a problem, yet always appeared punctually to collect her rent.

As it was, I rather liked Seaford. It felt calm and unfussy. Along the esplanade I passed a row of well-maintained beach huts and a Martello tower. Between them, a tiny seafront cafe serving the richest and most welcome homemade tomato and basil soup. I was their only customer, and I devoured three bowlfuls.

I reached Newhaven at 4pm, much later than I had planned, and headed straight for the harbour. Newhaven lies at the mouth of the River Ouse in East Sussex, and unlike the Kent ports further east at Folkestone and Ramsgate, Newhaven is still an important harbour providing cross-channel connections to the continent for both passengers and freight.

The harbour comprises of east and west piers, with a light on each. On the west pier, the original light was built in 1883, but was rebuilt in 1976 after both the pier and lighthouse suffered storm damage. The east pier originally had a wooden lattice tower with wooden lantern room, but this was rebuilt in steel in 1928, and eventually demolished following vandalism in 2006. Now a 41-foot circular steel pole, painted white with three horizontal green bands, stands in its place.

I could not reach either light up close. The walkway along the west pier was closed off, while the modern east pier light is now controlled by the harbour authority and is inaccessible to the public. I cycled to a large car park close to the west pier to get the best view of both lights.

Leaving Newhaven shortly before six, the route to Brighton was a straight dash along the coast, passing through Peacehaven and Saltdean, before descending down onto Brighton Marina. At the end of the west arm of the breakwater, there is a modern light mounted on a cylindrical concrete tower, displaying a quick-flashing red light. It is not a landmark of great beauty, but it was no less a lighthouse than several I had seen so far, so I was glad to mark it as 'bagged'.

I was due to stay with Jacqueline and Andy, who offered to put me up after responding to a request for help from Shift.ms. They lived on an elegant street a mile from the seafront, together with their three children, Dylan, Lauren and Natasha, who turned out to be, unquestionably, the most polite and well-mannered kids I have ever met.

I arrived at around seven, and by half past, at their recommendation, I was sitting in the nearby Preston Park Tavern with my food ordered and a pint of Hop Pocket in my hand.

Days 3 and 4

As I made my way back to the seafront the next morning, I was struck by how well Brighton caters for its cyclists. Almost every road in the city centre has a dedicated cycle lane, many with their own set of lights and right of way. The promenade, too, separates pedestrians and cyclists effortlessly, and although it was busy, I was cycling out of the city towards Shoreham in no time.

Shoreham Port is one of the largest cargo-handling ports on the South Coast, and there are a number of navigation lights in evidence. However, I was here to see the grey limestone tower on the seafront, with its cast-iron and copper lantern. It was built in 1846 and began life as a fixed oil-burning light, but was converted to gas in the 1880s, with a rotating light using a mechanism similar to a long-case clock. The lighthouse remained gas powered until 1952, when a new fixed electric light was installed. It currently has a range of ten miles.

The NCN Route 2 follows the seafront from Shoreham to beyond Worthing, but as the winds had now become gale force, it became impossible to continue on it. I found myself employing the principles of barely remembered weekend sailing lessons, tacking my route away from the seafront with a series of right turns, and then turning back again towards the sea a few-hundred yards later with a series of left turns. Progress was painfully slow, with just the occasional sympathetic nod from a solitary dog walker to encourage me. At one point I was overtaken comfortably by a stray wheelie bin, which had broken free from its owner's driveway.

In the five miles to Worthing I learned one valuable lesson. Each time I tried riding my bike in these winds, I elicited pained looks of sympathy from the few people I passed, as if they felt they should offer to give me a push. But if I got off the bike, I gave the impression that I had all but completed my journey and was just pushing my bike the final few-hundred yards to my destination.

So I continued, cycling when I was able to keep away from the seafront, and pushing when it seemed the better option. Despite the slow pace I reached Littlehampton at around 4pm and made straight for the harbour.

Littlehampton once had a pair of small wooden weatherboarded leading harbour lights that were affectionately referred to as the salt and pepper pots. They were built at either end of the east pier, with the high light completed in 1848 and a shorter low light completed in 1868.

Concerned that an invasion force might use the lights as navigation aids, they were demolished in 1940. After the war ended, a pair of lights was built in the same location in 1948. The current rear range light is a futuristic-looking, white-painted, concrete tower whose light is visible for ten miles. The current front range is a simple fixed green light mounted on a black column.

I rather liked Littlehampton and was delighted when the Facebook post announcing my arrival had attracted the attention of Philip, an old friend from London. I first met him 30 years ago, when I rented a corner of his girlfriend's living-room floor each weekday night to avoid having to find a place of my own. After a comfortable night only yards from the harbour, we met for breakfast, and while I contemplated my greying beard and expanding waistline, I was irritated to see that he looked exactly the same as he did back then. He may have moved out of London, got married, had children then divorced, yet he seemed as relaxed and untroubled by the world as he did all those years ago.

Leaving Littlehampton behind, the seas and wind were calmer, and I was happy just to let my GPS guide me to the next lighthouse at Southsea, some 40 miles further along the coast. Initially, the route took me inland to Yapton, and then meandered back to the coast at Bognor Regis, before heading inland once more into Chichester.

Chichester is a wonderfully preserved Georgian cathedral city with wide, prosperous streets surrounded by ancient city walls. I was last here to visit my friend Kate, a nutrition expert, who had moved out of London a few years earlier to an extraordinarily old, beautiful, beamed and low-ceilinged town house. My route took me straight past her front door.

Over lunch in the city centre, I noticed that NCN Route 2 followed another long section of the dreadful A259 road that had caused me such grief with Bank Holiday traffic on the first day. I was confident I could do better, and set off along a series of small lanes, cycle paths and tracks through Bosham and Chidham, before finding myself on a wide, apparently abandoned stretch of traffic-free road. I cycled its length joyously, revelling in my ability to use my nose to find the best route. But after following the road for a couple of miles, it stopped abruptly at the entrance of the Baker Barracks, guarded in number by armed soldiers of the Royal Artillery.

I retraced my steps and followed the route I should have taken from the start. After Havant, I managed to stay away from the main road, with large expanses of water to my left and unspoiled views across to Hayling Island.

I approached Southsea Castle along the splendid Eastney Esplanade, from where I got my first view of the Solent and the Isle of Wight. The castle was built in 1544 and was part of a series of coastal fortifications constructed by Henry VIII. It was extended and largely rebuilt in the early 1800s and the lighthouse, commissioned by the Admiralty, was constructed on the western gun platform in 1828, rising 34 feet and built into the castle's outer walls. The stone tower is painted white with black bands, and its flashing white light can be seen for eleven miles.

Day 5

I was up and off the next morning, excited at the prospect of organising a boat trip out to the Palmerston Forts. These four remaining granite and iron forts were built in the Solent between 1867 and 1880, after Prime Minister Lord Henry Palmerston commissioned them to defend the Royal Navy fleet in Portsmouth harbour against a Napoleonic invasion. The French invasion never materialised, and they came to be referred to as 'Palmerston's Follies'.

All four forts originally housed lighthouse towers on their roofs, and two have since been converted into luxury hotels. The concierge was based down at Gunwharf Quays, so I headed there full of enthusiasm. My excitement was short-lived, however, after one of the Solent Forts hotel group crew informed me that the only way I could visit would be to book a Sunday lunch package at £160 per person. Alternatively, I could opt for a two-night, two-dinner 'trio of forts experience', but she declined to mention the price for this, having seen my face drop at the cost of lunch.

I settled for a long-lens photo of Spitbank Fort from Southsea, and later saw Horse Sand Fort and No Man's Land Fort from the Isle of Wight ferry, and finally St Helens Fort from Nodes Point on the Isle of Wight.

The fast ferry to the Isle of Wight reached Ryde at around lunchtime. My plan was to circle the island clockwise, getting to Shanklin, where I was due to stay, by mid-afternoon. Compared with the relatively flat terrain around Southsea the previous day, the terrain was altogether more challenging, and the other cyclists I encountered all wore skin-tight Lycra, riding bikes with tyres a third of the width of my own.

Having spotted St Helens Fort from Nodes Point Holiday Park, I climbed a steep hill up onto Culver Down, which represented my best opportunity to see the Nab Tower, a strange-looking light built on a circular concrete and steel fortress at the western entrance to the Solent.

The Nab Tower was built during the First World War and was intended to be one of eight such fortified towers, with nets and cables strung between them to form an anti-submarine barrage across the Solent. Only the Nab Tower was completed, and after the war it was identified as an ideal location for a lighthouse to replace the lightship that had been based nearby since 1812.

A small steel tower and lantern, painted red, was added in 1920 and it was staffed by three keepers, relieved monthly, from then until the station was automated in 1983. It was converted to solar operation in 1995.

After Yaverland, I was able to hug the coast all the way to Shanklin along the Red Squirrel Trail, an exhilarating stretch of track right at the sea's edge. Large waves cascaded onto the track every few moments, so I found myself slowing down and speeding up to avoid getting drenched. If this had been one of my son Tom's computer games, I reckon I would only have lost a couple of lives by the end.

Arriving at Shanklin along the seafront, I made for Hayes Barton, a welcoming guesthouse with generous, comfortable rooms and excellent food. Chris and Joan are wonderful hosts, and Chris is also a lighthouse enthusiast who volunteers as a tour guide at nearby St Catherine's lighthouse. By contrast with the mean-spirited Solent Forts hotel group, Chris and Joan put me up for two nights, gave me breakfast and dinner on both nights, and refused to charge me a penny.

Day 6

With Chris's help the following morning, I devised a route for the day that incorporated the Needles Lighthouse and St Catherine's Oratory, ending with a private tour of St Catherine's Lighthouse.

I started later than planned, having decided I could fit in a quick visit to the local launderette. I hadn't appreciated how long the wash would take, or how many 20p coins would be required to dry everything. Once I set off towards the Needles it began pouring with rain, and I discovered that my wet-weather gear was back at the guesthouse, so I returned to Hayes Barton once again.

Setting off for the second time, I felt determined to get back on track, but three miles short of Newport, on another stretch of the Red Squirrel Trail, I suffered my first puncture. Needless to say, my tools, repair kit and inner tubes were all back at the guesthouse. I pushed the bike to Newport, and by the time I found the Wight Mountain cycle shop, I must have looked a sorry sight.

I felt a little embarrassed to ask for help with something as simple as a puncture. Unprompted, however, they replaced the inner tube, serviced the brakes, adjusted my chain and gave my bike some oil. They had seen coverage of my lighthouse adventure in a monthly cycling magazine that had just been published, declined to charge me anything and wished me a safe onward journey.

It was now past 2pm, and other than a pannier full of clean kit, I had accomplished very little. I gave up on getting to the Needles before dark, and headed south to St Catherine's instead, putting in turns of speed whenever I found the energy. As I freewheeled the last half mile down to the lighthouse, I was struck by how quickly the sloping green lowlands give way to crumbling, white rock landslips, and by the commanding views in all directions out into the English Channel.

Chris's private 30-minute tour of the lighthouse turned into an hour and a half, and it was only a call from his wife Joan, to say that dinner would be served in less than an hour, that brought it to an end.

St Catherine's Lighthouse was built by Trinity House in 1838 to guide shipping in the Channel, as well as vessels approaching the Solent. It is constructed of white stone, in three tiered, octagonal plinths. Originally nearly 130-feet high, the tower was reduced by more than 40 feet in 1875 because the light was often shrouded in mist and fog. When cliff erosion caused the fog

St Catherine's.

signal house, located near the cliff edge, to crack, it was mounted on a lower tower connected to the front of the lighthouse tower. The two towers together are affectionately referred to by locals as the Cow and the Calf.

It has a range of 25 miles and is the third-most powerful of all the lights maintained by Trinity House. The fog signal was discontinued in 1987, and the light itself was automated in 1997. Today, the lighthouse plays an important role as an automatic weather reporting station, as well as a GPS correction beacon.

At dinner later that evening, I sat next to a charming retired couple called Roy and Jean. They were Isle of Wight veterans and had been staying with Chris and Joan for the same week each year for more than a decade. This year they almost hadn't come because Jean's father had died the previous month, and they hadn't felt that a holiday was appropriate at a time like this. Roy was keen to tell me more about his late father-in-law: 'Kind man. Engineer. Good with children. Could work out the tension of a spring, you know?'

However well meant, this touching epitaph left me feeling suddenly overwhelmed with sadness. That the life of such an evidently good man could be summarised in fewer than twenty words, and with four glib, detached phrases, brought a tear to my eye. I wondered what my own epitaph might be: 'Pleasant chap. Family man. Could identify any lighthouse off the UK coast, you know?'

I fell into bed, irritated that I'd only managed to 'bag' one lighthouse today. I felt lonely for the first time, and thinking back to my conversation with Roy and Jean at dinner, I questioned what this undertaking, and my life, was all about.

Day 7

With so much left undone from the day before, I needed to be up and out early to stand a chance of seeing the remaining three Isle of Wight lights and still catch a ferry across to Southampton before dark. After such attentive and warm hospitality, it was quite a wrench to thank Chris and Joan and leave Hayes Barton for the final time.

St Catherine's Oratory is a tall medieval octagonal tower – the only medieval lighthouse surviving in England – standing on one of the highest parts of the island. It is all that remains of an oratory built in 1328 as penance by a local landowner for stealing wine from a merchant ship that had run aground. A coal-fired light was originally displayed through eight openings on the top floor, forming a lantern. In the 18th century, four buttresses were added to the base of the tower to strengthen it, giving it the appearance of a medieval space rocket.

The views were breathtaking, but it was easy to see why it had been so ineffective as a beacon. Even on a day like today, a handful of low-lying clouds were shrouding the tower in a fine mist, obscuring its view of the sea at frequent intervals.

From the Oratory tower there is a straight fifteen-mile sprint to the Needles Headland, which forms a chalky peninsula to the west of the Isle of Wight, rising from jagged chalk rocks to 400-foot-high cliffs. These rocks have always proved a hazard to shipping making its way up the Solent to Portsmouth and Southampton, and a lighthouse was originally built up on the cliffs at Freshwater in 1785.

This tower was often obscured by mist and fog, and was replaced in 1859 by the current lighthouse, built at sea level on the outermost of the chalk rocks. Designed by James Walker, it was constructed from granite and cost £20,000 to build. It is currently painted in broad red-and-white bands, and emits a range of five red, white and green lights in total, each one marking a separate hazard or safe channel. Its lights are visible for seventeen miles.

The Needles Headland boasts unmissable sea views, and air so fresh that it prompted Tennyson to declare that it is 'worth sixpence a pint'. This wasn't quite my experience, however. After the solitude of the southern coast, I found myself entering a world of gift shops, teacup fair rides, carousels, games kiosks

The Needles Headland.

and hundreds and hundreds of athletes competing in the annual Isle of Wight Challenge, a gruelling 65-mile run which is held on the same May weekend each year.

I took in the lighthouse from the safety of a large wooden viewing platform, and was keen to move on. It's a dramatic sight, and one of the most recognisable and best-known lighthouses around our shores, but as a visitor attraction it was not for me.

My final target on the island was a strange-looking light at Egypt Point in Cowes, from where I planned to catch the ferry across the Solent to Southampton. Egypt Point is the most northerly point of the Isle of Wight and was one of Queen Victoria's favourite places when she stayed at Osbourne House, her summer residence. The lighthouse was built in 1897, a simple lantern supported on a 25-foot-high, red-painted metal column. The original light and lantern were replaced with a modern polycarbonate navigation light in 1969, which was in use until the lighthouse was decommissioned in 1989.

I found it, but at the cost of cutting it very fine for the ferry back to the mainland. I managed a quick selfie without dismounting, before pedalling for all I was worth to the chain ferry across to East Cowes to meet the Red Funnel service to Southampton. I was the last person on – and made it with less than a minute to spare.

Emerging from the Red Funnel ferry at dusk, I was met by Gavin Millar, a keen cyclist, avid sailor and partner to a fellow lighthouse obsessive, Katherine. Gavin and Katherine had read about my adventure in the ALK newsletter, and had offered to put me up. I studied at Southampton University after I left school, so I was delighted to discover that Gavin and Katherine not only lived in a part of town that I knew very well, but also that their house was just a few doors down from a wonderful pub where I had worked during my student days, and briefly managed after I graduated.

Over a couple of pints of Perridge Pale at the South Western Arms, I discovered that Gavin and I had plenty in common. Like me, he had spent childhood holidays visiting his grandparents on the coast, only for him they were near Bamburgh in Northumberland, and it was the Longstone Lighthouse that flashed through his bedroom window.

In June 2012, Gavin launched his Solway Dory sailing canoe from his back garden in Southampton and set off to see how far around Britain he could get before his scheduled return to work in September. So began a voyage that took him a thousand miles around the British coast.

We returned from the pub to a fabulous homemade fish pie that Katherine appeared to have conjured up from nowhere. I retired to bed late, questioning why I had chosen to leave Southampton after university at all.

Sleep did not come quickly, as I reflected back over my first full week of cycling. However good it felt to have racked up 25 lighthouses, it was really my physical health that gave me the most satisfaction. So far, it seemed, cycling nearly 260 miles had not provoked any new MS symptoms, and any tiredness I felt seemed entirely natural and manageable. A long way to go, but an encouraging beginning.

WEEK 2

Day 8

I thought I had got up early, but creeping downstairs to make myself a cup of tea I found Gavin fully dressed, my clothes washed and drying out on the line, and breakfast already laid out. Katherine had left for work an hour earlier, so over toast and cereal Gavin and I shared stories of sailing, cycling and how much Southampton had changed since my university days.

By car, my next lighthouse near Beaulieu would have involved a busy, industrial stretch of dual carriageway through Millbrook and Totton. It was a road I was familiar with from day trips to the New Forest. By bike, however, I could take advantage of the Hythe ferry, crossing the water from Town Quay at the east end of Southampton Docks to the pier and marina at Hythe opposite.

A ferry has operated between Southampton and Hythe since the Middle Ages, and the route is marked on a map from 1575 by Christopher Saxton. The service was owned and run by the Percy family for the majority of the last century, but its future was uncertain when I crossed, relying on a single catamaran on loan from the service between Gravesend and Tilbury on the Thames.

Pausing in Hythe to plan out my route to Beaulieu, I realised that I had accepted, and would now have to decline, a kind offer of a bed for the night here from Colin and Sandy, keen lighthouse enthusiasts whom I had met through ALK. I needed to keep up the pace if I was to reach the Channel Islands by the weekend.

Progress towards Beaulieu was slow, and although the roads were flat and the views heart-stirring in places, I was exposed to strong winds and held up queues of cars behind me, waiting for a gap to overtake. Turning off the main Beaulieu Road towards Lepe, though, was a different story. The lane was quiet, the hedges on each side provided welcome shelter, and I picked up my speed.

My target was Britain's youngest lighthouse, whose official title is Beaulieu River Millennium Beacon, built in 2000 to help navigate the approach to the Beaulieu River from the Solent. The lighthouse's cement-rendered brick tower has an octagonal lantern and weathervane on top. It displays a white light to indicate the safe channel, with red and green sector lights on each side, and also serves as a daymark during daylight hours.

Back in Beaulieu village, I stopped for far too long for lunch at the Old Bakehouse Tea Rooms, and by the time I got going again my legs were stiff and I was behind schedule once more. I was making for Hurst Castle, where I had arranged to meet several members of the Association of Lighthouse Keepers. They established a museum of lighthouse artefacts there, after Trinity House's museum in Penzance closed in 2005. Mondays were the one day of the week when all the volunteers would be there, and I needed to reach Keyhaven for the ferry across the water by 3pm at the latest if I was to meet up with them.

My route to Keyhaven took me through Lymington, a delightful town I wished I had more time to stop and explore. Situated on the west bank of the Lymington River, it is now a major yachting centre with three separate marinas. But it began as an Anglo-Saxon village, recorded in the Domesday Book as 'Lentune'. Throughout the Middle Ages and until the early-19th century, Lymington was renowned for its salt making, and more recently established a thriving ship-building industry.

Keyhaven is a hamlet with a pretty harbour, lying at one end of the shingle bank known as Hurst Spit. You can walk along the spit to Hurst Castle in around half an hour, but I was waiting at the quay for the short ferry crossing, where my

ALK friends had told me to introduce myself to the ferryman, Bob. The harbour seemed desolate and exposed, and for the first time I worried about where I would leave my bike and panniers. But as Bob pulled up at the quay, he insisted that there would be room on his boat for me, the bike and my luggage, and between us we managed to haul it all on board. The water was remarkably still and peaceful, protected from the Solent by the shingle spit, and so the crossing was remarkably quiet.

As we neared the castle, a heavy fog descended, concealing the current Trinity House lighthouse altogether. I could make out the castle's Tudor entrance through the mist, conjuring images of a time when weary travellers arrived after long journeys on horseback, rather than heavily laden bicycles.

My ALK friends seemed very pleased to see me, and for the first time since Dungeness, I posed in front of my bike for official photographs. John Best, a longstanding ALK member and volunteer at the museum, showed me around the castle, and helped me to clamber up onto the castle walls to see the two former low lights. The ALK museum and archive is expanding, and I was delighted to see that their current project was the restoration of the original red octagonal lantern from the Nab Tower, which I had seen from the Isle of Wight. It was nearing completion and was to be their prize exhibit.

The restoration work is carried out by a small team of volunteers and enthusiasts, headed up by Keith Morton, the ALK Project Manager at Hurst Castle. Lighthouses are a passion for them, and their knowledge, skill and dedication are remarkable.

The current Hurst Point Lighthouse was built by Trinity House in 1867 to guide vessels through the hazardous western approaches to the Solent. It has a tall, white-painted, circular stone tower with lantern and gallery, as well as keepers' accommodation and other associated buildings around its base.

The lighthouse was extensively modernised in 1997, including the installation of an accurate system of red, green and white directional lights that mark the channel between the Needles and the shingle banks. Unlike many earlier directional lights around our coast, the ones at Hurst can be realigned in the event of movement of the shingle.

Hurst Point.

There have been a number of lights at Hurst Point, from as early as 1733. Two of the former low lights still stand, dating from 1866 and 1911, which were built into the castle walls.

Somehow, the castle staff, the ALK volunteers, my bike, luggage and I all managed to pile on to the tiny ferry back to Keyhaven. John Best had kindly offered a bed for the night, and by the time I had cycled the hour-long route to his house in Christchurch, supper was already prepared. We talked about many of the lighthouses I would visit, and the people I should look up on the way. He may not have cycled to them all in a single journey, but I couldn't find a lighthouse that John hadn't reached at some point in his lifetime. I had a lot of catching up to do.

Day 9

After the fog of the previous afternoon, the glorious heat and sunshine on the south coast the following morning was unexpected, though extremely welcome. After crossing the River Stour at Iford, my route took me back to the coast at Boscombe, before following the seafront on dedicated cycle lanes all the way to Sandbanks, through Bournemouth, Branksome Beach and Canford Cliffs.

Sandbanks is a small coastal resort on a peninsular crossing the mouth of Poole Harbour. It's renowned for its exclusive homes and famous, well-heeled residents. In 2005 a modest bungalow sold for £3 million, and again in 2007 for £4 million. Earlier this year, another sold for £13.5 million. I blew my budget for the day over coffee and cake at the Sandbanks Beach Cafe, but it was worth every penny.

With accommodation in Sandbanks beyond my means, I found a friendly, welcoming hotel on the cliffs above Poole – an ensuite room with a balcony with spectacular sea views, all for £39. I sat outside with a beer in hand, gazing out to sea while catching up on a week's worth of *The Archers*. I have been a fan since I was a teenager, from the days when Nigel Pargetter was Mr Snowy, the ice-cream man, and when Laura Archer fell into a ditch and died of exposure.

Looking out to sea, I focused on a flashing light that, after a little research, I realised was the Needles Lighthouse. I had covered 72 miles since I had stood in front of the Needles headland, yet from this balcony the lighthouse was less than twenty miles away.

Day 10

The Condor ferry to the Channel Islands was late to arrive, and late to depart. The company had recently upgraded its fleet and I learned that the new ferries were suffering regular teething problems. It was an expensive enough crossing at £120, but an additional £15 secured me a seat at the bow, with panoramic views through pillar-less glass windows. It enabled me to get a good long-shot photo of Casquets Lighthouse, on a dangerous rocky outcrop eight miles north-west of Alderney. I hoped to find a boat trip that might get me closer to Casquets, although I had been warned that this was unlikely and the ferry would probably be as close as I could get.

Casquets was one of the lighthouses that I pictured whenever I thought about this expedition, because of its three separate towers, as well as the working light's distinctive narrow red-and-white painted stripes.

Each of the three stone towers originally displayed a coal-fire light when they were first lit in October 1724. They were named St Peter, St Thomas and the Dungeon, and their formation was designed to avoid confusion with other French lights close by.

They were converted first to oil lamps with metal reflectors in 1790, and then to a rotating mechanism in 1818. Various improvements followed throughout the 19th century until 1877, when the north-west tower was raised to 75 feet and the lights in the other two towers were decommissioned.

The lighthouse was converted to an electric light in 1952, with a range of 24 miles. All three of the original towers still stand and are in use. While the north-west tower alone provides a light, the south-west tower is now used as a helipad, and the east tower houses the original foghorn and other equipment. The single remaining lighthouse was automated in 1990.

The St Helier service stops first at St Peter Port, Guernsey's main harbour and ferry port. As we entered the harbour I was tempted to photograph the three principal harbour lights, but I knew I would be returning to explore Guernsey's lighthouses properly in a couple of days.

Casquets.

The ferry takes another hour on to St Helier, where I was met by Gil Blackwood, an impossibly fit, retired psychiatrist who had been persuaded by his daughter to partition off a wing of the condo he shares with his wife Christine and offer overnight stays on Airbnb. Although not yet officially open, he had kindly offered to put me up. Better still, he is a keen cyclist and offered to act as my guide around the Jersey coast.

When I think of the word 'condo' I picture a modest apartment, perhaps with a balcony, in a large, sprawling Victorian seafront building. Gil and Christine's condo was nothing of the sort. Upper King's Mount is an exclusive part of town, on a steep hill, offering panoramic views across green pasture back to the harbour and seafront. Each room is elegantly proportioned, and the hallway alone was as large as a cricket square, with enough room for a medium pacer's run-up.

Gil showed me to a suite of rooms which were utterly splendid. After travelling for most of the day, I would have been happy to sink into a bath and then see out the remaining hours on the bench on my balcony with a book. But Gil had other ideas. No sooner had I dropped off my panniers than he appeared at my door in full cycling kit, keen to get cracking.

In a glorious four-hour cycle around the west coast, we covered nearly 25 miles, pausing at four lighthouses. Gil's speed and stamina put me to shame, and while he pedalled with ease up every hill, I followed a good half a mile behind, almost invariably on foot.

Our first stop was Noirmont Point, a rocky headland to the east of St Aubin's Bay, where there is a black-and-white striped squat tower built between 1810 and 1814 to defend the island from Napoleon. It was only in 1915 that a lantern was fitted to the roof of the tower, with a range of thirteen miles. These days it is solar powered.

A brisk twenty-minute ride from Noirmont Point took us to La Corbière, a reef extending half a mile into the sea close to St Brelade's Bay on the south-west tip of the island. The rocks at La Corbière are passed by all marine traffic heading to St Helier and have always proved a danger to shipping. There are records of wrecks dating as far back as 1309, but it was not until after the mail steamer *Express* hit the reef and sank in 1859 that a lighthouse here was proposed.

La Corbière.

Designed by Sir John Coode, La Corbière was Britain's first reinforced concrete lighthouse and was completed in 1874. It has a white-painted tapering tower and was originally fitted with a paraffin oil lamp.

The island was occupied by the Germans from June 1940, and the light was largely extinguished until liberation in 1945, lit only when needed to guide German ships around the treacherous rocks. It is said that the lighthouse's loud and distinctive foghorn was sounded continuously for a whole day to mark the island's liberation. The lighthouse was converted to electricity in 1970 and automated in 1976. In 2015 the foghorn was decommissioned, and removed altogether a year later.

The lighthouse is connected to the mainland by a causeway that is accessible only at low tide. The stunning location makes it one of Jersey's most famous landmarks, and it has always been high up on my shortlist of must-see lighthouses.

Cycling to the lighthouse at Grosnez Point was glorious, as we followed the sea along the arrow-straight and flat Grande Route des Mielles for almost eight miles. Jersey has some wonderful, gravelled cycle tracks, but with roads like this they seemed unnecessary.

Once we got beyond L'Etacq the terrain changed dramatically as we headed up a steep valley with crops of potatoes and vegetables on each side of a quiet narrow lane. For a couple of miles I didn't see Gil at all, and by the time we reached a road junction at the brow of the hill I was ready for a decent break, while he was rested up and itching to move on.

Grosnez Lighthouse, at the north-west tip of Jersey, is a modern, white metal column, with a small polycarbonate lantern on top, constructed in the 1990s. It plays an important role, however, because its red sector marks the dangerous Paternoster Reef to the north-east.

Up until now Gil had seemed enthusiastic about my adventure, and I was confident of winning him over to the fraternity of lighthouse enthusiasts. But staring dubiously at this small white column, not much larger than a pillar box, he looked distinctly unimpressed.

Our final target for the day was to be Sorel Point, at Jersey's most northerly headland, a further eight miles by road. We ventured inland a little and followed tree-lined lanes offering welcome shelter, passing a number of substantial manor houses and a couple of large country hotels. This was clearly where the wealthy and successful made their home.

We got to the lighthouse at around 5pm, by which time I was ready to drop. It's a desolate spot, flanked on one side by the Ronez Quarry, and the lighthouse itself is a strange, squat concrete tower, just ten-feet tall and shaped like a pillbox. It was built in 1938 by Jersey Harbour Authority and was originally painted in a black-and-white chequerboard pattern, serving also as a daymark. When the light was renovated and converted to solar power in 2009 it was repainted entirely white, along with the adjacent rocks.

The ride back to Gil's condo followed an almost straight line north to south across the island, and neither of us spoke at all until St Helier came into view. I joined Gil and Christine for dinner, over which I learned about their life on Jersey and Gil's career as a consultant psychiatrist turned Airbnb host. As night fell I retreated to my balcony with a mug of tea, unwilling to let the day end.

Day 11

I woke early to heavy rain and a gale that rattled the French windows in the drawing room below me. The forecast showed it clearing by mid-morning, so I took the opportunity to soak in a very hot, deep bath. There were plenty of signs that Gil and Christine were not yet seasoned guesthouse proprietors. On a shelf next to the bath was a dish containing dozens of miniature bars of soap, shampoo sachets, conditioners, bubble baths and hand cream. In the kitchen was a similar dish brimming with teabags and coffee sachets of every description, alongside hot chocolate powder, Horlicks, cocoa, milk and sugar packets. A schoolboy error. If Emily had been with me, these would all have been squirrelled away into her suitcase for the kitchen cupboard at home.

I mentioned to Gil that perhaps he should limit the complimentary drinks and bathroom products a little, for fear that many guests would simply take home what they hadn't used. He seemed highly amused by the idea, admitting that this was exactly how Christine had acquired them all in the first place.

After stopping to chat with a reporter at the *Jersey Post* offices, Gil and I cycled anti-clockwise around the south and east coasts of the island, taking in the lights at Demie de Pas, La Greve D'Azette, Mount Ube, Gorey and St Catherine's. With the exception of the original St Catherine's Breakwater light, now sited outside the maritime museum in St Helier, I can't claim that any of these are either beautiful structures or of great architectural merit.

The light at Demie de Pas, for example, is a modest, black-and-orange painted, concrete, cone-shaped tower with a light, fog signal and radar beacon mounted on top. A little way offshore, it guides shipping away from one of a series of dangerous rocks south of St Helier harbour. Its principal white light has a range of fourteen miles, but the area inland of the light is especially hazardous, so it also casts a red light back towards the shore.

Neither this, nor the next few, were lights to pause or marvel at. The light at Greve D'Azette, one of a pair of range lights, has a lattice steel tower that is built alongside the promenade wall. It is hardly a tourist attraction, so I was surprised to see a sizeable crowd gathered around its base. Only when we reached the promenade did I see that the base of the tower also serves as a bus stop on the main route into town.

Mount Ube lighthouse, a mile or so inland, is the rear range of this pair of lights. When lined up at night they guide shipping through the safe channel towards St Helier harbour. It was remarkably similar to the light on the promenade.

At Jersey's easternmost tip lies Gorey, once Jersey's principal harbour. On the pier is a white-painted metal tower with a small lantern, displaying red-and-green lights.

We had just St Catherine's to conquer before taking the ferry to Guernsey that evening. The harbour at St Catherine's dates from the 1840s, part of a plan to establish a port on Jersey's east coast to serve large naval bases on Jersey and Alderney. The current breakwater light is another white-painted metal tower, but when it was erected in 1950, the original 1857 light was re-sited outside the maritime museum in St Helier. This is a much more edifying lighthouse, with its elegant, 30-foot-tall octagonal tower. It felt like the first 'proper' lighthouse since La Corbière, and made a fitting end to the day's cycling, as well as a suitable point to thank Gil and part company with him.

Back in St Helier, I caught the slow overnight ferry – eventually destined for Portsmouth – to St Peter Port in Guernsey. Arriving at the harbour for the second time in a week, in my pocket I had the name of a hotel which had kindly agreed to accommodate me. When I arrived at the hotel's entrance, I realised just how extraordinarily generous the offer to accommodate me had been.

Day 12

Old Government House was once the official residence for the governor of Guernsey and is now the island's only five-star hotel. The fundraising team at Shift.ms had put out a plea for accommodation on Guernsey, and the manager of the hotel had responded. It is part of the Red Carnation Hotels group, which also includes a wonderful hotel in a side street near the British Museum in London where I have stayed many times. It is my favourite hotel, so to find myself staying at another in the group was very welcome news.

My plan was to make Guernsey my base for three nights, enabling me to use one of the days for a boat trip to Alderney to visit the beautiful lighthouse at Quénard Point. This morning, however, I planned a relatively flat ride around the east coast, taking in the range lights at St Sampson and stopping to get as close as I could to the offshore light at Platte Fougère.

These days the harbour at St Sampson is better known as a yachting marina, but this was once a substantial dock, exporting granite from local quarries. The entrance into the harbour was marked by a pair of range lights, with the front light on Crocq Pierhead. Built in around 1874, its small cast-iron tower, with domed roof, casts a fixed red light with a range of five miles. It's a little creepy, with more than a passing resemblance to a Dalek, albeit missing its sink plunger and associated weaponry. The rear light at St Sampson takes some spotting, because its fixed green light is mounted on the clock tower of the former harbour master's office building.

St Sampson is a pleasant enough place, but I needed to press on, because I wanted to see the light at Platte Fougère and wasn't entirely confident of where might offer the best view. By midday I had reached Fort Doyle, at Fontenelle Bay on the northern shore of Guernsey. Built in the first part of the 19th century, Fort Doyle was designed to protect the island against French invasion. But it wasn't until the Second World War that Fort Doyle saw enemy action, when the occupying German forces fortified the area with three coastal-defence guns, anti-aircraft guns and mortars.

These days the fort is renowned for its spectacular sea views, so I made my way to a long bench on a circular stone platform that once housed a cannon, from where I could gaze out to the black-and-white banded octagonal tower of the Platte Fougère Lighthouse.

After retracing my steps back to St Peter Port, I had hoped there might be a scheduled boat trip that would take in the tall, imposing lighthouse at Les Hanois. Having established that these were rare at this time of year, my only option was to cycle up to the headland at Pleinmont, involving the steepest climb since Fairlight, in Sussex. I was clearly getting a little fitter, because I made it two-thirds of the way up before dismounting and pushing.

The going got a lot easier once I reached St Martin, one of the most expensive parishes on the island for property. This is a green, lush part of Guernsey, with quiet lanes perfect for cycling. The easy-going flat cliff paths on the Pleinmont headland gave me a spectacular view looking out to the lighthouse at Les Hanois. In fact, the views are spectacular in all directions, and I read that on a clear day you can see Jersey, as well as the French coast. However, it was now approaching dusk, so I felt privileged at least to have seen what I came for.

Designed by Nicholas Douglass, the lighthouse at Les Hanois was first lit in December 1862, in response to a series of shipwrecks in the first half of the 19th century on the treacherous rocks off the western coast of Guernsey.

The lighthouse is important in the development of lighthouse engineering, because all the stones in each course, as well as all the courses, were dovetailed together to form one solid mass. It resulted in an almost solid tower, and this method of construction became the pattern for all sea rock towers thereafter.

The lighthouse is an imposing, tapered, granite tower, with a helipad mounted on top that was added in 1979. It was the first rock light to be converted to solar power, in 1996, and its light displays two white flashes every thirteen seconds, visible for twenty miles.

I had covered barely twenty miles all day, but I was glad to have seen so much of the rugged coastal scenery for which Guernsey is known. I felt underdressed in the hotel's Crown Club bar, and even more so in its splendid dining room. But I had built up a hearty appetite and ordered liberally from the extensive menu. Perhaps unwisely, I also selected a number of the wines that had been 'paired' with each course.

Les Hanois.

My evening's entertainment was provided by a diner at a neighbouring table. A portly and clearly well-to-do gentleman, he was undoubtedly the noisiest and messiest eater I have ever encountered. He barked orders at waiters frequently, spitting out mouthfuls of food each time he did so. He demanded fresh napkins with each course, which he spread liberally around much of his upper body. At one point, a claw he was pulling from a crab flew out of his hand and landed at my feet. I wondered if it was all part of some elaborate stunt for a television show, but I learned later that he was a Guernsey resident and regular diner here.

My day ended with a typical Red Carnation gesture. I had been awaiting the publication of a feature about my bike ride in the *Sunday Telegraph* but had been unable to track down a copy. Back in my bedroom, a pristine copy of the newspaper lay on my bed, along with a handwritten note saying: 'See page 17 – Great article!'

Fame at last!

Day 13

I was up early the following morning for the boat to Alderney. The contract for the scheduled ferry service between Guernsey and Alderney had been awarded the previous year to Bumblebee Marine, a family enterprise run by father and son Chris and Dan Meinke. Their vessel is a newly built, bright-yellow, ten-metre catamaran, capable of carrying no more than a dozen passengers.

As I reached the quayside it started to rain, and the sea began to swirl as the wind picked up speed. There were six of us waiting hopefully, and despite the change in the weather the Bumblebee emerged out of the gloom.

Our skipper for the crossing was Chris, a relentlessly cheerful chap, who warned us that the going might get a bit choppy. He wasn't kidding. The heavy rain had driven me, and my five fellow passengers, to take shelter in the catamaran's tiny wheelhouse. But rain was the least of our troubles, because no sooner had we emerged from the harbour at St Peter Port than we started to be thrown about the wheelhouse with each wave that hit the side of the boat.

The bench seats in the wheelhouse are quite high, and not one of us could touch the floor with our feet while seated. It meant that any movement of the boat caused us to slide along the bench until the person on the end fell onto the floor. We took it in turns to sit at the end of the two benches, and for a few minutes it felt exhilarating, like the most popular ride at the fun fair. But before long it felt relentless, and it dawned on me that this was how it was going to be.

My balance is not great at the best of times, and I felt my centre of gravity shifting with every wave we encountered. I tried to compensate by clenching muscles that I didn't know I had, and grabbing hold tightly of anything that was fixed to the floor or ceiling. Somewhat improbably, I discovered that individually clenching my left and right buttocks helped considerably, just as long as I did so in time to the rise and fall of the boat. And so I maintained a rhythm as best I could, shifting my balance between left and right buttock, left and right arm.

Nor was our skipper exempt from the ordeal. Now, Chris is not a tall man, and when seated on his captain's stool, his feet didn't quite touch the ground either. In most conditions this would not be an issue, but today it meant that he was struggling to stay upright as much as we were. Frequently, we would hit an especially fierce wave, Chris would be thrown from his stool onto the floor, he'd roar with laughter and then claw his way back to his position. It was a great testament to his nautical skills, however, that no matter how roughly he was flung, he never once let go of the wheel.

After 90 minutes we reached dry land and docked at Alderney. I felt thoroughly sick, and although my target was the lighthouse at Quénard Point, all I really wanted to do was find somewhere to sit down and remain still for a while.

The single garage on the island offered bike rental, and for just £10 I managed to hire a small electric bike whose battery, I was assured, would endure a complete circuit of the island. But first, I cycled straight to the centre of town in search of breakfast and a strong cup of coffee.

I was extremely fortunate to find Gloria's Food, a wonderful family-run cafe and bistro, in a small street leading from the main shopping area. I ordered a full English breakfast and got chatting to Gloria herself about what I was doing on Alderney, and how I hoped to get closer to Casquets Lighthouse than I had managed on the ferry crossing from Portsmouth.

News travels fast on Alderney. While I was tucking into a really first-class breakfast, much was being done behind the scenes. Gloria's son tried, without success, to fix me up with a local boatman to take me out to Casquets. He had also found my website, donated £50 to Shift.ms and tipped off the features writer at the *Guernsey Press* that I was here.

Within minutes I saw a young woman running up the hill towards the cafe as if her life depended on it. I wondered what on earth made anyone rush about on an island like Alderney, until I realised that she had come to see me. She produced a voice recorder and asked me if I was the intrepid lighthouse cyclist. Pleased as I was to be newsworthy, I was surprised that my visit appeared to be her biggest scoop for many weeks.

I stayed at Gloria's Food for far too long, and it took a fair effort to pack my bag and get on my bike for the ride to Quénard Point. After two weeks on my bulletproof Thorn Nomad, this tiny-wheeled electric bike felt very strange indeed. But I was determined to make maximum use of the battery assistance, and within minutes was loving travelling at speed without any effort at all on my part.

The lighthouse on Alderney is spectacular, the first 'proper' tower lighthouse I had seen since La Corbière on Jersey. It holds a commanding position, with far-reaching views over the channel in three directions.

Also known as Quénard Lighthouse after the headland on which it was built in 1912, Alderney Lighthouse is at the island's north-east point. It is 105-feet tall and painted white with a central black band to make it more visible to shipping during daylight hours. It looks out over a hazardous stretch of water known as the Alderney Race, between Alderney and Cap de la Hague in Normandy, that includes the strongest tidal streams in Europe.

The lighthouse was automated in 1997, and its light was downgraded from 23 miles to twelve miles in 2011.

Cycling back towards Braye Beach and the Bumblebee, I stopped at Fort Tourgis, an abandoned fort that had been built by the British in 1855, to provide defence for Alderney and its harbour against French naval power in the Channel, which now lies in ruin.

It was adapted by German occupying forces during the Second World War to resist potential British assaults to recapture the only part of the British Isles to be occupied by Germany. After the war it was used by the military up until the 1960s, then became a boarding school for a while before falling into disrepair. Despite various plans over the years to redevelop the fort as flats,

Quénard Point, Alderney.

houses, a luxury hotel, even a casino, the site remains eerily still and abandoned, but offers a spectacular vantage point over the island and its waters.

The crossing back to Guernsey was considerably calmer, and we had the wind behind us all the way. When we were nearing St Peter Port, Chris detoured towards the Tautenay, Roustel and Bréhon Tower lights, to make sure I got closer to each than I had managed the previous day. I'm not sure that I'd count any of these three lights as bona fide lighthouses, and I recognised that if these counted then dozens more dubious lights, beacons and towers lay ahead of me over the coming weeks.

Day 14

I had to be up early and down at the harbour by 8.30 for the short crossing to Sark. There is a fabulous lighthouse set into the cliffs at Point Robert on the island, and I had hoped to take one of the island's famous pony and trap rides there after disembarking at Maseline Harbour. Unfortunately, this would mean missing the ferry back to Poole, so my only option was to see the lighthouse from the Sark ferry, then stay onboard for the return journey to St Peter Port.

I was fortunate, at least, that the ferry route passed immediately in front of the lighthouse. On board I met a photographer called Gary, who had been using a camera mounted to a small drone to take some incredibly close-up images. He fired up his laptop to show me them, and I was able to view the lighthouse's lantern and buildings from every angle, even through the windows on both floors. In fact, I wouldn't have been able to get nearly as close if I had made it there in person.

Sark Lighthouse was built by Trinity House in 1913 to guide vessels passing through the Channel Islands away from the pinnacle of Blanchard Rock. It comprises a white octagonal tower, with keepers' accommodation underneath, set into the cliff face at Point Robert at the north-east of the island.

Sark was considered a cushy and desirable posting for lighthouse keepers because it was classed as a 'rock station' by Trinity House. That meant it attracted a higher wage, despite being considerably less remote than most other rock stations, and it was one of very few rock lights where a keeper could retire to the pub when they were off-duty.

Sark was automated in 1994, and its rotating optic was replaced with two LED lanterns in 2017. Currently it has a range of eighteen miles.

Returning to St Peter Port, there were still a few lights around Guernsey that I had yet to see. Somehow, I had missed Platte Lighthouse, incorrectly assuming that it was just a shortened name for the light at Platte Fougère. Then to St Martin's Point, where a flashing white light is mounted onto a short post on top of a square stone building. And lastly to the rear range light at Belvedere, similar to the Dalek-like squat tower at St Sampson, although flanked on either side by a pair of white-painted wooden lattice structures that look a lot like cricket sight screens. These serve as daymarks, while the light in the tower itself is visible for ten miles.

Point Robert, Sark.

Only the three harbour lights remained. I had seen and photographed each of them a number of times now, having embarked here on my ferry route to Jersey, as well as on each of the day trips to Alderney and Sark. But until now, I hadn't got up close to any of them.

The most imposing is the Castle Breakwater Light, which guides vessels into the harbour in conjunction with the rear light that I had just visited on the hillside above at Belvedere. It's a circular, 40-foot granite tower with lantern above, showing a fixed white light, followed by a fixed red light, both operated by electricity.

A second harbour light on White Rock Pier shows a flashing green light and, on Victoria Pier, there is a tall, square, wooden tower with octagonal lantern that shows three lights: a narrow fixed white light with a flashing green sector light to the north and a similar red sector to the south.

With these three harbour lights, I had seen all of Guernsey's lighthouses with barely an hour to spare before the Condor ferry back to Poole was due. Not for the first time, the Condor service was running late. I smiled when I remembered the reporter from the *Guernsey Press* telling me that the service had been so unreliable of late that they only bothered reporting when the ferries were actually on time.

We berthed at Poole after midnight, where I booked in for the second time at the Riviera Hotel.

Castle Breakwater, St Peter Point.

WEEK 3

Day 15

For the second time the view across to the Isle of Wight only heightened my sense of anxiety about the progress I was making. I may have clocked up more than 25 Channel Islands lights since my first visit, but I could still sit on the end of my bed and look out across the water to the Needles Lighthouse.

I set off for Anvil Point Lighthouse, beyond Studland Bay on the Isle of Purbeck, via the charming chain ferry service between Sandbanks and Studland that crosses the entrance to Poole Harbour. The landscape on the other side felt very different from the affluent and well-heeled Sandbanks. A single broad, straight road, lined with sand, runs for the three miles from Shell Bay to Studland. Trees on either side have been twisted and shaped by the wind, and only heather, gorse and other hardy vegetation covers the heathland beyond. This is Studland Bay, a national nature reserve since 1946, and a haven for birds and other wildlife.

It was barely 10am as I cycled alongside Little Sea, an acidic freshwater lake formed by the sand dunes that cut it off from the English Channel. But the twitchers were already parked up and in position, such is the reserve's renown for sightings of many of the rarer species of grebe and warbler.

Pausing in Swanage to consult my map, I noticed that Purbeck is really a peninsular, and not an island at all. It burgeoned as a tourist destination in Victorian times, although quarrying had been the region's principal industry for many centuries before. When the Great Fire of London in 1666 led to the large-scale reconstruction of the city, it was Purbeck stone that was used extensively for paving its streets.

The seafront at Swanage is rather charming, with its long, white sandy beach and well-tended grassland and gardens on the opposite side of the seafront road. A row of wooden beach huts afford their owners an enviable view of the sea, although youngsters eager for a swim need help crossing the fairly busy road first. Like every other seaside town, there were the requisite game arcades and a handful of ice-cream parlours. Yet Swanage seemed to belong to another era and was all the more charming for it.

Anvil Point Lighthouse perches on the headland at Durlston Country Park and Nature Reserve, home to a fine castle, extensively restored in recent years, as well as the Great Globe, one of the largest stone spheres in the world. Built in Greenwich from Portland stone in 1887, it weighs almost 40 tonnes and is three metres in diameter. It's a remarkable object, attracting quite an audience this morning, but my real goal was, of course, the lighthouse.

Built from local stone in 1881, it was designed to provide a waypoint for vessels passing along the English Channel coast. Although its squat tower is just 39-feet tall, the light itself is nearly 150 feet above sea level. Originally lit by a paraffin vapour burner, it was modernised and electrified in 1960, at which time the original clockwork-driven Fresnel lens was removed and donated to the Science Museum in London. In May 1991, the lighthouse was fully automated.

In 2012, an LED lamp was installed above the rotating Fresnel lens installed in 1960, and this now serves as the main light at Anvil Point. It displays a white flashing light every ten seconds, which is visible for nine miles.

Retracing my route to Swanage, I followed a narrow and gently inclining lane through Woolgarston towards Corfe Castle. The verges on each side of the lane were extremely tall, but every few-hundred yards the road opened up to majestic, undulating scenery in all directions. I was aware of Dorset's reputation as

Anvil Point.

a beautiful county, but along this lane at least I was continually taken aback by the landscape.

I descended into the village of Corfe Castle at speed, and on an emotional high. It's funny how a place you have never visited can evoke a specific emotion or reaction, simply through association. For me, Corfe Castle can only mean *Nuts in May*, Mike Leigh's perfect 1976 television play with Alison Steadman and Roger Sloman. I pictured a Morris Minor and a couple arguing over who should hold the castle's guidebook. I was tempted to stop, but with Weymouth still twenty miles away I needed to press on.

My mother always told me that you should never go to a supermarket when you're hungry. For a cyclist, the equivalent rule is that you should never pull in at a decent-looking pub when you still have some distance to travel. The pub was the Greyhound Inn. The beer was locally brewed and called Dorset Knob. The lunch was a fabulous local crab sandwich, with a side portion of hand-cut, twice-cooked chips. By the time I got back on my bike I felt bloated, sleepy and ready to drop.

To say that I misjudged my afternoon would be an understatement. The first six miles to East Lulworth were almost entirely uphill, and the steeper I climbed, the windier it got. I climbed nearly 1,300 feet, and although reaching East Lulworth itself involved a short stretch downhill, the road quickly climbed again on the other side of the village. It was scenic, certainly, but this was army territory, and the road was punctuated with warning signs, red flags and forbidding wire fences.

It was not until I reached the village of Preston, a few miles north of Weymouth, that the route levelled out and I felt confident that I would reach Weymouth in daylight. As the town centre came into sight, I suddenly found myself at the front of a group of racing cyclists, apparently donning the yellow jersey. At a roundabout by a fish and chip shop I was congratulated, handed a bottle of water, and told that there was not much further to go. At the seafront a crowd of supporters gathered by a finishing line with streams of colourful bunting.

I have no idea what the event was that I had gatecrashed, but I was grateful that it spurred me on to my B&B on the harbour front.

Day 16

Weymouth's splendid esplanade of Georgian terraces is very pleasing on the eye, but the town's treatment of its cyclists is simply shocking. Where Brighton's promenade accommodates pedestrians and cyclists harmoniously, Weymouth regards cyclists with utter disdain. The local council has stuck forbidding 'No Cycling' signs to every lamppost, railing and wall. In fact, the money they have spent on these signs would go a long way towards establishing safe shared routes for pedestrian and cyclist alike. The same council also publishes a laughably useless cycle route map of the town, where every road in the town centre or near the seafront is shaded brown, indicating a 'busy or high-[high-speed] speed road suited to confident cyclists only'.

The town had lost its role as a channel port earlier in the year, after Condor's new ferry was deemed too large to berth here. I read that the council was discussing efforts to turn the quay into a leisure destination, rather than a ferry port. We can assume that whatever leisure activity is being proposed, it will not include cycling.

My first destination was the Isle of Portland, connected by road via a long causeway running between Weymouth and Fortuneswell. The island is home to no fewer than four lighthouses, the most famous being Portland Bill. Although only nine miles from my B&B, the route included one of the steepest climbs of the journey so far, and took two hours where I had allowed just one.

It was worth it, though. Two former substantial lighthouses still stand near the current tower. A few-hundred metres short of the headland stands the imposing former lower light, now a bird observatory. Behind it, further inland and up a steep hill, the former higher light is now a private house. Its squat tower may not be as imposing as the lower light, but the views from it are simply spectacular.

The main event, however, was Portland Bill Lighthouse itself. Built in 1906 to replace the two earlier lights, it's one of the most substantial and recognisable lighthouses on our coast. I took advantage of the guided tour of the lighthouse, and from the lantern it was easy to see why the two vast bays on either side of the headland need such protection.

It was designed by Sir Thomas Matthews, then Trinity House's engineer-in-chief, and has a tapered circular tower, nearly 140-feet tall, with lantern and gallery. It is painted white, with a single broad red band at its midpoint. It displays a group flashing light, which is visible for 25 miles. The lighthouse was automated in March 1996.

Portland Harbour was originally built for the Royal Navy, and it remained an important naval base until the end of the Cold War. At one time it was the largest man-made harbour in the world.

It was home to the prison ship HMP *Weare* at one time, and is now the residence of the *Bibby Stockholm* barge for asylum seekers. There's a prefabricated cast-iron lighthouse on the breakwater, which shows a white flashing light every two-and-a-half seconds, visible for ten miles.

Returning to Weymouth, I hoped to reach Bridport by nightfall. By dusk, I was exhausted and found refuge in the Crown Inn,

Portland Bill.

in Puncknowle, where the landlady insisted that I chain my bike up in the pub's dining room, limiting the number of diners she could accommodate. I discovered Palmers Copper Ale, a local brew described as a 'session ale' and 'the Head Brewer's drink of choice'. I couldn't help but agree.

Day 17

Over breakfast in the Crown Inn, I plotted my route to Exeter, where I had arranged to stay with old friends Jonathan and Penny Harris. My next lighthouse was beyond Exeter, in Teignmouth, some 60 miles away. So today would be my first entirely 'light-less' cycling day.

Blanche, the owner of the Crown, thought otherwise. With my pot of coffee, she handed me an article from the local newspaper, which speculated that an ancient building in nearby Bridport might have once served as a lighthouse. The Chantry is the oldest building in the town, with parts dating to the mid-13th century. The article argued that a semi-circular stone sconce on the building's south wall may have been the support for a torch or fire-basket, leading some historians to suggest that it served partly as a lighthouse or seamark.

I was a little dubious, not least because the Chantry is more than two miles from the sea. However, I imagined returning home triumphantly after successfully conquering every lighthouse around our coast, only to discover that I had left out an important, hitherto unrecognised landmark. Without hesitation I cycled straight into Bridport, located the Chantry and took at least a dozen pictures. I must admit that it didn't look much like a lighthouse to me, but several fellow lighthouse enthusiasts came to mind whom I could irritate with evidence that I had 'bagged' one more lighthouse than they had.

As I freewheeled into the village of Uploders, I passed the entrance to a substantial private house, with tall, meticulously manicured border hedges. A young woman, dressed in what I can only describe as a skimpy French maid's outfit, was balanced on the top rung of a step ladder, leaning precariously to reach a few stray wisps of hedge with a pair of garden shears. Unbelievably, the cut of her dress revealed a pair of red lacy knickers.

For a moment my mind froze. Had I really seen what I thought I had seen? Was my mind playing tricks with me? I was freewheeling at such pace that there was no time to pause or go back. Besides, what would I say or do if I did? Down in the village itself, I found my answer. After passing a suffragette, a pirate, Sherlock Holmes and Her Majesty the Queen, I discovered that my visit to Uploders coincided with their annual Scarecrow Festival.

The 40 or so miles to Exeter were ghastly. I found myself hugging the rumble strip along the side of the busy A35 for nearly ten miles, and by the time I managed to escape onto quieter lanes beyond Wilmington, I was shaking with fear. The last ten miles were mercifully quick, however.

Jonathan and Penny live in a gorgeous, leafy part of Exeter, set a couple of streets back from the River Exe. They left London to move here, and it wasn't hard to see why. Jonathan was managing director of the children's education publisher Letts. He nurtured my early publishing career, and rewarded me with a decent salary, a directorship and a splendid jet-black Volvo 850 Estate, which my colleagues referred to as 'the hearse'. He has always been one of those sickeningly irritating people for whom everything he touches turns to gold. While I eventually left Letts somewhat aimlessly, he did so to set up a new publishing business, as well as his home, down here in Exeter.

Jonathan and Penny are extraordinarily good company. We caught up on nearly two decades' worth of news over lamb and lentils, washed down first with a pot of tea, then a few bottles of St Austell Brewery's Proper Job, and finally a bloody good bottle of red. As I lay in bed reminiscing about the stories we had shared, I spent a little too long wondering how much more accomplished my commercial publishing career might have been if I'd hung on to Jonathan's coattails for just a little longer.

Day 18

Jonathan was up and out by the time I came down for breakfast. He had left at dawn to travel up to Lord's for the first day of the first Test match against New Zealand. I envied him.

My own agenda for the day was a lot more complicated, having agreed many months previously to deliver a speech and present an award at the Fresher Publishing Creative Writing Awards at Bournemouth University.

Leaving my bike in Exeter, I took the five-hour coach back to Poole. Emily had posted a suit and a pair of black shoes to my friend Emma the day before, so that I could look reasonably presentable on the night. When I eventually reached Poole, Emma was there to greet me, clothes parcel in hand.

Emily had clearly been in a hurry when packing my clothes, and the jacket and trousers she had selected were from two different suits. In fact, the trousers were from a suit that had mistakenly been put through the wash and had shrunk dramatically. The black shoes had no laces and the shirt needed cufflinks.

I fashioned a pair of cufflinks out of paperclips, kindly supplied by the hotel reception, which at least meant that I could turn up wearing a respectable shirt. That apart, my only option was to wear my cycling trousers and shoes. I'd need to weave an apology and explanation into my speech.

While being introduced to this year's publishing graduates at the university, I took a call from Zoe, my eldest daughter. My son Tom, who had been enduring a particularly nasty, cowardly spate of bullying at school, had gone missing. What should she do?

I gave my speech, but my heart wasn't in it. My mind was completely focused on Tom, and I must have seemed like one of those people you meet at a party who pretends to be interested in what you have to say, but who isn't quite looking you in the eye. I don't recall whom I spoke to, or even who won the prize. I remember being asked to read the winning short story, but I couldn't tell you what it was about. I looked a mess, in my slightly stained utilitarian cycling trousers. In fact, every student in attendance was better dressed than me. I wanted to be home. I wanted to be there for my son. Not here. Not on my bike. No more lighthouses.

I chose to walk back to my hotel along the seafront. I got news that Tom had been found and was safe and well. But I was tormented by a flashing light out at sea, which reminded me that, yet again, I could see the bloody Needles Lighthouse.

Days 19 and 20

After travelling back to Exeter the next day and spending a second night at the Harris household, I was keen to get going. The first twelve miles out of Exeter followed the Exe Estuary Trail, alongside the River Exe, and were the most beautiful of my journey so far. I recognised Oystercatchers and Terns, but felt ashamed of my inability to identify more of the birdlife I encountered, though these tranquil off-road lanes and tracks made the two recent day-long coach journeys seem a distant memory.

Despite being heavily laden, I was averaging more than fifteen miles an hour for the first time since leaving home, and by mid-morning I was on the seafront at Dawlish Warren – or 'Cornish Sporran', as my brother Will had called it on a family summer holiday when we were both very young.

At the far end of the esplanade at Teignmouth, the lovely little lighthouse is a popular local landmark. As I stopped to take photos I met Brian, a chatty, bearded man in his seventies from Bristol. He told me that he drove down in his campervan every year at this time, always parked next to the lighthouse, and always sat in front of it with his lunch and a book. There was no nicer place on earth, apparently.

The entrance to Teignmouth Harbour has always been treacherous, with a number of dangerous currents, rocks and shifting sands. The small, limestone lighthouse was built in the mid-1840s, lit by three gas burners and showing a fixed red light, with a range of seven miles, to guide ships into the mouth of the harbour. The lighthouse has long since been electrified and still operates to this day. It shows a fixed red light visible for three miles.

There are several other modern and unmemorable lights around the harbour, which I paused at only briefly. Of slightly more interest is the Lucette Beacon, on the opposite side of the harbour. It's not really a lighthouse, I suppose, just a beacon on top of a white metal column. But it clearly has some age, and I was happy to count it.

Beyond Teignmouth, I was in familiar territory. I cycled past the entrance to Babbacombe Model Village, where I have spent many hours over the years searching for superheroes, Daleks and cartoon characters, all hidden in plain sight among the most fantastically realistic recreation of a fictitious British town in miniature.

In Torquay, I remembered a one-night stopover on our way to the Scilly Isles, when Emily and I, together with the three children and our Labrador Willow, all crammed into a tiny room in a cheap hotel high up on the hill above the town.

In Paignton, I passed the theatre on the seafront where we had taken the kids to a variety show a decade earlier, having suffered four consecutive days of rain in a leaking family tent. The show promised a 'sensational summer experience', which was quite a claim, but the children seemed to enjoy it. Sadly, the venue was only half full, and the master of ceremonies had to shout, 'Yes!' very loudly and start clapping to let the audience know when each act had come to an end.

From the harbour at Paignton I took the small ferry across the bay to Brixham, affording me a perfect view of the breakwater lighthouse on arrival. This small cast-iron tower was built in 1916, after the breakwater at Brixham was extended by more than a thousand feet. It shows an occulting red light, visible for three miles, which is powered by electricity. Like in Teignmouth, there are other simple and modern lights marking the entrance to the inner harbour.

I was making good progress, feeling fit and keen to keep moving. I still reckoned on being able to reach two more lights before dark, and planned to find somewhere to stay in Dartmouth. On the headland beyond Brixham lies Berry Head Nature Reserve, a stunning headland, surrounded by water on three sides. It's an area of some renown, being a Special Area of Conservation, National Nature Reserve, Site of Special Scientific Interest and Scheduled Ancient Monument. It's home to a substantial colony of guillemots, a Napoleonic fort and, most importantly, a splendid lighthouse.

Berry Head Lighthouse was built by Trinity House in 1906 under the supervision of Sir Thomas Matthews. It has a small, squat tower, just fifteen-feet tall – one of the smallest lighthouse towers in the British Isles – but at 190 feet above mean high-water level, the headland itself provides all the elevation necessary.

These days it flashes a white light, twice every fifteen seconds, which is visible for nineteen miles.

My last lighthouse of the day was at Kingswear, a small, pretty village on the bank of the River Dart, directly opposite Dartmouth itself. The eight miles from Berry Head were a bit of a slog, involving several narrow lanes where I managed to hold up lines of cars for a good few miles.

Descending into Kingswear, I found Beacon Road, running alongside the river, which sounded promising. I could see the lighthouse marked on my map, but as a result of erosion, a long stretch of the coast path had collapsed, and forbidding signs warned me that both the beach and lighthouse below were now inaccessible.

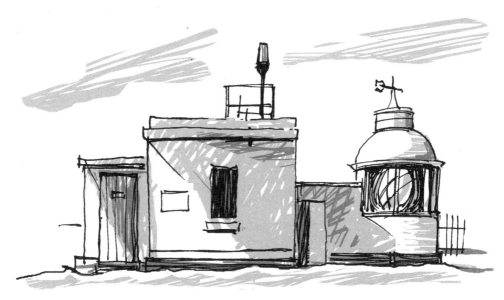

Berry Head.

A group of sandy teenagers suggested otherwise. They pointed out the path that they had emerged from, and within minutes I was down on the beach in front of a very odd little conical-shaped lighthouse. It was built as recently as 1981, from glass-reinforced plastic. Operated by the Dart Harbour and Navigation Authority, it has quite a complicated light pattern, with a white light showing the safe channel, visible for eleven miles, as well as a red sector to the left and a green sector to the right through tiny little windows set into the lantern.

Back in Kingswear, I joined the Lower Ferry crossing over to Dartmouth satisfied with my day's work. But in Dartmouth every pub, B&B and hotel appeared to be full. I found sanctuary at the Stoke Lodge Hotel, a few miles out of town, and by 7pm I was showered and sitting outside with a pint of Tribute and a food menu considerably beyond my budget and pay grade.

There are times when you've just got to do something and worry about the consequences later. This evening was just such an occasion. Money wasn't tight yet, nor was it in plentiful supply. But with few budget items on the menu, I threw caution to the wind. I ordered Crab & Butternut Squash Risotto, followed by Pan Fried Sea Bass Fillet with Crayfish Velouté, washed down with a bottle of house white. I staggered up to bed £60 lighter, but with an enormous grin on my face.

Day 21

I set off from Stoke Fleming determined to make the 50 or so miles to Plymouth and, after last night's extravagance, just as determined to survive on snacks from my panniers alone.

The early morning began with a freewheel downhill to Slapton, via Blackpool Sands. It's a route I know very well, having camped nearby with the family several times. We first discovered Blackpool Sands in 2003, after I lost my temper on the beach at Dawlish, about thirty miles back towards Exeter. It had been a hot day, and the beach at Dawlish was packed, strewn with discarded beer cans, as well as throngs of teenagers playing loud music. I lasted about fifteen minutes before bundling everyone back into the car and committing to drive for as long as it took to find the beach of our dreams. It turned out that the beach of our dreams was Blackpool Sands. The approach by car from above this beautiful, sheltered cove is as stunning as the beach itself. Ask any child to draw a picture of their perfect beach, and it's likely that Blackpool Sands is what they will draw.

I knew I had arrived at the perfect spot the moment we piled out of the car. As we walked onto the sand, the first words I heard came from an elderly man in an olive-green deckchair, who asked: 'Do you think it's too early for a gin and tonic?'

My sort of beach.

After Blackpool Sands, the road to Torcross runs along a narrow strip of land, separating the freshwater lake of Slapton Ley from the beach at Start Bay. Torcross itself is a small, attractive seaside town with a harrowing history. It was evacuated in 1943, along with many other villages in the area, to make way for 15,000 Allied troops who needed the area to practise for the D-Day landings.

In the early hours of 28 April 1944, nine German torpedo boats intercepted a three-mile-long convoy of vessels travelling from the Isle of Portland to Slapton Sands to undertake landing rehearsals for D-Day. Two tank landing ships were sunk and 946 American servicemen died. Poor communications led to badly timed shelling on the beach, killing about 300 more men. Over 1,000 lives were lost over the course of the operation, most of them through US Army friendly fire. A Sherman amphibious tank and several plaques stand at Torcross car park, between Slapton Ley and the beach, as memorials to the men who lost their lives.

The climb out of Torcross towards Start Point Lighthouse was not as demanding as I expected, and I wondered if I was starting to get fitter. Despite fellow cyclists warning me that the Devon coast would likely represent the toughest stretch of the whole journey, I felt relaxed, carefree, and in a more positive state of mind than I had been for several years. It's remarkable how constraining just the diagnosis of multiple sclerosis can be, and how rapidly it can lead to a negative mindset. Naturally, cycling for the majority of each day was tiring me out, but nearly three weeks into the expedition I was suffering no new or lingering symptoms that I could pin on MS.

These were glorious miles, cycling along the prettiest of fern-lined lanes, with the occasional glimpse of the sea to my left and typical Devon pasture to my right. When I reached the car park on the headland above Start Point, a mist had descended. And by the time I had walked down to the lighthouse itself, I was in thick fog. I didn't see the lighthouse at all until I was within 50 feet, its foghorn punctuating the otherwise peaceful surroundings.

I've dragged my children around this lighthouse many times, but I will never tire of the view from the tower. You can see the entire length of Start Bay as far as Dartmouth in the distance. You also get a decent view of what remains of Hallsands, a small fishing harbour lost to the sea in 1917 following extensive dredging offshore for the sand and gravel needed to build the naval dockyard at Keyham, near Plymouth.

Start Point is one of the most exposed peninsulas on the English coast, with a sharp headland running almost a mile out to sea on the south side of Start Bay. The lighthouse, at the end of the headland, was designed by James Walker in 1836. Constructed of granite, its tower is of gothic design, with a castellated balcony immediately below the lantern room. Nowadays, the lighthouse displays a group flashing light, three times every ten seconds, which is visible for eighteen miles.

Start Point.

Leaving Start Point, I knew that the 30 miles or so on to Plymouth were going to be tough, with as many as ten climbs of 300 feet or more. But time was on my side, for the moment at least.

To make up for the previous evening's indulgence, I was determined not to spend any money at all today. I'd avoided the fee at the Start Point car park by walking my bike alongside me. Lunch had comprised of flapjacks and tea from existing supplies, and I reckoned on being able to survive on the same for supper.

After an hour of excruciatingly slow progress, I got a text message from the Thompsons, lovely friends from Kent, who were themselves staying with farming friends near Yealmpton, just a few miles ahead of me. Jo had been following my progress avidly and was proving to be a big fan.

As I reached the driveway to an attractive Devon farmhouse, I was met with colourful streams of bunting, balloons, Jo's children Jessie and Edward, as well as Jo herself, beaming her infectious smile. This was a regular May half-term fixture for the Thompsons, and seeing handfuls of children running excitedly around the farm, I felt as though I had somehow transported myself into the plot of an Enid Blyton story.

Jo's farming friends – Stuart and Jo – were lovely and insisted that I stayed for supper. Where just an hour earlier I had planned a supper of a cereal bar and a mug of tea, now I was sitting down to a substantial roast dinner. It was nearly 8pm when we finished, and I got up, reluctantly, to leave.

Stuart suggested I stay overnight, but I was keen to press on. Enjoying my evening with two such lovely families, a wave of homesickness began to overwhelm me, and I sobbed copiously for much of the last ten miles into Plymouth.

I found a cheap, rundown hotel by the harbour, where the dozens of fixed and flashing lights from my bedroom window brought me back to my senses and beckoned me onwards.

WEEK 4

Day 22

Plymouth has been an important port for many centuries. It was from Plymouth that the Pilgrim Fathers departed for the New World in 1620 and established Plymouth Colony, the second English settlement in what is now the United States of America.

It's an important city for the Royal Navy, too, and the naval base in neighbouring Devonport is the largest in Western Europe today. The city's strategic importance meant that it was bombed heavily during the war, and the city centre had to be completely rebuilt in the 1940s and 50s.

The bay at Plymouth, known as Plymouth Sound, looks safe enough to the naked eye, but the dozens of beacons and flashing lights visible from my hotel window suggested otherwise. In fact, if you wanted to investigate the source of every flashing light visible from Plymouth Hoe, you'd need at least a week. For now, I had less than a day, thanks to a wonderfully kind invitation to spend a week at the Lizard Lighthouse, the most southerly point on the British mainland, on the South Cornwall coast.

The opportunity came from Emma, who had taken out a six-month rent on one of the keepers' cottages. She wrote:

I'm just sitting here with the *Sunday Telegraph* and reading about your epic adventure. I am currently renting a cottage for six months at Lizard Lighthouse. If you would like to stay a night or two you are more than welcome.

The Lizard rental was Emma's own epic adventure, once her son had left home for university and her daughter had embarked on a gap-year adventure to South East Asia. But after just a month in Cornwall, Emma's daughter had been involved in a moped accident in Cambodia, had suffered serious head trauma and returned home.

Although her daughter was recovering well, Emma wasn't in a position to return to the Lizard, which prompted her incredibly generous offer. What began as an invitation to stay a night or two quickly turned into the whole of my children's school half-term week. It meant that Emily and the children could drive down from Kent to join me. A week off. A holiday. With the family. In Cornwall. In a lighthouse. And not just any lighthouse. A lighthouse I didn't know and had wanted to visit all my life.

It required pausing the journey here in Plymouth, catching a train to Truro, then cycling the 27 miles to the Lizard by nightfall where, all being well, Emily and the children would be waiting for me. After the week at the Lizard, I would retrace my route, by bike and train, to start back again in Plymouth at the weekend.

That left me the morning to chalk up the majority of the poles and beacons around Plymouth Sound, as well as the famous lighthouse on the promenade at Plymouth Hoe.

I started on the promenade. It is said that it was here, on the lush green lawned headland, that Sir Francis Drake insisted on finishing his game of bowls before heading out to defeat the Spanish Armada in 1588. This morning, a local funfair was being unpacked and unfolded from trailers for the upcoming Bank Holiday weekend.

I thought that nothing would distract me from my path to the lighthouse, but I found myself looking down in awe at the Art Deco lido, which had just reopened for the summer season. Built in the 1930s, it's a saltwater swimming pool of a type that is increasingly rare. There are a handful closer to home on the Kent and Sussex coasts, but many are in poor repair, some abandoned altogether. This one is remarkably well-preserved and gives a sense of Plymouth's splendour and prosperity before the war.

The lighthouse on the Hoe is one of the most popular tourist attractions in Devon, and although I was at the entrance at the 10am opening time, there was already a queue of people wanting to look around it. The views from the lantern are extraordinary, both out to sea and over the city itself. With views like these, I'd happily make Plymouth my home.

When the rock base underneath John Smeaton's lighthouse on the Eddystone Reef was found to be unstable in the 1880s, plans were made to dismantle the tower and rebuild it on the Hoe at Plymouth. Smeaton's Tower at Eddystone was officially decommissioned in 1882, once the new lighthouse, designed by John Douglass, was completed. A new base was constructed in Plymouth to accommodate the lighthouse, and then the tower was dismantled and rebuilt on the Hoe, stone by stone. It's a prominent and much-loved landmark to this day.

I had counted upwards of 30 lights from my bedroom window the previous evening, most of which my research

Smeaton's lighthouse on Plymouth Hoe.

indicated were modern, metal-framed lights of one sort or another. I spent most of the rest of the day checking them off, and there were plenty that had merit, even if they stretched the dictionary definition of a lighthouse.

Although the modern pair of leading lights on the Hoe, below Smeaton's Tower, were of little interest, I found a charming little light at Cattewater Approaches. No more than about six-feet tall, it has a small black reflector that gives its domed roof a beak, and I dare say that late at night, after an evening on the town, you would be forgiven for mistaking it for a lone penguin.

The range lights near the Royal Western Yacht Club were unremarkable, with the rear light set into the roof of the yacht club building itself. I was starting to understand why the only two lighthouses in Plymouth that people ever mention are Eddystone and Smeaton's Tower.

On the opposite bank, at the entrance to the marina at Mount Batten Point, there is a substantial, red-painted lighthouse lantern set into the ground. It looks a little unloved, with its red paint peeling away, but the optics inside are splendid. With so many lighthouse optics removed and replaced by tiny, modern lenses, this is a rarity.

Following a punishing cycle uphill to see the circular concrete tower at Staddon Point and its neighbouring offshore beacon, I'd had enough. Although I was knocking these lights off the list quite quickly, I felt little enthusiasm for the task. My mind was focused on catching the train to Truro and seeing the family for the first time in a month. I decided to leave the rest of the Plymouth lights for my return in a week's time.

The train service from Plymouth to Truro is part of the mainline service between Paddington and Penzance. It's a decent, twice-hourly service, although their policy concerning bicycles seems a little random. Each train has a dedicated compartment for oversize luggage and bicycles, with a maximum capacity of just six bikes. Unless there is a vacant bicycle rack when you board, you can't get on the train.

It doesn't take much to make me anxious at the best of times, but this was off the scale. I was on the platform with nearly half an hour to spare, but there were already two other cyclists waiting. What were the chances that there would be three vacant spaces on the next train? How many trains would I have to wave off before finding one with space? I paced up and down the platform, my bicycle at my side, worrying about where the carriage with the goods compartment would stop. Could I beat the other two to it? Why were they looking so relaxed? Had they pre-booked spaces? The whole problem seemed insurmountable, until the train pulled in and the three of us wheeled our bikes into a completely empty goods carriage.

Emerging from Truro railway station, I reckoned I had about a 25-mile ride, about three hours, to the Lizard. It didn't count as far as the adventure was concerned, because I would be covering these same miles all over again the following week. So I took the most direct route, along NCN Route 3, and opted for speed and stamina rather than scenery.

In Helston, I found a supermarket and bought one of every variety of pizza they had. Less than an hour later, Zoe, Tom and Lottie were giving me the guided tour of the lighthouse grounds and cottage. Tom had already set up camp in the little living room, with dozens of his little games cartridges piled up on each arm of the sofa. Complicated wiring, chargers and consoles everywhere.

I put on a pair of normal, everyday jeans, laid every pizza out on the kitchen table, opened a bottle of Malbec and felt like a proper dad again for the first time in a month.

Days 23 to 26

Half-term week at the Lizard was special. At Emma's recommendation, we walked over the cliffs to Kynance Cove, where we spent a windy few hours on the beach, alternating between homemade pasties and flapjacks from the splendid beach cafe.

Lottie had brought her multicoloured pocket kite – designed to fly in all conditions, and with a *no-knots guarantee*. We paused on the springy, gorse headland above the cove to give it a go, but it spent more time on the ground than in the air, and after one particularly aggressive tailspin, its ribbons became plaited – permanently – with the kite's single string.

We discovered the beautiful sandy beach at Poldhu, owned by the National Trust, where we made the classic mistake of laying down our towels to claim our spot away from the crowds at low tide, and then having to move everything in a hurry – twice – as the tide came in.

We spent an almost perfect day meandering the gardens and beach at Trebah. But throughout, Tom was very quiet. Silent, in fact. The bullying he had been suffering at school hadn't stopped. The school was apparently sympathetic but said they could only intervene if Tom was prepared to put forward a name, something he steadfastly refused to do. He was certain that a formal complaint would only make matters worse, and so Tom was reduced to spending his days in solitude, silence and frequently in tears.

As a parent, there can be few more difficult or upsetting challenges to face. Emily and I had each tried to talk with him, but there was no question of him telling us who was involved. I spent a lot of half-term week just squeezing his hand, wishing it was all different. From my own perspective, I didn't feel I could wave the family off home and continue on my journey until or unless we were able to ease Tom's suffering.

Like many dads, I just wanted the name of the nasty little brat who was causing my son such misery, so that I could turn the tables on him and make every day for the rest of his life utter hell. Emily wasn't as convinced as I was that this would be a constructive course of action to take.

My state of mind wasn't being helped by an author whose book I had helped to publish a few months earlier. She turned out to be exceedingly high maintenance, emailing me several times a day with a series of petty requests, comments and suggestions from her readers. While I was walking hand in hand with Tom, in silence, through the tropical gardens at Trebah, she texted to say that she had just forwarded an email of complaint from a reader that I needed to address and respond to straight away.

If this was all designed to test me, and to mess with my head, then it was proving very effective. As I read and replied to my author's email, my phone fluctuated between one bar and no signal at all. The email failed to send. Several times. But on the fourth attempt, it suddenly felt as though I had emerged into the light. What on earth was I doing? Why was I allowing this paltry email, from this small-minded and ungrateful writer, to affect me so badly? To ruin the short time I had with my family? All this, at a time when my family – my son – really needed me.

I vowed to myself, there and then, that I would email the author to inform her that she would need to find a new publisher and distributor for her book. Then I caught up with Tom, and sat him next to me on a bench while I gave him the speech of my life about the consequences of bullying, of allowing bullies to go unchallenged, of the others who would suffer at his hands if we didn't take action. He listened, in complete silence, for a long time.

And then he gave me a name …

On Friday morning we packed our bags in silence. I shifted, seemingly without warning, between sadness that Emily and the children were about to say goodbye for what would be a couple of months at least, to exhaustion at the emotional toll that the week had taken, to excitement that the journey was about to restart.

Before setting off, Lottie and I took a tour of the Lizard Lighthouse, something we had spectacularly failed to do in the four days since we arrived. We learned that there had been considerable local opposition to the idea of building a lighthouse here, thanks to the healthy profits to be made from salvaging cargo from the numerous ships that wrecked or ran aground off the point.

The first lighthouse here was completed by Cornish philanthropist Sir John Killigrew in 1619. Its maintenance and upkeep was to be funded by the tolls collected from ships that passed the point. However, these were deemed to be voluntary, and as a result the lighthouse fell into disrepair. By 1630 it was derelict.

More than 100 years later, in 1748, Trinity House supported a proposal by Thomas Fonnerau to construct a new light at Lizard. The original proposal was for four towers, although this was eventually scaled back to two. They were completed and first lit in August 1752.

The two octagonal towers stand 62-feet high, joined by a row of two-storey keepers' cottages. The lanterns were originally

Lizard.

coal fired, but were replaced with Argand lamps in 1812 and then electrified in 1878.

In 1903, a rotating optic with a high-powered carbon arc light was installed in the eastern tower, and the western tower's lantern was decommissioned and removed. The carbon arc light was replaced with an electric lamp in 1936, and today the lighthouse displays a white flashing light, which is visible for 26 miles.

As the tour came to an end, I saw Emily's car fully packed and ready to leave. I felt my emotions get the better of me and started to cry. As I waved the family off, I decided that it was time to give up. By train, I could be home by nightfall. In fact, I could probably get back before the others. I could demand a meeting with Tom's school on Monday morning and fire off an email to the author who had become the bane of my life.

But what then? How would I feel tomorrow? Or the next day? Or the following week, having given up with less than a third of my adventure completed?

Determined to fight on, I needed to distract myself from the doubts and anxiety in my head. Before my MS diagnosis, I used to love hiking and long-distance walking. I could keep myself going for ages, just by repeating a count of one to eight in line with my steps, one-two-three-four-five-six-seven-eight. And then start back at the beginning, one-two-three-four-five-six-seven-eight.

I found that I was able to do something similar with the rotation of my pedals. I counted eight rotations, and then I counted eight more. And then 8 more. And then another eight. I covered the ten miles back to Helston in 45 minutes, and barely two hours after that, I was boarding a train back to Plymouth at Truro station.

I was in Plymouth by early afternoon, where I found a guesthouse close to the hotel where I had stayed the previous week. I still had a handful of unexciting lights and beacons to see on the western side of Plymouth Sound, and I knew that if I didn't force myself back out this afternoon I probably wouldn't bother with them at all. An afternoon with too much thinking time and I'd talk myself into heading home again.

I found and ticked off two lights at Millbay Pier, followed by a small metal column at Eastern King, and then a red-and-white striped navigation light at Devil's Point. Only the last of these merited more than a token selfie.

Although not in my guidebook, I noticed a light on my map near Maker, opposite Devil's Point. I crossed the River Tamar to Mount Edgcumbe Park on the Cremyll Ferry, and was standing by the light barely ten minutes later. The house and gardens at Edgcumbe, with spectacular views over the water to the city, were much more interesting than the light I had come to see.

It's fair to say that if I hadn't been looking for ways to occupy my thoughts, I wouldn't have bothered to track this light down. But I was glad of the distraction, and keen not to think about Emily and the children, back at home without me. I retraced my steps and caught the ferry back to Admiral's Hard in Plymouth.

That left just two of Plymouth's peripheral lights, neither of which looked promising. The first turned out to be a small pyramidal tower near Mayflower Marina, mounted onto a corner of a multi-storey complex of riverside apartments. At least the other light, at Mount Wise Pier, had some age. Its fixed lights shine from a square weather-boarded structure, a bit like an old-fashioned bus shelter. It also acts as a daymark, with the seaward face painted in red-and-white stripes. Few would consider it a lighthouse, but at least it has been designed and constructed with purpose and care.

I had one final mission in Plymouth, which was to see the Plymouth Breakwater light, as well as the most famous lighthouse of them all: Eddystone. For now, though, I just needed sleep. Since breakfast I had toured the Lizard Lighthouse, seen the family off, cycled to Truro, taken the train to Plymouth and then cycled another 30 or so miles. Having avoided giving head space to any dark or sad thoughts all day, I phoned home but got no answer. I phoned Emily's mobile, only to discover that with Devon-and-Cornwall-bank-holiday-weekend traffic, they had travelled barely 75 miles all day, and had spent most of it in stationary traffic near Bristol.

Day 27

I was at Cattewater Harbour at dawn, having been granted passage on a boat about to embark on a six-hour fishing trip. With luck, it would get me up close to the Plymouth Breakwater Lighthouse, and deliver at least a decent long-lens shot of Eddystone.

I found an all-night shop and bought a handful of pork pies, scotch eggs, crisps, chocolate and water. Who knew what I might need for six hours at sea? I also packed my tiny portable radio and earphones, because England were playing New Zealand in the second Test at Headingley and I didn't want to miss a ball.

There were ten of us booked on the boat, and we met, bleary eyed, by the harbour steps. We were told to look out for the *Explorer*, a light-blue vessel skippered by Ken Bridge, who has been operating fishing and pleasure boats in Plymouth for 45 years.

My nine fellow passengers were here for the fishing, and bream, bass, ling and pollock were on the menu. They were all amateur fishermen, although a party of seven were taking it very seriously indeed. They were dressed in barely used full-length green waders and the sort of yellow waterproof jackets that you only ever see in advertisements for fish fingers. My guess was that trade at the local chandlery had been unusually brisk the previous afternoon.

Then there were Rob and Sam, an about-to-be-married couple in their early twenties who were clearly enjoying still being able to holiday during school term times. Rob had obviously been extolling the thrills of deep-sea fishing, although I think it's fair to say that Sam was yet to be convinced.

Ken is a jovial skipper and host, and I sensed a barely concealed smile as the party of seven climbed aboard in their matching seafaring apparel. He greeted Rob and Sam heartily, expressing a little concern that six hours in rough seas might be a bit much for the young lady. He greeted me equally warmly, but didn't know quite what to make of me. We had spoken by phone the previous afternoon, and he had willingly offered me a place on the boat for a tenner, as long as I promised not to fish. It was a promise I was happy to make, although now I was here he was worried that there wouldn't be much in it for me.

Having reassured Ken that a photo of the breakwater light and seeing Eddystone were genuinely the only rewards I sought, we steered gently out of the harbour. I hadn't appreciated quite how far out the breakwater is sited, nor how substantial a structure it is at 1,500 metres long.

Initially, a lightvessel was moored at the western end of the breakwater, but in 1841 the Admiralty commissioned a 78-foot tower, constructed from Cornish white granite. It was first lit in 1844, displaying a white flashing light that is visible for one-and-a-half miles. In 1854 a second white light was added, from a window lower down in the tower, indicating the safe harbour entrance channel.

The original plan was for a similar lighthouse to mark the eastern end of the breakwater, but this was not considered cost-effective. Instead, a beacon was erected, which included a spherical cage designed to accommodate up to six shipwrecked sailors.

In percentage terms, this was my most productive day so far. It was barely 9am, and with both breakwater lights reached I had already achieved two-thirds of my target for the day. But it counted for nothing unless I also saw Eddystone, arguably the most famous offshore lighthouse of them all.

For now, though, I was at a bit of a loss. We would be trying out a number of fishing spots before having so much as a chance of seeing Eddystone, the cricket didn't start for another couple of hours, and I'd forfeited my right to a fishing rod. I guess most people's advice would be just to sit back, relax and take in the view. But advice like that rarely serves me very well, and within fifteen minutes my mind wandered to money worries, whether I'd have any work when I eventually returned home, what action Tom's school would take with his tormentor, and whether my bike was safe in the foyer of the guesthouse. And that was just the beginning. Believe me, I may not be the best at multitasking, but I hold the record for the number of simultaneous worries and anxieties that it is possible to dwell on in a single moment.

We anchored near a wreck, apparently renowned for plentiful shoals of black bream and bass. Ken produced a tray of strong tea in mismatched mugs, and then patiently equipped the party with rods, weights and bait. The party of seven were confident that they knew it all and required no assistance. Rob and Sam gladly accepted Ken's help, and Sam seemed genuinely pleased to be kitted out with a mackerel line, which required no bait, only shiny, reflective metal lures with hooks at one end.

We fished for nearly an hour. Sam caught at least a dozen mackerel, Rob one decent-sized sea bass, and the party in fancy dress absolutely nothing. Ken was permanently on the move, unhooking Sam's mackerel, offering suggestions and tips to the party who knew it all already, washing mugs and producing more tea.

With all the rods reeled in, we moved to the site of another wreck. The procedure was the same, except this time I had an irritating last wicket stand by the New Zealanders to occupy me – 350 all out. A much more respectable total than it should have been.

At around midday, Ken invited me into the wheelhouse. He had a folder of photographs of Eddystone to show me, both early and contemporary. The lighthouse clearly meant a lot to Ken, a constant symbol of his 45 years in these waters. Soon afterwards, he pointed dead ahead, and there it was, just a small dot on the horizon. With my zoom lens I could see all the missing detail, *if only this damn boat would stay still for just a second.* I took 30 photos, at least, of the sky, the sea, the deck ... I seemed to catalogue the entire seascape comprehensively, apart from the lighthouse itself.

Ken secured agreement from everyone to head towards the lighthouse, promising excellent fishing close to the rocks. This was all that nine of the ten members of the party needed to hear.

It was a calm afternoon, but there was a silence in the waters around the Eddystone rock that was both eerie and calming at the same time. It's almost impossible to imagine the feat of engineering demanded to construct a tower here, on this isolated rocky outcrop. To be sitting in this boat, in the shadow surrounding the base of this tower, was humbling. It really was …

The current Eddystone Lighthouse is the fourth to mark the small but dangerous Eddystone Rocks, fourteen miles south-west of Plymouth. The first tower, built by eccentric Henry Winstanley, was completed in 1698 and was the first tower rock lighthouse at sea in the world. When waves 90-feet high crashed over the lighthouse during its first winter of operation, Winstanley returned and rebuilt it, almost doubling its girth and raising its height to 120 feet. Built of wood and stone, it survived only four years, before both the tower and Winstanley himself perished during a hurricane in 1703.

The second tower was designed by architect John Rudyerd, who favoured a cone-shaped design over Winstanley's octagonal shape. Completed in 1709, it stood for nearly 50 years until it was destroyed by fire in 1755.

The third tower, designed by John Smeaton, is the one currently sited on Plymouth Hoe, following its decommission in 1882. His inspiration is said to have come from the shape of an English oak tree, something in nature proven to withstand gales and storms. It is a shape that has been adopted in the construction of rock lighthouses ever since. Work began in 1756, using 1,493 blocks of local granite. He also pioneered an ingenious method of securing each block of stone to its neighbour, using dovetail joints and marble dowels.

Smeaton's Tower was lit for the first time in October 1759 and stood for 120 years. In fact, it was because of cracks in the rocks supporting the lighthouse, rather than in the tower itself, that a new lighthouse was required in the 1870s.

The fourth and current lighthouse was designed by Trinity House engineer-in-chief Sir James Douglass. It's another granite tower, broader in its base than its top, which was first lit in

May 1882. Its revolving optic was operated by clockwork, with a large weight on a chain that needed to be wound for fifteen minutes each hour. Two Argand oil lamps were converted to paraffin in 1906, and the lighthouse was eventually automated and fully electrified in 1982. It flashes twice every ten seconds, and has a range of seventeen nautical miles.

After Eddystone, my cup of happiness was full, and I was content to put the anxieties in my chattering mind aside for a while. It felt like a reward for the various poles, beacons and columns I had diligently ticked off my list during my two visits to Plymouth.

Back in the harbour, the final tally of fish was counted, and Rob and Sam were clear winners. In fact, the guys who knew it

Eddystone.

all and needed no help had barely scraped together a barbecue's worth between them. Still, those waders will come in handy for something, I'm sure. And the rubberised sailcloth jackets will look great on the back seats of their Range Rovers at home.

By early evening I was pedalling steeply out of Plymouth for the last time. I had arranged to meet up with an old friend in Fowey the next day, and unless I got some miles behind me this evening I was unlikely to make it. I vowed to keep going until I found a decent-looking pub with rooms.

I struck gold in Menheniot, a pretty village a couple of miles outside Liskeard. The White Hart looked splendid with its recent coat of pale-yellow paint, and dozens of hanging baskets and window boxes boasting flora of every colour in the rainbow. I found welcoming staff, a comfortable room, decent food and several pints of immaculately kept Tribute bitter.

Day 28

Looe is only eight miles from the White Hart, but the route for cyclists was not an easy one, and once again I held up traffic along a series of minor roads. Looe starts alongside the East Looe River, a couple of miles from the harbour, but the town centre itself seemed a long time coming. Even when I eventually reached the pretty shopping streets, I was happy enough to take my time, and got side-tracked by a wonderfully artistic display of award-winning Cornish pasties at the Cornish Bakehouse. It was still early in the day, but I was becoming used to a daily pasty and this looked like too good an opportunity to miss.

Looe has been a popular holiday resort since Victorian times. The town also still boasts a small fishing fleet, with 120 people employed in the industry. I was heading for the Banjo Pier, best reached by chaining up the bike and walking across the small family beach. I took off my shoes and enjoyed feeling the warm sand on my feet. The water was crystal clear, and frighteningly cold. Several families were swimming happily, clearly hardier than me.

Looe's Banjo Pier Lighthouse is unexciting. Although apparently built in 1860, its red cylindrical lantern, mounted on a twenty-foot cast-iron pole, seems more modern. There's a small iron-railed gallery surrounding it, with a fixed metal ladder providing access. It displays a red-and-white occulting light, which is visible for fifteen miles.

Polperro is only five miles on from Looe, although I chose the slightly longer, easier route following NCN Route 2. It's much smaller than Looe, although hundreds more people seemed to be milling about than the town has capacity for. It is also devastatingly pretty, so it's easy to see why the visitors come. Its lanes are narrow, barely more than the width of a car, yet somehow cars and pedestrians share the road amicably enough. The steep banks on either side of the town are lush and green, and the view down to the harbour can't have changed much in 100 years.

Although I found a simple red lantern on the end of the western pier of the harbour, I was more interested in the light at Spy House Point, just outside Polperro. It was built in 1911 to guide vessels away from the dangerous East Polca and Peak rocks, and is a small, black-and-white painted, cylindrical brick tower mounted on stone paving. It emits quick flashing lights, red to the west and white to the east, which are visible for eight miles.

The road from Polperro to Polruan was typically Cornish and absolutely breathtaking. Gorse bushes sprouting vivid yellow flowers lined the route, with frequent gaps to take in lush, green rolling hills to my right, and cliffs and the sea to my left.

Polruan is another beautiful Cornish village, but it felt quieter and more relaxed than either Looe or Polperro. I suspect that's because on the opposite bank of the river lies the more fashionable harbour town of Fowey.

The ferry across the River Fowey cost £4, including my bicycle. The crossing took only a few minutes, and we landed at Whitehouse Pier, where two of the four lights I had come to see were waiting for me. At the end of the quay itself is a modern, undistinguished light mounted on a metal frame on top of a concrete structure.

More interesting is the red-painted cast-iron cylinder, mounted on a narrow, red column, a few metres away. It emits a white flashing light, visible for eight miles, as well as sector lights – green to the right and red to the left. It's both unusual and noteworthy, although as I wheeled my bike towards the town centre it dawned on me that I had an incinerator bin in the garden at home that looked very similar.

Fowey is arguably the most attractive harbour town in Cornwall, and it is easy to see why it has inspired so many writers over the years, including Daphne du Maurier and Kenneth Grahame. But it has also served as a major port for centuries, first for the navy and more recently for the export of china clay.

I was here to meet up with Sarah, a dear friend from my days selling maps and travel books at Stanfords. The last time I had seen her was at her wedding, more than fifteen years ago.

I took refuge in the Brown Sugar Cafe in South Street, and then sent Sarah a text to let her know I was here. She's a graphic designer, and her studio was nearby. I was so pleased to see her, and we picked up effortlessly on news and gossip about friends and former colleagues. She is also a lighthouse enthusiast and was able to point me in the direction of Readymoney Cove, from where I could take the coast path up on to the headland to see the principal Fowey light at St Catherine's Point.

A couple of hours passed and I didn't want to leave, but I was keen to get to St Austell this evening and there were still two lights to see. A steep, stepped path from Readymoney Cove took me up on to the headland, and after a prolonged hunt I found an extremely disappointing light close to the castle ruins, looking little different from the sort of lamp you'd see on top of an old fashioned ambulance.

Further along the headland, I spotted a small wrought iron gate, almost entirely covered with brambles. It took an age to inch my way through, and then on to a dark, overgrown path. This time, though, it was worth the effort, and I was rewarded with the bright-red cast-iron lantern built in 1904. It's a handsome structure, and sits on an octagonal base with red-painted iron railings around it. Its white flashing light can be seen for eleven miles to mark the safe entry channel into the harbour. It also emits red flashing sector lights, which are visible for nine miles.

My work in Fowey was almost done, but as I was up on the headland already, I decided to walk on to see the Gribbin

Daymark. It's not a lighthouse, nor has it ever served as one, but it is a substantial daymark, 85-feet tall, built in 1832 'for the safety of commerce and the preservation of mariners' – so it held some relevance, after all.

With St Austell still eight miles away, I had not yet arranged anywhere to stay. The hot tip for budget travellers appeared to be the local youth hostel. I hadn't stayed at a youth hostel for the best part of 30 years, and I hadn't appreciated that I still qualified. The YHA had set up a temporary hostel at the Eden Project, Cornwall's global garden housed in tropical biomes, with plants collected from many diverse climates and environments throughout the world.

I booked what was described as a bed in a 'pod', one of a group of sleeping pods made from shipping containers, each technically able to sleep four people. I say 'technically' because space was at a premium. Once inside the door, there was room only to get into whichever bed was yours, and one further step into an open-doored shower and toilet. If you were sharing this with three other people, it would certainly help if you already knew them intimately. If you didn't, then you certainly would by the time you left.

Fortunately, feedback from previous travellers had brought the cramped conditions to the attention of the management team, and single travellers were now being assigned their own pod. This changed everything. I could assign one bed to my luggage and another to me. Far from feeling cramped, I felt I was staying in relative luxury.

A central marquee served as reception, bar, cafe and meeting area. I'd arrived too late for an evening meal, and the nearest pub was further away than I was prepared to travel. So I fashioned a meal from crisps, cake and a pork pie left over from the previous day, washed down with a couple of bottles of beer. Just like the youth hostels of my (genuine) youth, the protocol seemed to be to sit with your fellow travellers and share stories of your journey to date. I chose to slip away quietly, back to my pod, where I fell asleep watching the cricket highlights on my phone.

WEEK 5

Day 29

My YHA pod was surprisingly comfortable, and with the shipping container affording almost no natural light, it was nearly 9am before I woke up. However, the pouring rain and gale-force winds provided little incentive to leave the relative shelter of the forestry surrounding the Eden Project.

I sat in the marquee reading until 11am, when I abandoned any hope that the weather was about to clear. The ten miles to Mevagissey were quick, such was the strength of the wind behind me, for a change. But the harbour front was so blowy that I had to get off the bike and push the last half mile.

I love Mevagissey. It was once the centre of Cornwall's pilchard-fishing industry, and the village's distinctive inner and outer harbours are still used by several-dozen small fishing boats today. It's an extremely attractive village, nestled in a small valley between the steep slopes of the surrounding hillsides. Although its narrow streets are full of gift shops, craft workshops, galleries, cafes and pubs, it feels more of a working village than others along this stretch of coast and is all the nicer for it.

From the haven of the aptly named Lighthouse Cafe, the steamed-up windows suggested that the weather had not cleared. Judging by how each new customer entered, theatrically sighing while shaking out each layer of clothing as it was removed, it had in fact got worse. I inched my way around the harbour, onto the pier, and just about made out the white tower on the end.

The Victorian Pier Head Lighthouse was built in 1896 to protect the outer harbour. It has a hexagonal cast-iron tower, painted white with a black band around the base. The lantern houses a white light that flashes twice every ten seconds. The light is visible for twelve miles, and there is also a fog signal mounted on the gallery that sounds every 30 seconds in reduced visibility.

Leaving Mevagissey, there should have been time enough to cycle the twenty or so miles on to St Anthony's, famous for the distinctive lighthouse that my generation remember because of Jim Henson's TV show *Fraggle Rock*. It wasn't the mileage that concerned me, but the nine hills that my route planner indicated stood in my way. Even after a month on the road, I had acquired no satisfactory strategy for cycling uphill. Regardless of the gear I selected, or how carefully I paced myself, whenever my route began to climb I started to feel giddy and faint, and my legs would tremble and quiver uncontrollably. I suspect that MS played a part, because balance and surefootedness have always been an obstacle, but whatever the cause I just felt more confident pushing the bike up hills.

A few-hundred metres before St Anthony's Lighthouse is a quay, from where I could make a ten-minute ferry crossing to Falmouth on the other side of the bay, where I was booked to stay. However, the last ferry of the day was at 6pm, and missing it would mean an additional 30-mile cycle around the bay, via Truro.

I took a punt. Foolish, really, as barely an hour into the ride I realised that I could have cycled straight to Falmouth and then caught the ferry to St Anthony's first thing in the morning. It was too late, though, and I was committed. The rain was relentless, as were the winds. It was hateful cycling, requiring a stop every half mile or so to clean and de-mist my glasses. Several times I considered abandoning my plans and finding somewhere local to stay. But it became increasingly obvious that there was nowhere *local*, and that I was on a beautiful but entirely empty peninsular, with just the occasional farmhouse and parked-up camper van for company.

Against the odds, I reached St Anthony's at around 5pm. It's a remarkable building, and I was envious of people who book the former keepers' accommodation for a holiday. It was exactly as I'd imagined, and I couldn't help but hum the *Fraggle Rock* theme tune that was such a part of my childhood.

The lighthouse was built in 1835 to mark the entrance to Falmouth Harbour, guiding shipping away from the Manacles, a series of treacherous rocks off the Lizard peninsula. It was designed by Trinity House's consultant engineer James Walker, and has an octagonal granite tower, 62-feet tall, with balcony and lantern, and two-storey keepers' accommodation attached.

Originally powered by eight Argand oil lamps, its flashing pattern was delivered using revolving parabolic reflectors, powered by clockwork. Mains electricity was installed in 1954, and the lighthouse was automated in 1987.

These days it shows an occulting white light, visible for sixteen miles, as well as a red sector to mark the Manacles, visible for twenty miles.

Through tears of nostalgia, mixed with rain that refused to give way, I was glad to have made it, and I cycled on to the quay pleased with my accomplishment. However, my contentment was extremely short lived. Due to the winds and sea conditions, no ferry was running.

Exhausted, hungry and nearly 30 miles from Falmouth, I tried to come up with a plan, but I had absolutely nothing to offer. Far from clearing up, the skies were closing in and the rain and gales were as strong as they had been all day.

At 6.30pm, I concluded that my only option was to cycle through the weather as far as Truro, and on to Falmouth if it was still light. I never wish to revisit the four-and-a-half additional cycling hours that followed, even in my mind.

It was not until 10pm that I arrived at the Falmouth Lodge Backpackers hostel in Falmouth and was welcomed by Judy, an eccentric and Bohemian host, who has created her refuge in the image and style of the backpacking hostels she frequented in her own travelling days.

Everything I carried was soaked through, with the most serious casualty my phone. It was my connection with family,

St Anthony's.

and my means of plotting the journey and posting about it for the small but enthusiastic audience I had built up. The screen was dead, and I could see water moving about underneath the glass.

The fate of the phone seemed symbolic, representing how I felt at that moment. This was it. I was done. Spent. I would head home in the morning.

Day 30

Whatever decision I made about my next steps, it was patently obvious that I was going nowhere today. I would need to spend the day washing and drying clothes, finding a new phone, replacing guidebooks and recreating notes relating to client work. Fortunately, my Kindle and cameras were all stored in waterproof cases and were undamaged.

With panniers, wash bag, first aid kit, charging cables and stationery all drying out in front of Judy's kitchen Aga, I buried my phone in a bowl of rice – although it was evident that it had made its last call.

When I had arrived late the previous night, the downstairs dormitory had been full, but this morning there was only one other resident. He had long hair, with beard, tattoos and weathered skin that had clearly spent a lot of its life outdoors. I found him a little intimidating at first, one of those perpetual travellers who seem to stroll effortlessly through life, no matter what it throws at them. He was also impossible to age, and I had no idea whether he was 25 or 50. He was probably somewhere in between.

As I so often do, I had rushed to judge him, and he turned out to be enormously good company. His name was Nigel, and he had recently returned from Portugal, where he had spent several years working with boats. He fell out with his employer, came home and was now weighing up employment opportunities. There was a chance of boat-repair work here in Falmouth, but if this didn't come off then there were other opportunities to pursue in Swindon, as well as over on the Essex coast. He was in no hurry to decide.

Having briefly witnessed my mental state last night, he was also keen to help me out this morning. Noticing that my brakes looked ropey, he got some tools out, stripped them down and rebuilt them. When he was done, they were as responsive as on the very first morning.

He walked with me down into town, where I committed to a second, pricey mobile-phone contract, the only way I could think of to replace my phone without spending all the money I had left. As if to cement the extent to which I had misjudged Nigel, on the walk back he asked if I'd like to stop for a beer, and he admitted he was a bit lonely. He had a strange though endearing habit of changing a single syllable in lots of his words. He suggested we start at 'Witherspoons', and once two pints were ordered, he asked me what I thought of 'Jody'. I thought he was playing some sort of word game at first, and tried to join in, but I quickly realised that it was just Nigel. (Or 'Nagel'?)

Heading back to the hostel mid-evening, we only got as far as the Chain Locker, a lovely old pub on the waterfront, where I was in familiar territory with a couple of pints of Proper Job. Nigel seemed genuinely unbothered about his next steps, and it wouldn't have surprised me if he was in Falmouth this time next year, still considering his next move. We were from different worlds, but the conversation flowed liberally.

Back at the hostel, everything I owned was clean and dry. When I switched on my new phone, having restored an online backup, I discovered that Emily had spent the day contacting friends, family and supporters, urging them to get in touch with words of encouragement. A hundred or more texts, emails, messages and notifications downloaded in rapid succession. I didn't really have a choice now, did I?

Day 31

I left Falmouth in an altogether more positive mental state than the one in which I had arrived. I felt renewed and full of energy for the 30 miles to my next lighthouse in Penzance. It helped that the bad weather had passed, and the forecast for several days ahead was for warm sunshine.

In my original plans I would have been heading for the Lizard, but having spent last week there with Emily and the children, I could cycle inland for a while, and rejoin the coast near Marazion. The route involved eight uphill miles from the outset, but then delivered the reward of nearly twenty more that were either flat or downhill.

I reached Marazion by late morning, where I stopped for more than an hour with a pot of tea at Jordan's Cafe. There was a spectacular view out to St Michael's Mount, a tidal island linked to the mainland by a man-made causeway that is passable at low water. It is the Cornish counterpart of Mont-Saint-Michel in Normandy, France, with which it shares more than a passing resemblance. It has been in the ownership of the St Aubyn family for 230 years, although managed by the National Trust since 1954.

When I eventually got moving again I was able to leave the road and join the South West Coast Path, nestled between the seafront and the railway line. It took me in glorious solitude all the way into Penzance. I'd been here several times, most recently at the start of a summer holiday on the Isles of Scilly in 2009.

The harbour is just a few minutes on from the railway station, where a cast-iron lighthouse was built in 1855, after the pier was extended. Originally, its light was fuelled by colza oil, although sperm oil was used in stormy winter weather, which lasted longer and ensured that the keeper did not need to remain on site overnight.

It was electrified during modernisation in 1914, when a thousand-candlepower light was installed. It flashes red to each side, every five seconds, to mark the Gear Rock, with a white inner sector light to mark the safe passage into harbour. Its light is visible for nine miles.

It was still only early afternoon, so although I needed to find somewhere to stay in Penzance, I decided to cycle on to Newlyn to see the harbour light there. Newlyn is a busy fishing port, once famous for pilchards and herrings, but these days lands more than 40 species of fish and shellfish.

The harbour at Newlyn is more workmanlike than at Penzance, and the south pier, on which the lighthouse stands, is off limits. But there's a perfect view from the Victoria Pier opposite. It is another cast-iron tower, flashing a white light every five seconds, visible for nine miles. It was built in 1915, when Newlyn's pier was extended by 100 feet, and electrified in 1935.

Back in Penzance, I returned to the harbour and bought a return ferry crossing to the Isles of Scilly, departing the next morning. I booked in to the Duporth Guest House where the owner, a friendly chap called Steve, offered to look after my bike for the two days I would be away. His wife seemed less keen, and it was only when I realised that he planned to prop it up against the sofa in his private living room that I understood why.

I tracked down the DHL collection point where a letter from home was waiting for me. The most important news was that the head teacher at Tom's school had tracked down his bully, called in his parents and read them all the riot act.

The parcel also contained a month's supply of my MS medication, in pre-filled syringes. It was a complicated arrangement, because the formula needs to be kept below 5°C at all times. Right from day one, I had converted my front nearside cycle pannier into a makeshift cool box, and each night I had been freezing a series of ice bags in hotel and guesthouse kitchens to ensure that the medication remained cool during each day's ride. This new batch from home was encased in a leakproof cold polystyrene box, filled with ice packs, and the 30 syringes were still as cold as when they came out of the kitchen fridge the day before.

I've spoken with hundreds of MS patients since my own diagnosis, and it's remarkable how often the need to keep medication cool has curtailed their ambition to travel, and in some cases has taken away their confidence even to leave the house. I always hoped that this expedition would demonstrate that it is perfectly possible to adapt, and I had faith that my trusty front pannier would function as a perfectly serviceable fridge throughout the journey.

It wasn't easy finding accommodation on Scilly. Two substantial engineering projects in Hugh Town had swallowed up the island's guesthouse capacity, and I was struggling to find a bed at any price. After more than a dozen phone calls I secured the last bed on the island thanks to Lisa, owner of the Byelet, who offered me the use of a two-bedroom self-catering flat for the same price as her standard rooms.

Back at the Duporth Guest House, Steve greeted me heartily, but his wife gave me a Paddington-like stare. It was clear she already wanted her living room back.

Day 32

Early the following morning I was back at the harbour in a long queue waiting to board the *Scillonian III*, the ferry that has made the crossing between Penzance and St Mary's, on the Isles of Scilly, for more than 40 years. I discovered that most of the private schools were still on holiday this week, so the orderly line mainly comprised of well-intentioned but stressed and fussing middle-class families.

I felt conflicted, because I could so easily have been in this very queue with my own family. But there is something about congregations of middle-class families that I find almost unbearable. For a start, none of the adults talk to or acknowledge each other, apart from to establish where they send their children to school. There's evidently an unwritten pecking order, which provides a basis for establishing another child's suitability as a playmate for their own.

The rest of the time, conversations between adults are invariably conducted exclusively through their children. A frantic mother had a question for the official at the information window, but I happened to be standing in front of it. A simple 'excuse me' would have been fine, but instead she spoke very loudly to her daughter: 'I'm sure the nice man won't mind if we slide in front of him!'

That'll be me, then. Middle-class parents also leave absolutely nothing to chance, and don't allow a single moment for spontaneity. A succession of assertive mothers approached the poor chap assigned to help us all out to ask any number of inconsequential, banal questions:

Will our luggage be accessible during the crossing?
Can we reserve seats on the upper deck?
Will we see seals on the crossing?
Which side of the boat should we sit at to see them?
Is there Wi-Fi onboard?
Does the buffet onboard serve almond milk?

I smiled at this final question because I have travelled on the Scillonian several times, and I knew the buffet was more of a KitKat-and-instant-coffee sort of place than a skinny-decaf-latte-with-almond-milk one.

Nor were the questions limited to the crossing itself:

Where's the best place to eat when we land on St Mary's?
Should we reserve a table?
Is there a decent Vodafone signal on St Martin's?

And so it went on. For once, I was feeling entirely relaxed and in a good mental state compared with these bundles of stress and worry. I was confident that the Scillonian would have sold only as many tickets as there were seats, and that if there were seals to be seen, I would probably get the chance to see them. As for the facilities and opportunities awaiting us on St Mary's, I was minded to wait and see.

I shared a bench seat on the upper deck with an elderly couple whose only companion was a gentle golden retriever called Ben. The long-range photographs I took of the lighthouses at Tater Du and Longships did not go unnoticed, and it turned out that Geoff and Mandy had just spent a week staying at the keepers' cottages at Bull Point Lighthouse, on the North Devon coast. I would be at Bull Point myself in about a week's time, which Geoff regarded as a most remarkable coincidence.

I would also be seeing Tater Du and Longships close up at the weekend, but this crossing represented my best – and only – opportunity to see the lighthouse at Wolf Rock. It was some distance away, and Geoff offered his shoulder to steady the zoom lens of my camera. I got some great shots, but I would have liked to get closer.

Wolf Rock is a lone, hazardous rock located eight miles south-west of Land's End. It is said that its name came from the howling sound made when strong gales entered and escaped from the fissures in the rock.

After previous unsuccessful attempts at constructing a light, it was not until 1861 that engineer James Walker began work on a granite stone tower that copied the design of Smeaton's Eddystone Lighthouse. A substantial landing stage had to be built on the rock before work on the tower could begin, while the granite stones were dressed in Penzance before being shipped out to the rock. It was such slow work that it was nine years before the tower was eventually lit in 1870.

It's a magnificent, lean, tapering stone tower, displaying flashing red-and-white lights, which are visible for sixteen miles. It was electrified in 1955, and in 1972 became the first rock lighthouse in the world to be equipped with a helipad. The lighthouse was automated in July 1988.

The Isles of Scilly are a small island group about 25 miles off the south-western tip of Cornwall. There are five principal islands:

Wolf Rock.

St Mary's, St Martin's, St Agnes, Tresco and Bryher, each with its own distinctive culture, character and landscape. I was introduced to Scilly many years ago by a wonderfully eccentric friend called Adam, who had phoned me in Kent one Friday afternoon and invited me to accompany him for a week of walking and exploring the islands.

'Sounds lovely,' I said. 'When were you thinking of going?'

'Tomorrow. The ferry leaves Penzance at 10am,' was his reply.

I drove for eleven hours through the night in a 1971 Triumph Herald that I'd never taken further than the village shop. I was at the quayside in Penzance to meet him at nine o'clock the following morning. We stayed on Bryher, the smallest (and arguably the prettiest) of the islands, at a small B&B where we had to fend for ourselves for the last couple of days when the owner was helicoptered off to the mainland to give birth.

Some twenty years later, it felt very good to be back and, like most things on Scilly, very little had changed. The ferry arrived at the harbour in Hugh Town on St Mary's, the largest of the islands. The same group of worried parents proceeded to accost anyone available with a new round of questions:

How long will our luggage take?
How will we get to [insert name of island here]?
Should we have lunch first and then come back for our belongings?
Will our luggage be safe?
Will they be taking the luggage bound for [insert name of island here] first?

For once I was travelling light, having left all but a single pannier back in the guesthouse in Penzance. I was away from the middle-class mêlée and marching through the main shopping street in Hugh Town within minutes. I've made a few trips here over the years, so I knew where to gather the few essentials I needed for the couple of days I was here.

The Byelet guesthouse is on a hill in a smart residential street on the edge of town. Its owner, Lisa, was evidently born to be the island's most effective ambassador. She seemed to sense my arrival, somehow, and a tray of tea and scones that would have fed a small army were laid out in the garden waiting for me. She has run the Byelet herself for several years, and her father had been the head teacher at the main secondary school on St Mary's, educating the children from all of the islands.

Having explained the reason why I was here, Lisa suggested that I set off straight away to see Peninnis Lighthouse, so that I was back in time to take the evening boat trip to St Agnes, where I would not only be able to walk to the former lighthouse in the middle of the island, but also get a great view of Bishop Rock from the campsite at the far end of the island.

Since my last visit the school buildings on the edge of Hugh Town had been closed and boarded up, and a brand-new primary and secondary school built near Old Town Road, close to the island's southern beach. As I passed the entrance, I couldn't help but ponder what a delightful schooling the children from the Isles of Scilly must receive.

The lighthouse on St Mary's is on the outer headland at Peninnis Head, a peninsular that affords some of the most spectacular views the island has to offer. The lighthouse itself is unusual, with its white-painted steel tower mounted on a black-painted steel lattice base.

It was built in 1911, and guides vessels entering St Mary's Sound and on to the harbour at Hugh Town. One of the first gas-powered lighthouses to use acetylene (which drove the rotating optic, as well as fuelling the light), it was designed to be automated from the outset. It was converted to electricity in 1992 and emits a white light, flashing every fifteen seconds, which is visible for sixteen miles.

The evening boat trips to St Agnes are popular, not least because of the Turks Head, a thriving pub occupying the former coastguard boathouse, just a minute's walk from the quay. I recognised several

Peninnis Head.

faces from the ferry that morning, and as soon as the boat landed a race got underway to see which family could get to the pub first and bag the best table. A couple of families lagged behind, their smug smiles suggesting that they had pre-booked.

I only had time for a pint of Tribute and a couple bags of crisps, because the boat returned in a couple of hours and I had two lighthouses to see and photograph before it got dark. I headed up the track towards the former lighthouse, which comes second only to the Turks Head as the island's principal landmark.

Sited at the highest point on the island, it is visible from almost everywhere, and although disused still acts as a daymark to passing vessels. It's beautiful, it's in private ownership, and there is nowhere I'd rather live.

St Agnes.

Built in 1680, it is one of the earliest constructed by Trinity House. It has a four-storey, white-painted, conical stone tower, with adjoining white-painted keepers' cottages. Following conversion from coal fire to oil in 1790, a parabolic reflector was fitted at the same time, which established a flashing white light, visible for eighteen miles.

After the light at Peninnis Head was completed in 1911, the light on St Agnes was no longer needed and was discontinued the same year.

The campsite at Troytown Farm, at the western tip of St Agnes, is the most beautiful campsite on earth. Two small fields, a few steps up from a sandy beach, look out across the water to Bishop Rock, as well as a handful of small uninhabited islands. There are no vehicles, other than the tractors and Land Rover that serve the farm itself. A crude hammock has been fashioned from old fishing nets between two tall rocks by the shore. To cap it all, the farm sells homemade ice cream, unpasteurised milk and fresh clotted cream. Really, it's hard to imagine anywhere more idyllic for a family camping holiday.

The lighthouse at Bishop Rock is about four miles offshore, and I needed my trusty long lens once more. Using the campsite's gatepost to steady the camera I secured some fabulous pictures. The water was currently so choppy off the western coast that it would be another couple of weeks before the island's boat trips would venture out that far.

When Sir Cloudesley Shovel's squadron of the British Fleet was wrecked in 1707, causing the loss of 2,000 lives, the single lighthouse on St Agnes was deemed insufficient. As a result, Bishop Rock, the islands' most westerly danger, was identified as a suitable location for a new lighthouse.

Trinity House's engineer-in-chief, James Walker, first attempted a cast-iron screw-pile lighthouse, but a heavy gale in February 1850 swept away the whole structure just before it was due to be lit. Walker's second attempt was a granite tower, 150-feet tall, based on Smeaton's Tower at Eddystone. This was lit for the first time in 1858.

Concerns about the tower's foundations resulted in work starting on a third lighthouse, built around the existing one, in 1883. The work was undertaken by engineer Sir James Douglass.

The foundations were also strengthened with vast blocks of granite sunk into the rock and held by heavy bolts. This new tower, 160-feet high, was lit in October 1887, and is the one that is still in operation today.

Its white light, flashing every fifteen seconds, is visible for 24 miles. Originally fuelled by paraffin, it was converted to electricity in 1973, equipped with a helipad in 1976 and automated in 1991.

They had stopped serving food when I eventually got back to the Turks Head, but it had been worth missing a meal to see Bishop Rock.

Bishop Rock.

Normal service resumed on the boat back to Hugh Town, and competitive mothers compared recent holiday destinations with whoever would join the conversation. I was learning how to answer the seemingly innocent question, 'Have you been here before?' It is designed to engage you in tedious and lengthy accounts of the frequent, expensive holidays they have enjoyed on the islands, and of the properties they have considered buying. There is a simple answer that tends to silence the showing off: 'Have I been here before? I live here.'

Days 33 and 34

I walked down to a tiny broadcasting studio at Porthmellon, home to Radio Scilly, a community radio station launched by Keri Jones in 2007. For a while it laid claim to being the world's smallest radio station, serving the 2,100 island residents. I was due to be interviewed during the breakfast show, and I met the show's host, Lydia, at the top of the stairs.

I was on after Ken, head of the St Mary's Boatmen's Association, delivered his regular slot highlighting the boat trips scheduled for the day ahead. I had made the right call the previous evening, because tonight's trip to St Agnes was cancelled.

When my turn came, Lydia asked about my expedition, as well as my previous visits to the Scillies. She was either genuinely interested or a bloody good host. By 10am it was all over, and I met Ken again briefly as I waited in line for a boat trip to the eastern isles, taking in the daymark on St Martin's and Round Island, home to the only lighthouse on the islands that I had not yet seen.

This was really a trip for bird lovers, lured by probable sightings of Manx shearwaters, storm petrels, shags, guillemots and puffins. We paused off St Helen's, one of the 50 or so uninhabited islands in Scilly. But it wasn't always so, with remains clearly visible of one of the earliest Christian sites in the islands, an 8th-century chapel once home to Saint Lide. There are also the remains of an isolation hospital used to quarantine sailors with the plague. These days, the residents of St Helen's all have wings, and everyone on the boat seemed delighted to see dozens of puffins. Despite the abundance of seals, shags and guillemots, the puffins were the star turn.

Round Island, at the most northerly point on the Isles of Scilly, has only ever been inhabited by lighthouse keepers. As we circled the island it was not hard to see why. It's a bleak, barren rock that is constantly battered by waves and wind. We couldn't dock on the island – landing is restricted – but we got as close to the rocks as our skipper was prepared to venture.

The lighthouse was built by Trinity House in 1887 to protect shipping from the dangerous northern rocks and smaller islands. The sheer rock face made offloading building materials virtually impossible, and a flight of steps had to be cut into it.

Round Island Lighthouse is a white circular tower, 63 feet tall, designed by James Douglass. Originally oil powered, the lighthouse was electrified in 1966 and automated in 1987, after which its light pattern changed to a flashing white light, visible for eighteen miles.

As far as lighthouses were concerned, that was me done on the Isles of Scilly. The next crossing back to the mainland was the following afternoon, so I had the rest of the day and most of the next to rest and prepare for getting back on my bike on Sunday.

Round Island.

When I bade farewell to Lisa, she knocked a third off my bill and then donated a healthy sum to Shift.ms, taking my total raised so far above £5,000. She also presented me with all my laundry, cleaned and ironed, claiming that she needed to put a load on for the construction workers staying so it was no trouble adding mine. The workers assigned to the Byelet during the construction work were clearly the lucky ones.

Back in Penzance I was reunited with the bike, and excited at the prospect of reaching Land's End. It represented a significant milestone, as the most westerly point in England and home to another of our most iconic lighthouses.

Day 35

The road from Penzance to Mousehole follows the cliff edge and is part of NCN Route 3, ultimately connecting Land's End with Bristol. I was bound for Lamorna Cove, the nearest point to Tater Du Lighthouse.

A quick search for more information about Lamorna Cove unearthed nearly 200 one-star reviews on Tripadvisor. Apparently, an exploitative private parking company in Exeter counted using the car park to turn around as *parking*, and issued £160 fines to every car spotted doing so, using a series of drones and hidden cameras. It is a shame for the proprietors of the cafe at the cove, whose business must have suffered, such is the feeling of resentment from holidaymakers and locals alike.

The walk to Tater Du, along the South West Coast Path, was a bit of a scramble and it took nearly 40 minutes before I spotted the squat, modern lighthouse whose shape is so familiar. As a child, my parents had given me a copy of Derrick Jackson's excellent guide *Lighthouses of England and Wales*, and Tater Du was the most modern lighthouse in the Trinity House fleet at the time. I recall marvelling at its seemingly space-age architecture and its equally unusual name.

After a French trawler bound for Dieppe was wrecked between Longships and the Lizard in 1962, and a Spanish ship was wrecked off Boscawen Point in 1963, Trinity House planned an additional lighthouse at Tater Du, on the cliffs between the coves at Lamorna and Porthcurno.

Tater Du.

It's a strikingly modern, 50-foot-high circular concrete tower, painted white, with an adjoining single-story service building behind. It was completed in 1965 and was the first new Trinity House lighthouse to be built for 60 years. It is still the newest in the fleet, if you don't count Bull Point, which was rebuilt in 1972 after landslides caused the existing lighthouse to collapse.

The lighthouse was designed from the outset to be automated and unstaffed. Power is provided by batteries that are recharged from the mains. It emits a white light, flashing three times every fifteen seconds, which is visible for twenty miles. An additional red sector light warns shipping of the nearby Runnelstone Rocks.

Back at Lamorna, I had a long, steep climb to get back on to NCN Route 3, and then a leisurely eight miles on to Land's End.

Land's End peninsular is renowned worldwide for its hundreds of significant archaeological sites, but in other ways it is quite bleak and serves mainly to help tourists part with their cash. I have visited only once before, when it played host to a substantial *Doctor Who* exhibition when my son Tom was very young. We lasted less than five minutes inside, after a static Dalek suddenly came to life, shouted, 'Exterminate!' and sent him running back to the entrance. That was £40 I wouldn't see again.

I was here now because of the famous Longships Lighthouse, about a mile offshore. Without children in tow this time, I made my way straight to the viewpoint from where I could take a series of dramatic pictures looking down to the lighthouse on the rocks below.

Of the many rocks off the coast at Land's End, the group at Carn Bras, about a mile offshore, is the most dangerous. After a handful of attempts to erect beacons on the rocks, architect Samuel Wyatt designed a circular lighthouse made of granite in 1795 that served for nearly 80 years. In 1873 it was replaced by a more effective lighthouse designed by Trinity House engineer-in-chief Sir James Douglass. This was built on similar principles to Smeaton's light at Eddystone, with a tall, tapering, 115-foot-tall granite tower.

Originally employing oil lamps, the light was converted to electric power in 1967, and then to solar power in 2005. It was automated in 1998. It emits a white light, flashing twice every ten seconds, which is visible for fifteen miles.

I was not at Land's End for very long, and it was still only late morning. I hadn't yet thought where I might stay that evening, and the small town of St Just seemed a bit near, while St Ives, still 25 miles distant, a bit far. My map suggested that there were few other options along the way.

For now, my target was Pendeen Lighthouse, on a headland below the village of Pendeen, between St Just and St Ives. I took my time getting there, stopping in pretty St Just to wash down a fresh, local crab sandwich with a couple of pints of Trelawny at the Kings Arms, and then sleeping them off on a shady bench in well-tended gardens in Pendeen village. This final stretch is spectacular, with the low stone walls on either side of the lane offering panoramic views. Cornwall's colours differ from Devon's, with distinctive flowers in vivid hues of red, yellow and

Longships.

bright orange growing naturally in the hedgerows alongside the lanes and minor roads.

I didn't know the lighthouse at Pendeen, and as I approached my first impression was of another squat tower like the one at Berry Head. On arrival, though, I realised that I had been approaching the lighthouse from higher ground, and the tower is a lot taller than I'd thought.

The high cliffs along this section of the Cornish coast meant that passing vessels were often lost, unable to see either the light at Trevose Head (to the east) or Longships (to the west). A beacon alongside a chapel dedicated to St Nicholas served from the early-16th century, but this was lost during the Dissolution of the Monasteries.

Trinity House commissioned a Cornishman, Sir Thomas Matthews, to build a new lighthouse and fog signal on the headland at Pendeen. It was completed in 1900, a rubble stone and cement tower in a commanding position close to the cliff edge.

Pendeen.

An electric lamp replaced the oil lamp in 1926, emitting a white light, flashing four times every fifteen seconds, which is visible for sixteen miles. The lighthouse was fully automated in 1995.

I decided to press on to St Ives, and I loved the last ten miles, with wild landscapes of the lushest green bracken mixed with heathers in a variety of crimson reds and purples. Every few miles, in the most inaccessible terrain, lie the tall, ruined stone chimneys and roofless shells of former tin mines.

St Ives itself was heaving. I made my way to the seafront and tried to cycle along Wharf Road towards the harbour, but there were so many people on foot that the roads only seemed to clear for cars. It's a thriving place, and despite the crowds I loved it. It's a more modern resort than I'd imagined, with residential and commercial streets mixing several architectural styles, most of them post-war.

The oldest part of town seems to be around the pier, where the streets suddenly narrow and the houses were evidently built for nobler stock. John Smeaton was commissioned to build the East

Pier, which was completed in 1770. But a lighthouse wasn't built on the pier until 1830, when an unusual octagonal gallery was built on top of a square stone base. It was a gas light, visible for seven miles, which served for 60 years, until it became redundant when the pier was extended in 1890.

I discovered that Smeaton's Lighthouse was almost destroyed by fire in 1996, although it has since been fully restored. It's an interesting lighthouse, unlike any I have seen so far, but its appeal is not enhanced by the four large commercial wheelie bins stored permanently around its base.

When the pier extension was complete, an octagonal, white-painted cast-iron tower was built on the end. It was prefabricated in Bath and is almost identical to the one at Mevagissey. It shows two green lights, one from the lantern and one from about halfway down the front of the tower. Inexplicably for the first week of June, a range of brightly coloured Christmas lights hung from the gallery railings.

WEEK 6

Day 36

Seven miles out of St Ives, the harbour town of Hayle has a rich industrial heritage, having exported Cornwall's coal, copper, tin and iron over several centuries. At one stage, rival iron foundries were built at either end of the town. In 2006, Hayle was awarded World Heritage status in recognition of its historic industrial importance. Since the war, the town has relied more on tourism, boasting miles of fine sandy beaches and an estuary teaming with birdlife.

I reached the estuary by mid-morning, just as the tide was coming in, an event well worth experiencing. The incoming tide fills the estuary from both entrances, leaving a shrinking strip of sand in the middle. At high tide, the two beaches merge together, enabling the harbour to continue serving a small fishing fleet as well as numerous leisure users and charter boats.

I was here thanks to a pair of lights built on the western side of the river entrance. When lined up, they mark a safe channel into the harbour. I discovered the first of the two lights, the rear light, in a very poor state. Lying at the edge of a golf course, at one of the highest points in the dunes above the estuary, is a sad-looking square concrete box, covered in graffiti, standing on stilts. On its seaward side, it is in slightly better repair – painted white, with a broad, red horizontal band to serve also as a daymark.

The front light proved much harder to find, and I was running out of time before the tide came in. When eventually I found a decaying structure close to the beach, I concluded that it must have been the old front light I was looking for, took a handful of photographs, and returned to the bike only moments before the two waters met.

My work in Hayle was done, but the town continued to deliver. My route to Godrevey and Portreath passed through the King George V Memorial Walk, a long promenade alongside the water at Cooperhouse Pool. On one side lies the calmest water, on the other almost a mile of the most meticulous, perfectly maintained gardens imaginable, with lush grass cut shorter than a bowling green and a blaze of colour in every flowerbed.

Once the park and the town were behind me, the terrain changed and returned quickly to the wild Cornish coast depicted in the guidebooks. My target was the heathland at Godrevy, at the north-east entrance to St Ives Bay. It is managed by the National Trust, with Godrevy Island, home to the beautiful lighthouse – said to be the inspiration for Virginia Wolfe's novel *To the Lighthouse* – barely 300 metres offshore.

The island can only be reached by boat, but the lighthouse is so close to the coast path that it really didn't matter. I was happy to sit close to the shore and reel off 100 or more photographs.

The first half of the 19th century saw the development of fishing and industrial trade in St Ives, and with it an increase in ships along the north coast of Cornwall. The Stones, a dangerous reef opposite St Ives, caused many ships to wreck, but it took until 1854 before a lighthouse was commissioned.

It was designed by Trinity House engineer James Walker, and built in the middle of the largest of the rocks that make up Godrevy Island. The main structure is a white octagonal tower made from rubble stone bedded in mortar. A pair of cottages provided accommodation for the keepers, although these were demolished in 1933 when the lighthouse was automated.

The lighthouse was modernised in 1995 and converted to solar power. In 2012, the light was moved from the tower to a new steel structure on an adjacent rock. It shows a white flashing

Godrevy Island.

light, at ten-second intervals, visible for eight miles. It also shows a fixed red light marking the Stones reef.

I stopped for lunch at the National Trust cafe on the heath, where every other patron was a surfer. No one else in the cafe was more than twenty at most, and the wetsuits they were wearing only served to draw attention to their impossibly slim, fit frames. I was aware that the body-fitting cycling top I was wearing was having the same effect – although with my 50-year-old, seventeen-stone frame, it was somewhat less flattering.

Portreath is eight miles further up the coast, and was once an important port, sending copper ore to Swansea for smelting and bringing Welsh coal to power the steam engines used at the mines. The harbour was extended at around this time, and a circular stone tower, with a light on its flat roof, was built at the end of the Landmark Pier in 1812.

On the hill above the harbour, a 25-feet tall, white-painted conical tower was built to serve as a daymark. Together these two aids to navigation guided shipping safely away from the hazardous Gull Rock and Horse Rock. The light has long since been removed, but both structures remain and have benefitted from recent coats of white paint.

I liked Portreath and would have been happy to linger. It's a popular but unassuming place, with affluent Victorian and Edwardian terraced houses lining one side of the seafront road, and modern flats and houses on the other. The beaches here are said to be popular with naturists, but there was a strong, chilly breeze and everyone I encountered was fully clothed.

Close to 7pm I reached Newquay, and was pleasantly surprised that a hotel I had booked for just £10 seemed okay, although I was a little concerned that I was its only paying guest. I found a friendly evening porter, masquerading as the barman when required, who drew my attention to a £30 damage deposit. Evidently he decided that I was unlikely to cause trouble, however, and waived the charge. My room was unlike anywhere I had stayed before. There were a simple pair of bunk beds and a bathroom without a door. Absolutely everything in the room was screwed onto the walls and floors, including beds, table, chair and mirror. I discovered that, out of season, it's only ever booked for hen and stag parties, and only on Friday and Saturday nights. A booking on a Monday in June was rare, and the porter seemed genuinely pleased when two walkers arrived looking for a bed for the night, and a third came in to ask for directions. This was clearly the most he'd had to contend with for some time.

Exploring Newquay, I felt a little uninspired. I didn't get why it's the most popular resort in Cornwall, and I was clearly not the demographic it aims to attract. I cycled past a Co-op, where I discovered that all the unsold fresh food had been marked down in price, and I managed to pick up a chicken pasta salad for 39p and a ham sandwich for 29p. That was my supper sorted for less than £1, which, alongside my £10 hotel room, made Newquay just about the cheapest place on earth. I celebrated my good fortune by adding a bottle of Rioja to my basket, which I am ashamed to admit cost more than my dinner, bed and breakfast combined.

Day 37

I was happy to leave Newquay to the surfers and the stag and hen weekenders. I had a reasonably straight fifteen-mile stretch of coast road ahead of me, which an initial glance at my map suggested would be fairly easy going. My GPS indicated otherwise, however, warning me of at least eight ascents, and marking the route as only really suitable for fit, experienced cyclists.

I felt energised by the Cornish landscape, which at this time of year seemed richly and intensely colourful. Although I could see the lighthouse at Trevose Head a couple of miles ahead, I was drawn towards the smell of fresh coffee coming from the clubhouse of what was clearly a golf course for the well-heeled. I was banking on it being open to non-members, and was pleased to discover that it was.

The final approach to the lighthouse was largely flat, with the rough granite cliffs on my left contrasting with the oranges and the yellows of the wildflowers on the headland all around. The cliffs are renowned for the presence of several uncommon plants, including the shore dock, wild asparagus and golden samphire. It's a popular area for birdwatchers as well, with populations of fulmars, razorbills, peregrines and guillemots.

For such an apparently wild and inaccessible place, the signs warning motorists about parking penalties and the likelihood of being clamped or towed away seemed a little incongruous. On one stretch of road no longer than 300 metres, I passed at least eight bright-yellow enforcement signs. Who on earth is so keen to park here, and why?

The lighthouse itself was splendid, at the north-western point of the headland, on the top of grey granite cliffs, 150 feet above the sea. Although a lighthouse on this stretch of the Cornish coast was proposed as early as 1809, it wasn't until 1847 that Trinity House built the lighthouse here. Until then, ships and maritime traffic using the Bristol Channel had to rely on the Longships Lighthouse to the south or the old Lundy Lighthouse to the north.

Designed by James Walker, it has a white-painted tower whose lantern currently displays a white flashing light, visible for 21 miles. There is a single-storey keepers' cottage on either side of the tower. The lighthouse was electrified in 1974, and then fully automated in 1995.

My ultimate destination for the day was Boscastle, where I was booked in at the famous Wellington Inn. Between Trevose

Trevose Head.

and Boscastle, however, lay a series of Cornwall's most fêted resorts, which I would need to pass straight through if I was to reach Boscastle before nightfall.

Padstow is a particularly beautiful town, with its eclectic mix of fishermen's cottages and merchants' houses arranged around a very pretty harbour. Its popularity is partly down to its food, with Rick Stein owning several restaurants here.

The Strand was absolutely heaving, and I found myself on the quayside with dozens of others awaiting the little foot-passenger ferry that crosses the Camel Estuary to Rock, on the opposite bank. Although Padstow doesn't boast a lighthouse as such, several red and green lights are mounted on poles at the entrance into the harbour, as well as at one end of the north quay.

At the mouth of Padstow Bay lies the Doom Bar, a bank of sand immortalised by a beer of the same name. Legend has it that the Mermaid of Padstow fell in love with a local man and tried to entice him below the waves. Although he managed to escape by shooting the mermaid, she cursed the harbour with a 'bar of doom', which ultimately brought about the wrecking of ships and the drowning of men.

We crossed safely, and encountered no mermaids.

The coastal fishing village of Rock seemed considerably quieter than Padstow, although I must have missed the town centre, because I never saw what my guidebook described as a 'string of boutique shops, beachfront cafes and exclusive restaurants'. My route passed a small bakery and cafe, where the teenager serving was clearly hoping to close early. Despite the cafe being open for another hour, she encouraged me to take my pasty and mug of tea outside so as not to dirty the tables she had just finished wiping clean.

The final descent into Boscastle was exhilarating, and I put to the back of my mind the thought of having to climb back up this hill in the morning. The village is gorgeous, boasting some very attractive thatched and white-washed cottages. It has a natural harbour, set in a narrow ravine, and was once a prominent port, boasting its own fishing fleet, and importing limestone and coal, while exporting slate and other local produce.

The Wellington Inn is one of the oldest coaching inns in Cornwall, and guests have included Thomas Hardy, who fell in love in Boscastle, as well as members of the Royal Family. I had been here before, when walking the South West Coast Path, but since my last visit the village had made headline news when it suffered devastating floods in 2004. A month's rainfall fell in two hours, turning the main street into a river and trapping residents on the roofs of houses and cars. Although there were no fatalities, homes, businesses and cars belonging to more than a thousand people were swept away.

My first impression was that the inn's elegant, turreted frontage must have escaped the floods largely unscathed. However, photographs on the stairs and landings told a different story, and evidently much rebuilding and refurbishment work had been necessary. It is a peaceful and welcoming place to stay, and over a couple of pints of Betty Stogs the only thing gnawing away at my sense of calm and contentment was the thought of having to push the bike back up the hill in the morning.

Day 38

The ascent was less punishing than I feared, and within an hour I reached the crossroads where I had left the main road the previous evening.

I was heading to Hartland Point, about 30 miles north, one of the lighthouses I was most looking forward to seeing. Although this was destined to be one of my shortest days, the only viable route followed the main A39 for 27 of the 30 miles.

At Kilkhampton I pulled into a lay-by, where a catering van made me a splendid bacon and sausage sandwich, along with a cup of steaming-hot tea. In no hurry to move on, I drank two more cups. When I walked back to bin my paper plate and cups, the owner glanced towards my bike and asked if I was riding for charity. When I explained my connection with Shift.ms, he scooped up two handfuls of Mars, Snickers, Twix and KitKat bars, and thrust them into my hands. 'You'll be needing these, then', he added. It wasn't the first time I'd been met with such impulsive generosity, but it was one of the most touching. It was a gesture that propelled me at speed along the final ten miles to Hartland.

Arriving at the Anchor at around 2.30pm, I found the place locked and empty. For a while I wondered whether I'd booked a place that was no longer in business – I'd read about hotels that close down but remain on booking websites for months or even years afterwards. I decided not to panic quite yet, and given how much of the day was left, I committed to riding on to Hartland Point now, rather than in the morning, which had been my original plan.

When I first visited Hartland Point Lighthouse, as a teenager, it left a lasting impression. Built down low on rocks at the very tip of the point, it feels especially remote and exposed to the ravages of the sea. Back then, there was sufficient accommodation to provide homes for four keepers and their families. Before I set off from home, I was lucky enough to meet Peter Smith, whose father had served here. Peter was brought up at Hartland Point Lighthouse and had gone to school in the village, making the steep three-mile walk there and back each day. In fact, Peter's father was the fourth generation of lighthouse keepers in his family, and at one point his father had served at Lundy South while his grandfather was at Lundy North.

Having seen photographs of Hartland Point taken during Peter's childhood, I felt a little sad when I reached the car park on the cliffs above the lighthouse. Landslides had cut off the access road completely, and the only view of the light was from the Coastguard station about 100 feet above. Cut off and abandoned, it was a sorry sight. Several of the keepers' dwellings that I remembered from my childhood had been demolished, following automation in 1984, and have made way for a helipad. Yellow signs warned of dangerous rocks, liable to landslides, and a large mesh barrier prevented any possibility of walking down the access road itself. I sat on a rock overlooking what was left of the lighthouse and shed a silent tear – for Peter's childhood memories, as well as my own.

The lighthouse was built in 1874 on a large rock at the very tip of Hartland Point, by Trinity House's engineer-in-chief Sir James Douglass. Its white-painted tower is 57-feet tall. Coastal erosion meant that rock had to be broken from the cliff head behind the lighthouse to fall on the beach and form a barrier against the waves. This proved to be a procedure that had to be repeated at frequent intervals, until a permanent barrier and sea wall was built in 1925.

Originally, the tower showed a series of six flashes every fifteen seconds, with a range of seventeen miles. However, in 2012 the light was replaced by an external beacon with a much-reduced range.

The three-bedroom keepers' accommodation and tower, together with helipad, were sold in 2016 for £450,000. It's an enviable private residence now, although the rough access road is still liable to cliff falls, and only passable with a quad bike or utility vehicle.

Back in Hartland Village, I found the Anchor now open for business, although as in Newquay, I was its only customer. I was unsure whether to try to strike up a conversation with the

Hartland Point.

landlady or immerse myself in my book. In the end I did a little of each, a compromise that satisfied neither of us and clearly left her unsure about whether to hover behind the bar or retreat to the kitchen and leave me to my book.

Day 39

When I had set out from home more than a month ago, I only had two commitments in my diary. The first was the Bournemouth University publishing awards presentation in mid-May, which I had safely accomplished. The other was an all-day meeting with the Commonwealth Education Trust in Clevedon, near Bristol, scheduled for the following morning. My problem was that Clevedon was 90 miles north, and even if I made rapid progress I was bound to end the day at least 40 miles short.

It was time for a rescue plan involving Allan, my friend from Oxford. I would cycle as far as Ilfracombe, where Allan would meet me with his car. We would stay overnight with Allan's brother and family in Taunton, and then he would drive me to my meeting in Clevedon in the morning. After a second night in Taunton we would return to Ilfracombe, where I would resume the ride, but not before a day trip to Lundy, where we would 'bag' the island's three lighthouses.

After a short stretch of the A39, which must rate as one of the least cycle-friendly roads in the south-west, I descended into Bideford, an attractive town on the west bank of the River Torridge, where I bought two day-trip tickets to Lundy for the day after next.

With the day trip organised, I joined the brilliant Tarka Trail, named after the route travelled by Tarka the Otter in the famous novel by Henry Williamson. It runs for 180 miles in a figure-of-eight pattern, centred on Barnstaple, the largest town in North Devon. The stretch between Braunton and Meeth is a section of flat, tarmacked unused railway, providing 30 miles of traffic-free cycling – the longest stretch in the UK.

I took a brief detour to Instow, where a pair of range lights mark the safe, narrow passage where the River Torridge and River Taw meet. I took another after Barnstaple, in Braunton, to track down a modern light at Crow Point that I had seen from the riverbank opposite.

Mortehoe sits on the cliffs above Woolacombe and offers wonderful panoramic views out to sea towards Lundy. On the headland beyond the village lies Bull Point, where the relatively modern lighthouse forms one corner of a triangle of lights that includes Hartland Point and the two lights on Lundy Island.

The track leading from the edge of the village to the lighthouse was much longer than I remembered, and I began to wonder if I had either taken a wrong turn or missed the lighthouse altogether. Eventually, I saw a traditional building sporting the familiar Trinity House green-and-white paintwork, with a range of modern buildings and the lighthouse beyond. Despite its remote location, there were plenty of signs of life, with several cars parked up and washing hanging from a number of improvised lines.

When the first lighthouse at Bull Point was built in 1879, it stood more than 70 feet from the cliff edge. It served for nearly

100 years until much of the cliff edge surrounding the lighthouse fell into the sea in 1972, causing the fog signal station to collapse and leaving the boundary walls with deep cracks.

All but one of the original buildings and tower were subsequently demolished, and work started on a new lighthouse in 1974, using the generator and some of the equipment from the original light. It is functional, rather than pretty, with a squat, square, grey tower, whose light was automated from the outset. It displays a white flashing light, three times every ten seconds, which is visible for twenty miles.

After returning to Mortehoe, I had a leisurely descent into Ilfracombe along another section of former railway line. I had arranged to meet Allan at a large car park at the entrance to the town, but I arrived three hours early. I wandered over to a seafood restaurant in one corner and decided to wait for Allan at a table outside. Before long, I had ordered a seafood platter starter followed by skate with a lemon caper butter sauce.

By the time Allan pulled up in the car park, I had gorged some of Cornwall's finest seafood and enjoyed more than one glass of

Bull Point.

wine. Allan, meanwhile, had been sitting in stationary traffic on the M5 for nearly two hours and eaten a pasty and a bag of crisps.

'How long have you been here?' he asked.

'Oh, not long,' I replied.

I left it at that.

Day 40

With Allan's help I made my meeting in Clevedon with time to spare, and even managed to look respectable with the clean shirt and tie he had packed for me. The discovery that I could squeeze a finger or two between the collar and my neck was welcome, evidence of the weight I had lost after 40 days on the road. Having Allan with me also brightened my spirits, and I felt more positive and resilient than I had at any time since I set off.

I had worked with the Commonwealth Education Trust for a few months, helping to publish and distribute three wonderfully illustrated compendiums of children's short stories. The Trust was headed up by Judith Hanratty, now in her mid-seventies, who had more energy and resilience than I'll ever have. At Easter, she had apologised for not having been in touch for a fortnight because she'd had 'a couple of strokes and had been told to take a short rest'.

Despite her considerable experience and a most illustrious corporate career, Judith was very easy to sidetrack. We had planned this meeting for what was an important stage in the publishing project, but most of the morning was spent discussing the places I had been and the people I had met so far. She suggested various people who might help me over the coming weeks, including the chair of the Royal Cromer Golf Club, who would be busy staging a ladies' tournament when I visited, but who would gladly provide a pot of tea if I mentioned Judith's name. I'm not sure how valuable the meeting was from a publishing perspective, but I emerged with several new offers of help ahead of me.

Before reuniting with Allan, Clevedon was to offer a surprise. A very good friend from Kent, David, happened to be visiting his daughter and son-in-law, who had recently bought a house here. He had followed my progress from day one and was keen to catch up.

David is the business partner of Jason, the friend from Kent who tried to persuade me to see only a handful of lighthouses, in an Aston Martin, sustained by weekly supplies of clean underwear couriered by his PA. David and I met up in a tea shop on the waterfront and we spent a couple of hours catching up on news from Kent. When we eventually parted company, he couldn't resist telling me that he had a packet of pants from Jason for me in his car.

Allan met me in Clevedon, and since he'd left me that morning, he had found time to return to Oxford, pick up his son Cameron, and return ready for the day trip to Lundy Island the next day. It would be hard to find a better friend.

Day 41

We left Taunton at dawn to be sure of being back in Ilfracombe in good time for the crossing to Lundy Island, which lies in the Bristol Channel about twelve miles off the North Devon coast.

We had good reason for feeling extremely apprehensive, given our shared experience of making the crossing for my wedding day. Allan was particularly nervous; he had made that journey with his partner, Sharon, who was eight months pregnant at the time.

As it turned out, the crossing today was calm and unremarkable, except for a dense fog reducing visibility to just a few metres. Allan's son Cameron was, in a sense, also returning for a second visit, having been the soon-to-be-born baby from the wedding party. Now seventeen, he seemed a little bemused about why we were visiting the island and what the point was of my cycling expedition. I was determined to win him over, but we were clearly starting from a low base when he asked, 'What exactly is a lighthouse, anyway?'

He turned out to have a lot more sense than either Allan or me, however. We were both planning on stopping at the Marisco Tavern for a couple of pints before the hike to the far end of the island for our first of three lighthouses. Cameron, on the other hand, said that it would be much more sensible to stop on our way back, to be sure of seeing all three lights before the MS *Oldenburg* returned to the mainland. It was bloody irritating to be met with such common sense from a teenager.

The fog persisted, and we could see only a few yards of the straight, muddy track ahead of us. With no distractions we made good progress, and less than an hour after we'd disembarked we were close to Lundy North Lighthouse. I've been here several times before, and to my shame I even managed to poke about inside the tower on my first visit, after finding an unbolted window. But today the fog was so dense that I couldn't even find the metal staircase leading down the cliff to the lighthouse.

Irritatingly, it was Cameron who was the first to spot it. Sadly, the years had not been kind to Lundy North. The buildings adjoining the tower were badly in need of several coats of paint, and an outbuilding roof had been removed or had blown away, giving it the impression of a controlled ruin. The windows had been sealed shut with metal barriers, and the light itself had been removed from the lantern and replaced with a sealed beam unit strapped to a pole outside.

It was built in 1897 on a remote plateau at the northernmost tip of the island. It has a white-painted stone tower, with accommodation and equipment rooms both in front and behind. It was designed by Sir Thomas Matthews, who had succeeded Sir James Douglass as engineer-in-chief at Trinity House in 1892.

Following automation in 1985 it was controlled for a few years by the more accessible lighthouse at Lundy South. Following further modernisation in 1991 it was converted to solar power, and its current white flashing light is visible for seventeen miles.

We retraced our steps back to the village, more subdued and reflective than when we were heading north. Seeing Lundy North in that state made me wonder whether lighthouses will have to rely for their survival on heritage funds, fought for alongside other deserving public buildings such as theatres, piers, concert halls and fun fairs.

We had to turn off the main track to head west towards the Old Lighthouse, but the fog was still so dense that it was hard to be sure quite where to turn. I spent my honeymoon in the keepers' accommodation at the Old Lighthouse, and even now I would be confident inching my way between the Old Lighthouse and the Marisco Tavern. But there are far fewer helpful landmarks coming from the north.

Lundy South (left), the Old Lighthouse (centre) and Lundy North (right).

We played it safe and took the slightly longer route, via a path through the farmyard and campsite that I remembered from previous visits. I'm glad we did, because we saw no sign of the Old Lighthouse at all until we reached the stone wall that surrounds it. It was the perfect illustration of why this lighthouse had to be replaced.

It was built in 1819, on Chapel Hill, one of the highest points on Lundy. It has a tall granite tower, with adjoining keepers' accommodation. The tower showed two lights, a quick-flashing white light from the lantern at the top of the tower, and a fixed red light from a window at the base of the tower. Fog regularly obscured the light, and the lantern's optic rotated so quickly that it appeared to ships like a fixed light, with the upper and lower lights appearing to merge into one. The lighthouse was abandoned in 1897 and replaced with two new lighthouses at the north and south extremities of the island.

Being back here, I was struck by nostalgia, and hit by a wave of homesickness. Back in 1998, our wedding guests had headed home the day after our wedding ceremony, leaving Emily and me alone on the island for the week. The Landmark Trust staff looked after us royally, and as there were no day trips scheduled and no other people holidaying on the island, they encouraged us to stay in a different building each night.

Allan had also stayed in part of the Old Lighthouse over the wedding weekend, and he relived the moment when Reg, the island's agent, had woken up all our guests in a panic early on Sunday morning to warn them that more storms were coming and that the MS *Oldenburg* would be returning to Ilfracombe earlier than planned.

That left just Lundy South to see. With our return crossing still 90 minutes away, we had enough time to sink a couple of pints of Old Light in the Marisco Tavern before setting off to see it.

Lundy South lighthouse sits on a plateau directly above the quay where the MS *Oldenburg* embarks, so it made sense to take a detour on our way back to the boat. It has a broadly similar design to Lundy North, with a white-painted stone tower and adjoining keepers' accommodation. It was converted to solar power in 1994 and shows a white flashing light every five seconds, visible for fifteen miles.

By the time we had climbed the steps up to the lighthouse, the skies had cleared for the first time. My mood lifted with the fog, and I was heartened to discover that Lundy South was in a much healthier state than its northerly sibling. It had recently been painted, for a start, the light appeared to be intact and even the windows seemed clean.

It was also the first lighthouse of the day that actually impressed Cameron, who alternated between taking in the view from the helipad and climbing onto the roof of an outbuilding to see if he could get inside. Allan was still talking about the wedding: 'The storms are coming! The storms are coming!'

On the crossing back to Ilfracombe I made one last effort to win Cameron over to the cause by pointing out Hartland Point through my binoculars. It made little impression.

Day 42

After a second night in Taunton, Allan returned me to Ilfracombe for the third time in the week. He needed to be back in Oxford by lunchtime, so it was still dark when we pulled into the car park alongside the seafood restaurant where he had picked me up three days earlier. He'd offered to drop me at the petrol station on the hilltop above the town, to save a bit of pedalling, but as I hadn't had cause to cheat so far, I wasn't minded to start now.

I was close to tears when Allan and Cameron drove away. For a while I sat on the roadside, feeling weakness in my stomach and a good deal of anxiety. Until now I had just kept moving, and hadn't really paused to take note of my mental health. Sure, my drenching near Falmouth a fortnight earlier caused me to doubt what I was doing, but it had been fairly easy to put my troubles behind me and start again. Now, however, I really did feel like calling it a day. I'd cycled more than a thousand miles, I'd been away from home for six weeks, and I felt I'd demonstrated that having multiple sclerosis needn't mean giving up on your dreams. I could cycle back to Barnstaple, take a fast train to London and be back home in Kent by the end of the day. And everyone would still say how well I'd done.

What eventually got me to my feet was the realisation that I had been in Ilfracombe three times already, and I still hadn't seen the town's own lighthouse at St Nicholas Chapel, on the hill above the harbour. Whatever decision I made, I might as well go and find it while I was here.

The chapel here was founded originally in 1321, and it has maintained a light to guide shipping into the harbour since the Middle Ages. It is said to be the oldest lighthouse in the country. It ceased to serve as a chapel after Henry VIII dissolved the monasteries in 1540, but its role as a lighthouse remains to this day.

Whether the chapel offered divine inspiration I cannot say, but from its vantage point looking down onto the harbour, I decided to carry on. I followed the main A39 coast road to Lynmouth, which required such complete concentration that I was able to put everything else out of my mind for an hour or so. All but the last mile was tough going, when I was able to turn off onto a steep downhill plunge along a pretty toll road.

Lynmouth is a very attractive village, set at the foot of a gorge a few-hundred metres below the neighbouring town of Lynton. The two are connected by the funicular Cliff Railway, which opened in 1890 and is believed to be the highest and steepest railway in the world powered entirely by water.

Lynmouth has an unfortunate record as the site of the worst river flood in English history. One day in August 1952, nine inches of rain fell in a matter of hours, resulting in floods that all but destroyed the village. More than 100 buildings were swept away, 34 people died and a further 420 were made homeless. In the following months, 114,000 tons of rubble were cleared from the village, and the village itself took six years to rebuild.

At the harbour is a landmark known locally as the Rhenish Tower. It was built around 1832 to store salt water for indoor baths. I couldn't find it listed in any of my lighthouse resources and guidebooks, but it is said that at some point in its life it was fitted with an electric light for use as a beacon to guide shipping. The original tower was destroyed in the 1952 flood, but an exact replica was built in its place as part of the village's reconstruction.

To my dismay, the road out of the village to the lighthouse at Lynmouth Foreland was the highest and the steepest of my journey so far. I took Countisbury Hill in short stages, and the crest of the hill still seemed some distance away after toiling for more than an hour. I turned onto a gravel track leading to Lynmouth Foreland Lighthouse, which plunged so steeply downhill that I realised I could reach the lighthouse in a few minutes, but my only option would be to return the same way.

It's another of the lighthouses that I had always wanted to see, with its row of keepers' cottages set low down on the cliff edge. The cottages are available for holiday lets these days, but all I could think about was just how far you'd have to go if you needed a pint of milk. I was only three miles from Lynmouth village, but this felt like one of the most remote lighthouses I had yet seen.

It was constructed in 1900 and was the third light built to guide vessels passing through the Bristol Channel, following Hartland Point and Bull Point. Its white-painted circular tower is set a third of the way up a steep north-facing cliff, 220 feet above the high tide. Originally powered by oil, it was converted to electricity in 1975, when diesel generators were installed. It shows a white flashing light, four times every fifteen seconds, which is visible for eighteen miles.

Lynmouth Foreland was never a popular posting for lighthouse keepers, largely because its north-facing position meant that it only sees the sun during high summer. It was fully automated in 1994, and a pair of static LED lights have recently replaced the original Fresnel lens and optics.

Further along the coast road, I took a detour to follow the quiet, leafy and utterly deserted toll road into Porlock. I stopped for a while on the seafront at Minehead, where I noticed that

Lynmouth Foreland.

I had crossed the county border into Somerset, before pushing on towards Watchet via Blue Anchor Bay.

I recognised the harbour at Watchet the moment I arrived. Many years earlier, we had stayed with our extended family in a large house, a former hotel in fact, in a village called Waterrow, about ten miles inland from here. My father had suggested a fishing trip, and a group of us hired a boat from Watchet harbour for a day's sea fishing. I caught a ling, which we ate for supper, as well as a couple of dozen mackerel, which we discovered were the easiest fish on the planet to catch.

I also remembered the handsome red-painted hexagonal lighthouse at the end of the west breakwater. It was built in 1862, at a time when Watchet was a busy port, exporting iron ore to Ebbw Vale. When the harbour was damaged by a series of storms in 1900, the breakwater had to be rebuilt, and the lighthouse was removed and then rebuilt in 1905. It emits an occulting green light, every three seconds, which is visible for nine miles.

Watchet is a smaller town than I remembered, and the accommodation still available at 7pm on a Sunday night was beyond my means. So I pushed on once more, having secured a room at a guesthouse in Bridgwater, another eighteen miles further on, just a few-hundred metres from the Thorn workshops where my bike was built. I learned that it is frequented almost exclusively by Thorn owners visiting the town either to buy or service their bike, so I received a very warm welcome.

WEEK 7

Day 43

I couldn't stay overnight in Bridgwater without stopping by the Thorn cycle workshop to say hello. Workshop engineer Dave Whittle seemed happy to see me, and while I drank coffee he serviced my brakes, adjusted my chain and fitted a bracket to hold my saddlebag in place more securely. I think everyone at Thorn was reassured that both bike and rider were holding up well.

The ten miles to Burnham-on-Sea were my last along the A38, and when I turned off at Highbridge to join a cycle path running alongside the River Brue, it felt as though a great weight had been lifted from me. Burnham was a small fishing village until the late-18th century, after which its popularity grew as a seaside resort. It is a dream location for lovers of lighthouses, because as well as the unusual wooden lighthouse on the beach, there are two other lighthouses in the town.

It is said that the very first light here was attributed to a fisherman's wife, who kept a candle in the window of her cottage to guide the local fleet home. The first proper lighthouse was built in 1801, when a four-storey tower was attached to the verger's house close to the church. Known locally as the Round Tower, it showed a light through a window at the top. A good part of this building still stands, although it was halved in height when a new lighthouse was built in 1832.

This second lighthouse had a tall brick tower, a conical roof and a half-gallery on the front, which incorporated the keeper's quarters. It had a paraffin-fired light, displayed through a window near the top of the tower, which was visible for seventeen miles. It became the first lighthouse in the UK to be automated as early as 1922, and the adjoining keepers' cottages were sold at the same time. It was decommissioned in 1993 and has been a private house ever since.

Built by Trinity House engineer Joseph Nelson, its light was not visible by vessels at very low tides. So he built another one, the Low Light, on the sandy beach, an unusual, square, wooden-boarded structure that sits on nine wooden pillars. It looks like it is standing on stilts.

Although it fell into disrepair and was decommissioned in 1969, it was renovated and brought back into service in 1993. It remains the only working light at Burnham-on-Sea, and shows a white flash every 7.5 seconds, visible for 12 miles, as well as a directional light (white, red or green depending on direction) through two windows facing the water.

Beyond the village of Winscombe, my route joined the Strawberry Line, a beautifully scenic former railway line running through the Cheddar Valley that has been transformed into a cycle path and bridleway.

I reached Clevedon for a second time, this time by bike, where I met up with Dick Hannaford, a skilled sailmaker. He had seen the *Telegraph* article in May and got in touch to ask me to drop by his workshop when I passed through the town. I arrived to find him kneeling over one corner of a huge canvas sail, which entirely filled his immaculately clean workshop floor.

At 67, Dick said he was deliberately slowing down, choosing to take on only the projects that particularly appealed to him. He has an enviable reputation in the local area, and is as happy working on a protective boat cover as a world championship sail for a high-performance land yacht. Over coffee Dick thrust a sizeable donation to Shift.ms into my hand, and insisted on drawing me a map showing the easiest route to my next two lighthouses, at Black Nore Point and Battery Point.

The cast-iron hexagonal tower known as Black Nore Lighthouse, near Portishead, was built by Trinity House in 1894

The Low Light, Burnham-on-Sea.

to guide shipping in the Severn Estuary in and out of the docks at Avonmouth. It employed a clockwork drive mechanism that was only replaced by an electrical motor in the year 2000. It was decommissioned by Trinity House in 2010, before which it flashed a white light, twice every ten seconds.

Barely a mile onwards is the lighthouse at Portishead Point, known locally as Battery Point. A black metal lattice pyramid mounted on a concrete base, it was built in 1930 for the Bristol Port Company. It emits a white flashing light, three times every ten seconds, which is visible for sixteen miles.

These days, Portishead is a town of two halves, with the genteel and elevated streets on West Hill contrasting with the massive waterfront development on the marina. I found an elegant Victorian guesthouse in the old town, where my bedroom window overlooked the sea, directly above Battery Point Lighthouse.

Day 44

My original plan for the day was to cross the Avonmouth Bridge, using the dedicated cycle track that runs alongside the M5 motorway, and then head down to the docks to track down the North and South Pierhead Lights. A little research, however, resulted in an unwelcome discovery. There are more than forty navigation lights, beacons and masts listed along the tidal River Avon, between Avonmouth Docks and the Great Western Dockyard in Bristol.

The majority of these lights I could disregard, but I needed to be certain that none of these River Avon lights could reasonably be defined as a lighthouse.

I was able to rule out a pair of lights on Avonmouth Bridge straight away, having established that they were simply lamps bolted onto the structure of the bridge. I crossed off a further eight or more beacons inland of the Clifton Suspension Bridge. And by referring to the website of a German lighthouse fanatic, who had posted photographs of every single light along the rivers Avon and Severn, I managed to reduce the list of lights worthy of a visit from 40 to fourteen.

Nevertheless, even this shortened list included a series of near-identical and forgettable structures, and it took me more than four hours to complete. Even when looking back at the photographs I had just taken, I was already unable to distinguish one from another.

At least the pair of lighthouses at Avonmouth Docks were both traditional, 'proper' lighthouses. They were constructed after the dock piers were rebuilt in 1902, each with tapered towers with white-painted domed lanterns. The South Pierhead Light has an occulting light, visible for ten miles, while the North Pierhead Light flashes a white light, visible for eighteen miles.

I turned up at the headquarters of the Bristol Port Company hoping to be rewarded with permission to see the lighthouses, but as I anticipated, access was denied. Instead, I settled for a series of long-distance photographs from around various stretches of the Avonmouth waterfront.

Leaving Avonmouth, I was itching to cross the River Severn into Wales, but there was the small matter of a series of lights along the English bank of the River Severn. Consulting the German website for a second time, I reduced a list of nearly 50 lights to just nineteen – ten on the English side, which I would tackle this afternoon, and nine on the Welsh side, which I would hunt out tomorrow. Although none would really qualify as proper lighthouses, their designs varied sufficiently to make them worthy of a visit.

The ten lights on the English side of the river took me the rest of the afternoon, with only the lights at Berkeley Pill and the sweet little lantern at ground level at Sharpness sticking in my mind.

I headed back towards the Severn Bridge, which provides cyclists with a dedicated lane set back from the main motorway carriageway.

Pausing at the Salutation Arms, where their Tiley's Ordinary Bitter was very much to my taste, I reflected on the fact that since leaving Portishead this morning I had seen 26 lighthouses, only two of which would be universally described as such – the only two I had failed to see close up. It was not a day I would look back on with fondness, but by the end of it I was in a new country, Wales, which felt like a major milestone.

Day 45

I woke early in Chepstow determined to get the remaining River Severn lights behind me as quickly as possible. The rear range light at Beachley is built on land that forms part of the army barracks there, the entrance to which is patrolled by armed guards. A humourless soldier from the 1st Battalion, The Rifles, informed me that I would be arrested if I attempted to visit the light or even to take a photograph.

From the opposite side of the road, I decided to take the law into my own hands with a series of hastily composed photos while pedalling away as quickly as a heavily laden, overweight cyclist can. I laughed out loud at one of my pictures, which had a clear view of the light, but which also included a part of my left arm and hand, clenched into a perfect V-sign gesture that I had aimed at the soldier in question. For the record, the light looked similar to the ones at Berkely Pill that I had seen the previous day – a tall black lattice tower with a white circular lantern and gallery.

This was the only excitement in an otherwise tedious morning. By lunchtime I had seen all but one of the beacons and minor lights by the River Severn, having conquered a succession of lights whose names seemed to promise more than they delivered – Lyde Rock, Chapel Rock, Lady Bench, Old Man's Head, North Mixoms and Lower Shoots. The tower at Redcliffe at least had some age, its lattice steel frame having been built in 1920, although its lantern is redundant. These days its light is provided by eight bluish fluorescent strip lights, dating from the 1980s.

My final River Severn light was at Charston Rock, which guides vessels safely through a hazardous channel known as the Shoots. At Portskewett I turned onto a quiet lane leading to a picnic site by the river. It's a splendid spot, with dramatic views of both bridges across the river.

The light itself is modern, mounted on a small, white-painted stone tower, built on the rocks here in 1886. It looks like the white 'castle' or 'rook' on a traditional chess board, and was much the loveliest structure I had seen all day. It once served as the front of a pair of leading lights, in conjunction with the main tower at Redcliffe. Its modern light flashes white and is visible for eight miles.

Resting up on stepped rocks in the shadow of the Second Severn Crossing, I noticed a series of lights and beacons in the water in front of me. None were on the list I had made, and I was pleased to confirm that my shortlisting process had been robust.

With both Severn bridges in sight, the significance of reaching Wales struck me properly for the first time. Tracing my finger over my route on a small outline map I carried in my pocket, I surprised even myself at the distance I had covered. I had cycled almost every day for seven weeks, chalking up more miles than I had ever covered before, and so far felt in pretty good health. I was keeping up with my daily routine of MS injections, and using freezer blocks to keep my front pannier cool was now routine.

I got chatting to an elderly couple who were enjoying a picnic. Ray was a retired civil engineer and had worked on the construction of the Second Severn Crossing himself, before it opened in 1996. It was his last project before retirement. His wife, Val, had been a teacher in Cardiff. They visited this picnic area regularly, Val to enjoy the birdlife and Ray to marvel at his handiwork. When I explained what I was doing, and why I was here, they seemed puzzled. 'But there aren't any lighthouses anywhere near here,' Val offered.

I must say that I tended to agree with her.

Basking in the knowledge that the River Severn lights were now behind me, I decided to fit in a strange little light near the village of Goldcliff before nightfall.

The twelve miles to Goldcliff were flat and very quick, and followed NCN Route 4, which runs from London to Fishguard on the Welsh coast. A narrow lane led back out of the village, to a grassy bank alongside the shoreline.

The light at Goldcliff is not an object of great beauty. Built in 1924, it's a rusty, square steel box only a couple of feet taller than me. It has a simple light mounted on top. It once marked the southernmost part of the headland east of the River Usk, and displayed a white light, which was visible for six miles. It is no longer operational, and judging by its state of decay, it was decommissioned some years ago.

Goldcliff turned out to be a bit of a ghost village. The pub showed no sign of life, and I wondered whether it had closed permanently or just hadn't opened that day. The main street was deserted. With no phone signal and the pub shut, my only option was to cycle on another ten miles to Newport, where I was bound to have a choice of places to stay.

I may have had a choice, but I made the wrong one. I probably should have backed out the moment I reached the reception desk, which was positioned behind a heavy-duty set of security fortifications. What sort of clientele did this hotel attract?

Day 46

Back in my university days I met and fell hopelessly in love with a red-headed girl called Sarah from Newport, but sadly it was not a mutual thing. Nevertheless, it didn't stop me wanting to find out more about her hometown, albeit 25 years after we last met. It's a perfectly pleasant city, my hotel aside, and the locals are friendly, but I wasn't as enamoured by Newport as I had been of Sarah. I was happy to leave the city, even when I established that getting to the lighthouse at East Usk involved retracing a fair stretch of the previous evening's route.

Three miles upstream lies an RSPB sanctuary and wetlands centre, on whose shore is the sweet little lighthouse at East Usk. It marks the point where the River Usk meets the Bristol Channel. Built in 1893, it's a simple cylindrical steel tower, with gallery and hooded lantern on top. It's only 36-feet high, but unlike the disused light at Goldcliff, it's a proper lighthouse in miniature. The lantern houses a flashing white light, visible for fifteen miles, and there are also red and green sector lights on either side.

On the opposite bank of the River Usk I could make out the earlier light at West Usk. Although considerably less than a mile away as the crow flies, reaching it would require returning to Newport to cross the river and skirt around the docks to the south of the city. It gave me the opportunity to cross the river on the splendid Newport Transporter Bridge.

The bridge was designed by French engineer Ferdinand Arnodin and built in 1906. It's an extraordinary structure that works by carrying vehicles and passengers on a sort of gondola suspended above the water. It's the oldest and largest of the three ferry bridges left in Britain, and also the largest of the eight that remain worldwide. The crossing cost just £1.50, bicycle included, although for £4 visitors could climb and cross on the open steel walkway from which the deck was suspended, nearly 50 metres above me. As someone who fears heights, I was not tempted.

Approaching West Usk Lighthouse, I was looking forward to meeting Frank, its current owner, who runs it as a B&B. He had featured a few years earlier in an episode of *The Hotel Inspector*, when he and hotelier Alex Polizzi had clashed over his choice of decor and love of *Doctor Who* props.

The track leading to the lighthouse was hard going, a mixture of shingle and potholes, but as I neared the lighthouse I couldn't help but be spurred on by the rather unusual sight of a Tardis, clearly visible in the lighthouse's lantern gallery. Alex Polizzi obviously hadn't got everything her way.

I rang the bell and knocked loudly, but Frank was not at home. It was a pity, because he came across on television as a charming eccentric, and I would have liked to meet him and hear his story. I made do with a few photographs and made a point of sending the picture of the Tardis to Tom at home.

The lighthouse was built in 1821 to guide vessels through a dangerous tidal race at St Bride's, where the River Usk meets the River Severn. It was the first lighthouse to be designed by engineer James Walker, who designed a total of 29 lighthouses for Trinity House.

When first built, it had a 56-feet tall, circular brick tower with gallery and lantern. Towards the end of the 19th century, a two-storey circular building was added around the base of the tower, which provided keepers' accommodation. The lantern displayed two lights, one red and one white, which were visible for eleven miles. After being decommissioned in 1922, the lighthouse served briefly as a private home before falling into disrepair. When restored in the 1990s, a replica lantern was reinstated, and the building is now a luxury B&B.

My route to Cardiff was rewarding, following a succession of silent lanes and minor roads that hugged the Severn Estuary. It was only when I met the purpose-built Millennium Walk alongside Cardiff Arms Park stadium that I realised I had covered more than ten miles in just over half an hour. I cycled straight down to Cardiff Bay to check out my options for boat trips to a couple of offshore lights out in the Bristol Channel. There seemed to be regular rigid inflatable boat (RIB) trips out to Flat Holm, an island that marks where the Bristol Channel meets the Severn Estuary. But the rather strange-looking light at Monkstone was clearly not high up on tourists' list of boat trip destinations. I would need to come up with a plan for that one.

For tonight, though, I had just one more mile to cover. John and Judy, Emily's aunt and uncle, live in Penarth, and they had kindly offered me a bed for a couple of nights. I loathed the absurdly steep hill up into Penarth from the Cardiff Bay Barrage, but within an hour I was showered and in fresh clothes, with a glass of decent red wine in my hand and supper just a few minutes away.

West Usk.

Day 47

I left John and Judy early to head to Barry Island, where there's a lighthouse at the end of the dock's breakwater. It has always been popular with tourists – the town, not the lighthouse – but these days it is also held in affection by fans of *Gavin and Stacey*, which was filmed here.

I headed straight for the seafront, and was delighted to see several familiar landmarks from the series, including the fun fair, Marco's Cafe and the promenade building with the columns rising from the sea wall, where the final scenes of the original series were shot. I took a picture of the columns and posted it, without caption or comment, on my Facebook feed. My friend Sarah, who I had met up with in Fowey, simply replied, 'Tidy!'

After this brief comedic nostalgia, I realised that the Barry's Docks Breakwater Lighthouse was half a mile or so further east of the beach. I followed a fabulous tarmac cliff-edge track around the bay, from which I could see the islands of Flat Holm and Steep Holm clearly, and the Somerset coast indistinctly behind them.

The docks at Barry were opened in the 1880s after Cardiff's docks became congested. A breakwater was constructed, at the end of which was built a lighthouse with a circular iron tower with gallery and lantern and a roof painted deep red. It was first lit in 1890 and shows a quick-flashing white light that is visible for ten miles.

I made it back to Cardiff early in the afternoon, and was delighted, though somewhat surprised, to discover that John was ready to accompany me on my trip out to Flatholm Lighthouse (oddly, the lighthouse name is one word and the island two words) on a RIB. This was no leisure cruise, but an exhilarating, high-speed, back-breaking adventure designed for thrill seekers and stag weekenders. The website describes it as 'Cardiff's ultimate powerboat experience', and the only reason I was keen to go myself was because it represented my only chance of seeing the lighthouse today.

The craft seats twelve, and John and I were ushered up to the front. I was happy, although the organisers seemed highly amused for some reason, and mentioned something about hoping we had brought a set of dry clothes. A party of four behind us, regulars we discovered, also thought it hilarious that the two old-timers were at the front.

We left Mermaid Quay calmly enough, and we barely caused a ripple as we caressed the water across the bay towards the Barrage. After the inevitable safety briefing, I asked our skipper how close we might get to the lighthouse on Flat Holm, and also about the lighthouse at Monkstone. Although bemused by my interest, he offered to divert the tour to take in Monkstone as well.

Everything changed the moment we were through the Barrage. The RIB accelerated with the kind of force I had only experienced in a plane taking off. John and I were thrust to the back of our seats, the wind strong enough to contort John's face into a series of grimaces that would have suited Mr Bean. I assumed that my own face had followed suit.

Nor was the strength of the wind my only complaint. With the front of the boat rising and falling in the water, each wave caused a bath's worth of water to soak me every few seconds. I couldn't have been any wetter if I'd dived in. I managed to remove my glasses and secure them in a zipped pocket. I strapped my daypack to the leg of my seat. Then all there was left to do was clench my arm rail tightly, shut my eyes and wait for it all to be over.

After the longest twenty minutes of my life, we slowed right down, and I opened my eyes to discover that we were just metres away from Monkstone Lighthouse. Originally, this granite tower was unlit when it was built in 1839, and served as a day beacon to mark Monkstone Road, a submerged reef only visible during low spring tides. A circular cast-iron tower, with gallery, was added in 1925. This served until 1993, when it was replaced by a taller structure in fibreglass. It flashes a white light once every five seconds, which is visible for thirteen miles.

I would gladly have remained here, motionless, for the remainder of time, but the thrill seekers behind me were itching for more. Beside me, John sat absolutely still, bolt upright, with a stoic look on his face. He gave no indication of how he was holding up, and I had no words of comfort to offer. He mentioned something about it being important to have tried out attractions you recommend to friends and family, but that he probably wouldn't take this particular trip again. It was a more generous interpretation of our situation than I could offer.

Fortunately, Flat Holm Island was less than ten buttock-clenching minutes on from Monkstone. It lies right in the middle of the shipping lanes where the Bristol Channel meets the Severn Estuary, a route that all shipping headed for Cardiff, Newport, Bristol and Gloucester pass.

Although a possible lighthouse on Flat Holm Island was discussed as early as the 17th century, it wasn't until the late 1730s that a coal-fired stone tower was first built. It proved inefficient, the subject of numerous complaints. But it took until 1819 before Trinity House took over the lease and committed to improving the light.

The tower was raised to 90 feet, and a lantern was fitted with an oil-fired Argand lamp providing a fixed white light. Further improvements were made in 1866, including a larger lantern, new iron gallery and a further extension to the height of the tower. The light itself was also altered to an occulting pattern.

For much of the 20th century, the lighthouse was served by two sets of three keepers, each working one month on the island and one month ashore. The lighthouse was automated in 1988 and converted to solar power in 1997. Its flashing white light is visible for fifteen miles, and there is also a red sector visible for twelve miles.

Flatholm.

It was saying something that this single, hour-long RIB ride caused more discomfort to the small of my back, and backside, than nearly 50 days in the saddle. I was overjoyed to be back inside the Barrage wall, where the speed limit was just five miles per hour. John was still determined to remain stoic and positive, but I sensed he was glad it was over too.

John and I walked slowly up the hill into Penarth in silence, via the Barrage walkway where there is a modern, green-painted metal light on the north pier. Back at home, Judy asked John what he had thought of the trip. After a long pause he simply replied, 'Bracing!'

Day 48

I planned to cover the twenty miles from Penarth to Nash Point along minor roads, but I still managed to circle Cardiff Airport and then the substantial Ministry of Defence site at St Athan. The village square in Llantwit Major is gorgeous, however, and I was tempted to stop at the Old White Hart for coffee, or perhaps even an early pint. Barely 10am, it wasn't the first time I'd found an attractive pub in a pretty village at an inconvenient time.

John and Judy timed their departure perfectly to reach Nash Point to coincide with my arrival. The headland is popular with walkers and hikers, and we wandered along the broad path that runs directly in front of the two lighthouse towers. There still seemed to be plenty of family news to catch up on as we did so. The lighthouse buildings are licensed as a wedding venue, and as we passed one of the stone buildings adjoining the tower, a portly and red-faced man stuck his head out of the window and shouted: 'Shut the fuck up. Don't you know there are people getting married in here?'

A range of sandbanks known as Nash Sands, at the entrance to the Bristol Channel, make navigation for shipping hazardous. Trinity House engineer James Walker was commissioned to design a pair of lights at Nash Point in 1830. The high and low towers, set 330 yards apart, formed leading lights that indicated safe passage through the sandbanks.

The high light is a tall, circular, stone tower with gallery and lantern. Standing 122-feet tall, it shows an occulting white light, visible for sixteen miles. It also shows a red sector visible for ten miles.

The low light originally had a shorter, 60-foot-tall conical tower with lantern and gallery. It was decommissioned in the 1920s, and the lantern was removed some time afterwards.

Nash Point was the last lighthouse in Wales to be fully automated, in 1998.

Before saying goodbye to John and Judy, they treated me to lunch at the Horseshoe Inn at Marcross. We sat outside and kept hearing the absurdly loud foghorn from Nash Point. I thought about the effect that it would be having on the rude man from the wedding party, and grinned. But I discovered later that the

Nash Point.

foghorn was an important highlight of every wedding at Nash Point, so it was probably sounding at his request.

We ate well, and the pub served a bitter that was new to me, called Cwrw Braf from the Tomos Watkin brewery. I may not have been able to pronounce it, but it tasted pretty good. When we were done, it was hard to say goodbye to John and Judy, who had been such welcoming and genial hosts.

My final destination for the day was the Great House at Laleston, just outside Bridgend. Matthew and Suzanne, my brother and sister-in-law, had arranged to meet me there and treat me to a meal and overnight stay. I found them in the courtyard where they were already on their second pot of tea, and I helped them to get through two more. No one drinks more tea than my brother.

Matthew is a keen hiker and hillwalker, and he and Suzanne have always been able to find interesting places to visit, no matter where they are. I remember Matthew once visiting me at a grotty B&B in an unmemorable suburb of Leicester. I lived there for a few months when I managed to get onto a graduate trainee programme for Aldi, when they first entered the UK food market. With just a few hours' notice, Matthew had devised an eight-mile circular walk that took in several places of historical interest, including the site of the Battle of Bosworth Field. I only lasted at Aldi six months, but that walk is still fresh in my memory nearly 30 years later.

Over a dinner that included the most tender lamb I'd eaten in years, we caught up with family news, including making a tally of the nephews' and nieces' birthdays we'd each forgotten. My solution is usually just to write my nephew, Ed, a slightly bigger cheque each Christmas.

Suzanne says less than my brother, but what she does say always counts and often makes me laugh. A few years ago we arranged a short holiday in the Brecon Beacons that included as many members of our family as were prepared to come. I announced that it was market day in the local town and asked if anyone wanted to join me. Suzanne looked a little dubious: 'What sort of market is it? Is it a proper market selling local crafts and produce? Or is it a "nylon pants" sort of market?'

It turned out to be a 'nylon pants' sort of market, and I have not been able to look at many British market towns in the same way since.

Day 49

Breakfast at the Great House was as memorable as dinner, and I felt a stone heavier by the time I was back on my bike.

Porthcawl is a five-mile downhill freewheel from Laleston, where there is a lighthouse at the end of the stone breakwater by the harbour. Built in 1860, it has a tapered hexagonal tower made of cast iron, one of only two iron towers in Wales. It is painted white, with a black band at its base, and has a simple domed lantern that displays a fixed white light, visible for six miles. It also shows red and green sectors to the sides. Originally coal fired, it was converted to mains gas in 1974 and electrified in 1997.

We managed a series of hastily taken photos before the rain fell and we retreated to the Grand Pavilion Cafe. When the time came to say goodbye to Matthew and Suzanne, a wave of homesickness overwhelmed me. I'm not sure whether the condensation on my glasses was caused by the rain or my tears, but I cycled out of Porthcawl unable to see further than my front wheel.

I forced myself to cover seven or eight miles of NCN Route 4, before stopping to catch my breath. I diverted briefly to see a pair of range lights marking the entrance to the Tata Steel Works in Port Talbot, the taller of which was hard to distinguish from the electricity pylons close by.

Approaching Swansea, I made straight for the redeveloped Maritime Quarter, where the splendid Lightvessel 91, known as *Helwick*, is now moored permanently. It had first served close to the mouth of the Humber on the east coast, but spent the last six years of service off the Helwick sandbank in the Bristol Channel, south-west of Swansea. These days, *Helwick* is fully restored, and a prize floating exhibit for Swansea's museum in the marina.

I've always rather liked Swansea, having visited several times during late-summer holidays on the Gower Peninsula as children. Dylan Thomas was born here, and described Swansea as the 'ugly, lovely town'. But the Swansea of today is very different from the city when he was born, with much of it rebuilt after suffering heavy bombing during the Second World War. My own affection for the city is largely due to the manager of Radio Rentals in about 1979. One particular Gower holiday had been so wet that my father had gone from store to store, in what we all thought would be a futile attempt to hire a television set for ten days. Radio Rentals duly obliged, and the following morning the manager himself arrived at our holiday cottage with a portable television, set it up for us, and duly returned a week or so later to reclaim it. I think he charged my father £8 all in.

If nostalgia helped to mask the homesickness I felt that morning, then the Swansea Bike Path to Mumbles served to renew my enthusiasm and positivity. It's a wide, flat cycle path that hugs the coastline for the entire stretch between the Swansea Observatory and Mumbles, and runs the length of the old Mumbles tramway that carried the world's very first railway passengers. There are wonderful views across Swansea Bay to Mumbles Head, which marks the start of the Gower Peninsula, where an interesting lighthouse is located.

Mumbles Lighthouse was commissioned by the Swansea Harbour Trustees in 1791 to guide vessels into Swansea Bay, past the hazardous Mixon Shoal and the Mumbles rocks. After an initial structure collapsed, the lighthouse was finally completed in 1794.

Originally coal fired, an oil-powered light inside a cast-iron lantern was added later. It has an unusual two-tiered octagonal stone tower, with a gallery surrounding each tier. In 1905 the lighthouse was changed from a fixed to an occulting light pattern. It was converted from oil to mains electricity in 1969, then to solar power in 1995. LED lanterns were installed in 2017. It currently provides a group flashing white light, visible for sixteen miles.

From the comfort of the Beach Hut Cafe on Mumbles Pier, I was pleased to find a B&B in Llanmadoc, the village where I had stayed as a child, which meant cycling on another sixteen miles.

The rugged, untamed landscape of the Gower Peninsula stands in stark contrast to the vibrant urban renewal taking place within Swansea's Maritime Quarter, just a few miles to the east.

On Gower's south coast, steep limestone cliffs shelter a succession of secluded sandy beaches, while inland a gentle coastal plateau gives way to open moorland rich in gorse,

The peerless and bulletproof Thorn Nomad.

Dungeness: The lighthouse that ignited a childhood dream.

St Catherine's Oratory: Early space rocket or medieval lighthouse?

The Lizard: Our home for the end-of-May school holiday.

St Ives: The former and current harbour lights.

Hartland Point: Where the Bristol Channel meets the Atlantic Ocean.

Lynmouth Foreland: Remote and beautiful, but very little sunlight.

Burnham-on-Sea: one of the world's ten most beautiful lighthouses.

Mumbles: Gateway to the Gower Peninsular.

Whiteford Point: This wave-swept cast-iron lighthouse is a rare survivor.

Caldey Island: Home to a Cistercian monastery and this splendid lighthouse.

Llanddwyn Island: Spectacular views, but watch out for the tide.

Trwyn Du, or Penmon Lighthouse, with its hauntingly beautiful fog bell.

New Brighton: One of the Wirral's best-known landmarks.

Berwick-upon-Tweed: Ed and Allan at England's most northerly lighthouse.

Killingholme: A reunion of map-and-travel
booksellers.

Inside the Happisburgh optic.
(Photo © Patrick Tubby)

Ed departs from Happisburgh.
(Photo © Patrick Tubby)

Dovercourt: One of a pair of range lights now
on the Heritage at Risk register.

East Bank Lighthouse on River Nene: Once home to naturalist and artist Sir Peter Scott.

bracken and heather. This is common land, and one of the most important areas of lowland heath in Wales.

Llanmadoc lies on the north coast, where the saltwater marshes contain a natural abundance of samphire, sorrel and sea lavender, the perfect environment for the Gower salt marsh lamb so prized by chefs and restaurateurs. I had miles of open moorland ahead of me, and was rewarded with the sweet, nutty perfume of the golden-yellow gorse flowers with every intake of breath.

By 8pm I was showered, in clean clothes and walking down to the Britannia for supper. I was hoping I wouldn't be recognised. The last time I had been here, the previous summer with Emily and the children, I fidgeted and toyed with the wax candles on our table and set fire to the tablecloth.

Mumbles.

WEEK 8

Day 50

It felt fitting that on the 50th morning of my journey, I woke up in the village where I spent two such happy and significant summer holidays as a child. It was at about this time that the idea of cycling to every lighthouse took shape, influenced no doubt by the graceful wrought-iron lighthouse at Whiteford Point on the beach below the village.

When I stayed in Llanmadoc in the 1970s there were three pubs in the village, as well as a post office and village store. For such a small community, it isn't surprising that the Britannia is the only surviving pub, but it was encouraging to see a newly built and thriving community-run general store and cafe right in the heart of the village.

Leaving my bike at the cafe, I set off on foot for the lighthouse at Whiteford Point, following a series of pine forest paths running alongside an expansive stretch of sandy beach. My brothers and I used to improvise games of cricket on this beach, where whoever was batting could regularly hit the ball far enough to allow for an all-run six. Our games were wound up once my mother read that during the war the beach was used by the army as a shelling and mining range. Apparently, they were still discovering, and clearing, a few unexploded bombs each year.

Unexploded ordnance isn't the only hazard in the Burry Estuary. Dangerous currents run against the Atlantic Ocean to the west, resulting in many vessels being wrecked on the beach over the centuries. In January 1868, sixteen coal-laden ships were wrecked after a short crossing from Llanelli, when a sudden groundswell left them floundering off Whiteford Point.

The light at Whiteford Point was built in 1865 and is the only remaining cast-iron lighthouse surrounded by the sea in the United Kingdom. Its tall, tapered tower is constructed from eight courses of cast-iron plates, with lantern and gallery on top. Unusually, the lighthouse had three Argand oil lamps and reflectors, one pointing towards the south channel, one towards Burry Port and the last towards Llanelli. The light was visible for seven miles.

After the Llanelli Harbour Trust built a new lighthouse at Burry Holms, Trinity House discontinued the Whiteford Point Light in 1921.

At low tide, you can clamber over the rocks to reach the tower. Clearly, I had mistimed my walk, because with each step towards the lighthouse, the tide seemed to hasten its advance. I found myself about 50 yards shy of my goal, reluctantly settling for a handful of selfies and photographs from the safety of the beach.

Heading back to the village I crossed paths with Caitrin, a tall, spirited Scottish woman in her seventies, walking her elderly Labrador along a narrow stretch of beach that was holding out against the tide. A retired teacher, recently divorced, she had bought a small cottage near Rhossili and was enjoying her new-found freedom. She seemed unsure about quite where she was heading, or even how far she had already walked, yet seemed carefree and blissfully detached. I can imagine that life on the Gower Peninsular has had a similar effect on countless others.

My route out of Gower followed the estuary, where hen harriers and peregrine falcons are frequently spotted. I saw neither, although near Weobley Castle I was rewarded with the unmistakable sight of a red kite soaring effortlessly above me.

After Llanrhidian the road was flat, although a strong headwind made it tough going. On the promenade at Crofty, it took all my effort to overtake an elderly man who walked hunched over a stick. Barely 100 yards later, he managed to retake the lead.

Whiteford Point.

Everything changed once I crossed the estuary at Loughor Castle. With the wind now behind me, I barely had to pedal at all as I joined the Millennium Coastal Path, a glorious thirteen-mile trail that follows the north bank of the Loughor Estuary. The six miles I had just completed had taken more than an hour. The same distance along the north bank took about fifteen minutes.

I paused briefly at Burry Port, once a thriving harbour that accounted for the export of most of the coal mined from the Welsh Valleys. It was transported to Burry first by barge on the canal network, and then by rail. There's a small stone lighthouse on the west harbour breakwater, built in 1842. It is remarkably well preserved, having been restored in the 1990s when the harbour was transformed into a marina for yachts and leisure craft. It still functions, displaying a white flashing light visible for fifteen miles.

My day ended at Kidwelly, an attractive town on the River Gwendraeth above Carmarthen Bay, perhaps best known for its imposing and well-preserved Norman castle. I managed a quick tour in the late afternoon, recognising it immediately as the location used in the opening scenes of *Monty Python and the Holy Grail*, before hunting for somewhere to stay.

Day 51

I planned to reach Tenby by nightfall, a distance of around 40 miles, with only the little harbour light at Saundersfoot to stop at along the route.

The first ten miles to Carmarthen, all uphill, were difficult enough, but the ten-mile stretch along the main A40 that followed was a dual carriageway in parts, and no place for a bicycle. I gripped my handlebars so tight, for so long, that it took effort to release them when I finally left the main road at St Clears.

I swapped four-lane madness for single-track solitude and weaved my way back to the coast, passing through hamlets and small villages which, irritatingly, appeared to lack lunchtime pubs.

I reached Saundersfoot by early afternoon, finding a pretty harbour sheltering rows of yachts and small craft. It was built in the 1840s and used for the export of local coal and lime. There is a circular stone lighthouse on the far end of the south harbour wall, which dates to 1848. It's only eleven-feet tall, with a modest red lamp unit mounted on top. Despite being decommissioned when the local mines closed in 1947, it was rebuilt and relit seven years later, in 1954. It currently shows a flashing red light, visible for seven miles.

Tenby is just a few miles on, and it would be hard to think of a more attractive seaside town. In Norman times it was fortified, and most of the old outer walls remain, enclosing the medieval town. There was once a substantial castle here, and even now the keep tower that remains is an imposing sight. In Victorian times, Tenby was a fashionable seaside resort, and there are promenades on either side of the old town. The centre is a maze of narrow pedestrianised streets, and much of the high street is dedicated to small, independent stores of every kind.

In a quiet side street I found a launderette with a thriving fish and chip shop next door, both owned by the same family. The four of us waiting for our washing cycles to end each had meals spread out on paper on our laps.

As I made my way back to the guesthouse, weaving through joyful clusters of holidaying families, a wave of homesickness crashed over me once again. Each family, each child's laughter, each dog walker with loyal companion at their side tugged at my heartstrings, stirring an overwhelming and uncontrollable sadness within me. While breathtakingly beautiful, Tenby felt as though it was the last place on earth I wanted to be. It made no sense, and it left me feeling disoriented and conflicted.

That's not strictly true. It made perfectly good sense. Around half of all people diagnosed with multiple sclerosis have suffered depression at some point in their lives, often coupled with anxiety and a variety of related symptoms. It has plagued me, on and off, since I was eighteen. I must have tried just about every treatment, every therapy, every medication. Some have provided more effective relief than others, but none have proved able to prevent alarming mood swings, as well as extended periods of low mood.

Tonight, I just didn't feel strong enough to spend time alone. I passed a Baptist Church, where a male voice choir was about to start an evening recital, and I didn't hesitate to find the £5 entrance fee and a seat at the back. For nearly two hours I sat enthralled, despite the recital including a number of intentional tear jerkers, and I spent much of the second half sobbing as quietly as I could in the back row.

Day 52

A good night's sleep raised my spirits a little, but sharing the crossing from Tenby Harbour across to Caldey Island with twenty or more happy and carefree couples and families didn't help. The lighthouse on Caldey Island was one I had long wanted to see, but I didn't feel the sense of anticipation or excitement I had expected.

On the boat, I sat next to Ian and Janet, a middle-aged couple from Birmingham who were halfway through a week-long tour of the Pembrokeshire coast. I couldn't help noticing that Ian and I were wearing identical shoes. I chose my pair purely on the basis that they were reduced from £130 to £30, and I started to ask Ian whether he had done the same when I was kicked in the ankle by Janet, who seemed keen to cut me short. It turned out that they had been a present from Janet for Ian's birthday, and she clearly didn't want him to know how little she'd spent.

Caldey Island is one of Britain's holy islands, home to Cistercian monks, who continue a tradition that began there in Celtic times. Just two miles offshore from Tenby, the island is only a mile-and-a-half long and barely a mile wide. It is home to the current abbey, built in 1910 and considered to be the most complete example of the Arts and Crafts style in the country. These days, the monks rely increasingly on tourism for their livelihood, and fancy soaps, perfumes and handmade chocolate are marketed heavily. The chocolate is delicious, no doubt, but eye-wateringly expensive.

While most of the boat's passengers headed straight for the abbey, I marched on southwards, straight up the island's main track to the highest point, where the lighthouse is situated. Just a few minutes after disembarking, I realised that I was entirely alone.

Trinity House built the lighthouse here in 1829, to guide coastal shipping past the St Gowan Shoals and the Helwick Sands. It was designed by Joseph Nelson, who was also responsible for the lighthouses at Nash Point, Lundy North, Longstone and St Bees. It has a circular, white-painted tower, with a pair of single-storey cottages alongside for keepers and their families.

Originally oil powered, it was converted to acetylene gas in 1927, when the keepers were withdrawn. It remained acetylene powered until modernisation in November 1997, when it was converted to mains electricity.

It gives a flashing white light, visible for thirteen miles, as well as two flashing red sector lights, visible for nine miles.

As well as the lighthouse, there are spectacular views out towards Lundy and what must be the barest outline of the North Devon coast. But I wasn't feeling the thrill that seeing a lighthouse high up on my bucket list should have delivered, and all I really wanted to do was find shelter and crouch down in a ball, with my head between my knees.

Back in Tenby, a stall selling handmade lamb pasties did more to improve my mood than the lighthouse had done. I managed three. If you ever find yourself in Tenby, I recommend them heartily.

Caldey Island.

I collected my bike, riding away from Tenby with little enthusiasm. I vowed to keep going for three more days, until the weekend, before reviewing my mental state, at which point I would decide to either find a local doctor, head home for a break or abandon the rest of the journey altogether.

For now, I pushed on to the small Pembrokeshire village of Dale, beyond Milford Haven, ideally located for the two lighthouses at St Ann's Head, and close to where I could take a boat trip out to the island of Skokholm.

I found a guesthouse barely 100 yards from the Griffin Inn, a fabulous pub on the waterfront where, after a quick shower, I managed several pints of Cwrw Haf, the bitter I had discovered in the pub near Nash Point. I'd pay for it with a headache in the morning, but for that moment, the Griffin Inn was the finest place on earth.

Day 53

Dale is only a couple of miles from the lighthouse at St Ann's Head. After a short climb out of the village, the lane onto the headland was largely straight, flat and surprisingly wide for one with so little traffic. There are glorious, unspoilt views over Mill Bay towards Milford Haven to the east, and it is easy to see why St Ann's Head is the ideal location for a lighthouse.

Although Milford Haven is regarded as one of Britain's finest deep-water harbours, its approach is via Crow Rock and the Toes, a range of dangerous underwater rocks a few miles offshore. They have claimed many vessels over the years, and a coal-fired light was installed at nearby St Ann's Head as early as 1662.

A new pair of lighthouses were built by Trinity House in 1713, paid for by collecting dues at Milford Haven set at one penny per ton of cargo on British vessels, and two pence per ton on foreign vessels. One of these, the former rear light, still stands, and is now privately owned.

The moment I saw the former rear light at a distance, I was reminded of a New Year holiday walk we'd had near here with our friends Katie and Chris. I'd been given a GPS device for Christmas, new and innovative technology at the time, and much-coveted by walkers and hikers alike. Keen to show off, I suggested testing it by leaving the perfectly serviceable footpath for a GPS-guided shortcut back to the car. My revised route involved a boggy field and a heavily chained, wobbly five-bar gate, and on attempting to climb over it, Katie had a tantrum that I haven't let her forget to this day.

I cycled past the very gate and grinned broadly, before pulling up by the old lighthouse to take in the view. It's an impressive building, but after it was decommissioned in 1910 the lantern on top of its tower was replaced with a rectangular observation room, which does nothing for the building's aesthetics. However, the panoramic views over the headland, towards Skomer and Skokholm, must be majestic.

Just a few-hundred yards further towards the tip of the headland lies the current lighthouse, painted in the more familiar white-and-green Trinity House livery. It's an altogether more beautiful affair, an octagonal tower with lantern and gallery, and keepers' accommodation behind. It was converted from Argand oil to mains electricity in 1958, and fully automated in 1998. It flashes white and red lights, every five seconds, with the white light visible for eighteen miles, and the red seventeen.

There are several tall, modern lights marking the various approaches to Milford Haven that I needed to bag, including the three tall octagonal concrete towers at Blockhouse Point, and the corresponding rear range light at Watwick Point.

The current lighthouse at St Ann's Head.

The lighthouse at Great Castle Head, beyond the village of St Ishmaels, is a little more interesting, having been built for Trinity House by James Douglass in 1870. A small, square tower houses the light itself, right on the cliff edge. The tower has no lantern, and these days there are two sealed beam light units mounted on to the roof, one showing a flashing white light, the other a white, red or green light, dependant on direction. Both are visible for fourteen miles. The rear range light at East Little Castle Head is 100 years younger, and is another tall, tapered concrete tower.

My work in Milford Haven was done, but there was still one more lighthouse to reach today. I had found a two-hour RIB ride, called the Skomer and Skokholm Sea Safari, which departed from Martins Haven at 4pm. That gave me around 45 minutes to cover nine miles, a tough ask at the sort of speeds I was most comfortable at, but I was in with a chance. I cycled through Dale for the third time that day and made it on to the RIB with a few minutes to spare. Keen as I was to see the lighthouse on Skokholm, what pleased me most was that this was not a RIB ride anything like the one out of Cardiff Bay – it was an altogether more sedate affair.

Skomer is a small island less than a mile offshore that is renowned for its marine life. As well as the largest Manx shearwater colony in the world, there are thousands of puffins, as well as Atlantic grey seals, razorbills and gannets. The boat's log also reported several sightings of dolphins and harbour porpoises. We circled the island leisurely, with passengers asking to stop at every sighting of a puffin. Over the course of several boat trips, I've learned that puffins are always the star attraction.

We cruised a further couple of miles on to Skokholm, around a third of the size of Skomer. Day-trip passengers such as ourselves are not allowed to land on the island, but birdwatching stays of three or four days can be organised. Again, we circled the island slowly, counting seals, puffins, razorbills, guillemots and fulmars.

The coastline around Skokholm is more dramatic than Skomer, with cliffs up to 100-feet tall rising vertically from the sea. My attention was captured for a while by the comical sight of dozens of puffins taking flight, and by seals sprawled out on rocks in the same ungainly way that Woody, my black Labrador, lies on the hearth rug at home. Inevitably, my focus changed once the lighthouse came into view.

It could have done with a fresh lick of paint, but otherwise it was a beautiful sight. The building was bought by the Welsh Wildlife Trust in 2012, although the light itself is still maintained by Trinity House. There was a fundraising effort underway to renovate the site and open it for tours to island visitors. The wildlife wardens on the island now call the lighthouse their home, and I am extremely envious.

The lighthouse was built in 1915, by Sir Thomas Matthews, then engineer-in-chief of Trinity House. It has a white-painted, hexagonal tower, 58-feet high, with two-storey keepers' accommodation surrounding it.

It was designed to provide one corner of a triangle of lights, in conjunction with South Bishop and the Smalls, that together would guide shipping clear of the particularly treacherous coastline into Milford Haven. It is noted for being the last traditional stone-built lighthouse erected by Trinity House.

Skokholm.

It flashes a red or white light, dependant on the direction headed, which was originally designed to be visible for twenty miles. These days the light can be seen up to eight miles away, following automation in 1983.

We were back at Martins Haven at 5.30pm, and I should probably have booked another night in Dale. But to stand a chance of getting a boat trip out to see Smalls, the furthest offshore of all the England and Wales lights, I needed to be at St Davids Lifeboat Station at St Justinians by 9am the following morning. It left me with another 25 miles to cycle that evening.

I vowed to ride as though I were part of a race, chalking up each mile without looking anywhere other than straight ahead. But in Pembrokeshire, that's not an easy thing to do, and I found myself hugging the coast, passing a succession of glorious coves and beaches, seemingly empty, lit by the last of the evening's sunshine. I would gladly have stopped for a pint at the Druidstone Hotel. I could easily have whiled away a few hours with my book on the little beach at Norton Haven. The views of the bay from the Pebbles Cafe, outside Newgale, implored me to stop, while the tranquil little harbour at Solva would have tempted any seascape artist.

Eventually, I reached St Davids at around 9pm. Greg and Elin were new to the hospitality trade, and they had opened Ty Helyg B&B for the first time the previous week. The room rate blew my daily accommodation budget by some distance, but I quickly discovered that it was also the cheapest room in town. Greg and Elin turned out to be perfect hosts, and despite feeling exhausted I found myself sitting in their kitchen within minutes, sharing a couple of bottles of wine. Normally, even a review of a guesthouse that mentioned 'friendly and welcoming hosts' would give me reason enough to look elsewhere. This evening, however, my continuing low mood and anxiety made it a godsend.

Days 54 and 55

I was up early, nursing a sore head. I assumed that Elin's sympathetic look as I came downstairs for breakfast was down to the night before, but I quickly established that she had heard from the boatman that the trip out to Smalls was off. The weather had turned overnight, and there were now strong winds and unpredictable currents offshore. There would be another attempt at lunchtime the next day.

The news of the boat cancellation came as a deep blow, and my low mood was now affecting my ability to make any sort of decision. I could cycle on, but missing out on Smalls Lighthouse would be like going to Agra and giving the Taj Mahal a miss. I could stay another night in St Davids, but at the cost of eating through what were already looking like insufficient funds. Besides, I didn't like the thought of spending a whole day in my own company.

I shouldn't have been feeling like this. Making this journey was something I'd wanted to do all my life, so why was it affecting me in this way? The only memory that caused me to smile was of my son Tom telling me his favourite Tim Vine joke: 'I've just been on one of those once-in-a-lifetime holidays. I'll tell you what … never again.'

That was me.

I spent the afternoon sleeping, having filled the morning with phone calls to my MS nurse, my GP, my brother Will and to home. Typically, Emily's advice was to keep going and stay positive. Meanwhile, Will offered to set off for St Davids straight away. He could be with me by late afternoon, and we'd be home in Kent by midnight. My MS nurse suggested taking a few days to rest. My GP advised giving it a couple more days, but if the dark clouds didn't clear then she would be happy to prescribe some familiar medication the following week. So there it was. I could keep going or come home. Rest up or pedal on. I just wanted someone to make the decision for me.

When Saturday's boat trip was also cancelled, it was Elin who took on the role of route planner. With no improvement in the weather forecast for several days, it looked as though Tuesday would represent my next best shot at getting out to Smalls. Elin suggested pushing on to Fishguard, Aberaeron, or even as far as Aberystwyth. We could stay in touch, and whenever it looked as though a boat trip was likely to run, I could find somewhere to leave the bike and jump on a TrawsCymru T5 bus back along the coast again.

It wasn't ideal, but it made sense. I set off in the direction of Whitesands Bay, where I hoped to get a long-lens shot of the lighthouse at South Bishop, which would have to serve in the event that a boat trip continued to prove elusive.

The moment I reached the car park in front of the picture-postcard beach at Whitesands Bay, I felt an almost uncontrollable sense of melancholy and regret. It wasn't that South Bishop Lighthouse seemed so far offshore, although even with a long lens it was far from distinct. What troubled me was joy. Everywhere I looked I saw people enjoying themselves, something I was increasingly struggling to do.

I watched a family game of cricket underway, with a sandy tennis ball and stumps and a bat that appeared to be plucked straight from a set purchased at a beachfront toy shop. The children's laughter echoed across the sand, the game seeming to celebrate the very essence of a family summer holiday.

I started to well up, wishing it was me, with my children, playing the game. It was nonsense, really. My two daughters have never shown the slightest interest in any game involving a ball. Tom might have humoured me by agreeing to play, but his heart wouldn't have been in it. And the moment the first ball was bowled Poppy, our spaniel, would have chased after it and refused to surrender it.

Knowing that my feelings were irrational did nothing to ease them. I sat on the sea wall between the car park and the sand, lowered my head into my hands and began to cry. Quite noisily. I don't know for how long, but when I raised my head, a young girl and her mother were standing right beside me looking concerned. The mother asked if I was alright. Perhaps I should have said: 'No. I'm not alright. I'm exhausted. I've cycled about 1,500 miles and I don't want to cycle another metre. I'm making a journey that I've wanted to make for most of my life, and I'm starting to hate it. I set out to see every lighthouse around the coast, and I wouldn't be sorry if I never saw another lighthouse for the rest of my life. I'm missing home. I'm missing my children. I'm missing my wife. I'm missing my friends. I have multiple sclerosis, and I am sick to death of having to inject myself with drugs each day. My legs hurt. I'm running out of money. My career is a bit of a mess. I'm lonely. I'm probably depressed. I want to go home.'

But that's not how I was brought up. So instead I said: 'Fine, thanks. Just having a little wobble. Thank you for your concern, though.'

I pressed on, knowing that getting as far as Fishguard tonight involved reaching the lighthouse at Strumble Head first. I remember very little about those twenty miles or so, other than a steep hill out of what was evidently a pretty little bay at Abercastle. But even I had to concede that the final few-hundred yards downhill to the lighthouse at Strumble Head were spectacular.

The lighthouse is built on top of a small rocky outcrop called St Michael's Island, connected to the mainland via a metal latticed footbridge. It is unmistakably a Trinity House lighthouse, with its distinctive white-and-green livery, and I was keen to get up close.

After the harbour at Fishguard opened in 1906, the volume of shipping between Ireland and Wales increased, and Trinity House chose to build a lighthouse here in 1908. The light was designed to work in conjunction with the lighthouse at South Bishop, a few miles off St David's Head in St George's Channel. The white-painted, stone tower is 56-feet tall, with gallery, lantern and keepers' accommodation.

Originally, this was a paraffin light, with a revolving lens system supported on a bed of mercury, and an elaborate clockwork mechanism to drive its rotation. When the lighthouse was electrified in 1965, the system was replaced and simplified. The lighthouse was automated in 1980.

I had delayed the final few miles on to Fishguard because I reckoned the climb back up the hill from Strumble Head would be ghastly. But this was my internal voice talking, and once I made a start I soon reached the brow of the hill. The six miles into Fishguard included plenty of descents, and I was soon down at the harbour.

There are two lights at Fishguard, one on the northern breakwater, the other at the end of the Goodwick Sea Wall. The latter is also a breakwater, and is open to all. A rowing tournament was in full swing as I walked its length, involving dozens of local teams,

Strumble Head.

ranging from the semi-professional to somewhat shambolic bands of friends who looked as though they'd been coaxed out of the local pub to take part.

The Goodwick Sea Wall light is a white-painted, steel-lattice tower, mounted on a stone platform. It was built in around 1913, and currently has a red-flashing, solar-powered light on top, which is visible for ten miles. The lighthouse on the northern breakwater is more substantial. It dates to when the breakwater itself was constructed in 1906. It has an octagonal stone tower, a pair of galleries and a single lantern. Today it emits a flashing green light, visible for thirteen miles.

I couldn't get close up, because the northern breakwater is owned and managed by Stena, which operates the ferry service between Fishguard and Rosslare, in Ireland. I had to settle for a series of long-range photos from the eastern breakwater opposite.

I tracked down a pair of white posts, each showing a green range light, before finding an inexpensive guesthouse in a residential street behind the ferry terminal. I fashioned an evening meal from a variety of short-date pastries from the petrol station on the main road, found a repeat of *Dad's Army* on BBC Two and called it a day.

Day 56

I awoke to an email letting me know that the gales offshore were subsiding, and there was a chance of a boat trip out to South Bishop and Smalls the following afternoon. Unwilling to spend a day in Fishguard in my own company, I pressed on to New Quay to see the little harbour lighthouse there.

I discovered that New Quay is delightful. It reminded me a little of St Ives, though smaller, more genteel and with many fewer people milling about. Originally a fishing port, shipbuilding thrived here in the mid-19th century, following the construction of the breakwater in 1835. Heavy storms destroyed the breakwater and the original stone lighthouse in 1859. A second tower was also washed away. Today the breakwater is home to a polycarbonate navigation light, mounted on a wooden post.

I needed something to focus on, so kept pushing on towards Aberaeron without a break. I just couldn't afford to let my mind wander. If I did, pretty much anything I reflected on seemed capable of upsetting me. I smelled freshly cut grass, which precipitated guilt and anxiety about the state of the lawns at home. A Labrador at his owner's side, glad to be outdoors, reminded me of Willow, my own Labrador, and of how much I missed him. A queue at an ice-cream van. An empty school playground. A camper van pulling into a car park. Everything my eyes took in seemed to point to my own selfishness and neglect of the people I love. However unpleasant the A487, at least it demanded my total concentration.

Despite my state of mind, I acknowledged just what a remarkably pretty place Aberaeron is. Once a modest fishing port, the town prospered from the early 1800s, following the development of the harbour and the arrival of the railway. Shipbuilding also flourished, with more than 60 sailing vessels being built between 1810 and 1870. The architecture is Georgian, with a principal square of elegant Regency houses and buildings grouped around the harbour itself.

My day ended a little more positively. At the Monachty, close to the harbour, I enjoyed a couple of pints of Brains Bitter ('Traditional, honest ale!'), and phoned Greg and Elin, who were confident that tomorrow's boat trip was on.

WEEK 9

Day 57

A pre-recorded answerphone message announced that the Voyages of Discovery afternoon boat trip to the lighthouse at Smalls was on. I left my bike in the pub's beer cellar and took the first bus of the day bound for Fishguard.

It took almost exactly the same route that I had cycled, and I winced each time we overtook a cyclist, causing the wind to buffet around their wheels. The day before, that had been me.

In Fishguard, I was about to change on to the St Davids bus when I saw Elin waiting for me in her car. A typically kind gesture. She took me straight down to St Justinians, from where the boat trips depart, alongside the lifeboat station. There were about ten of us, all adults, unsurprising given that this was a Monday afternoon in school term time.

Our RIB was skippered by Daf, who with his wraparound sunglasses and grey-flecked beard looked like a fitter, more seaworthy version of me. He greeted me a little nervously, advising that there was 'plenty of swell' around Smalls, and he didn't rate his chances of getting very close to the lighthouse. Crestfallen, I took a seat at the back of the boat, resigning myself to another long-lens photo.

This was touted as the boat trip for seeing dolphins and whales, which partly explained why we were heading twenty miles out to sea. But while we saw gannets, puffins, oyster catchers and hundreds of seals, the dolphins and whales failed to appear.

Fortunately for me, the 'plenty of swell' failed to materialise too, and Daf got his RIB within touching distance of Smalls. In the tower's shadow, nestled among these unyielding rocks, a profound sense of tranquillity and stillness washed over me, dispersing the trials of recent weeks. And other than the sound of gently lapping water, it was almost totally silent. Even the faintest sounds we made seemed to be absorbed and reflected by the tower, returning them to us in hushed echoes. This moment demanded reverence, compelling us to be still, to listen intently and to cherish such a rare moment of uninterrupted serenity.

The Smalls are a group of rocks lying around 21 miles off the Pembrokeshire coast. They are particularly dangerous to shipping because they are never more than twelve feet above the water at high tides. When the sea is especially rough, which is often, the rocks are submerged completely.

The first lighthouse here was lit in 1776, and built to the design of Henry Whiteside, a musical-instrument maker from Liverpool. It had an octagonal oak tower, fifteen feet in diameter, supported on nine cast-iron piles around a central oak pillar. Its light came from oil lamps, and it had a single living room with lightroom and lantern above it.

Remarkably, it stood until 1861, when the current lighthouse was built to a design by Sir James Douglass based on Smeaton's lighthouse at Eddystone. Made of granite, the stones were prepared on shore, and construction took five years. It was first lit in 1861, with a white light, flashing three times every fifteen seconds, visible for 25 miles. A helicopter landing deck was added above the lantern in 1978, and the lighthouse was automated in 1987.

Sitting in a small, low RIB more than twenty miles offshore, the isolation of these rocks was undeniable. It must have been an exceptionally bleak and tough posting, being sent out here for two months at a time without the means to communicate with the mainland.

The lighthouse at Smalls was the scene of a tragedy that occurred during a particularly savage winter in 1800–1. At the time, the lighthouse was maintained by a team of two keepers,

Smalls.

Thomas Howell and Thomas Griffith. Apparently, it was well known that they disliked each other intensely.

The storms over this particular winter were so severe that the two keepers were cut off, and no relief ship was able to land for more than four months. Griffith died in a freak accident and Howell, fearing that he'd be accused of his murder, preserved his body in a makeshift coffin and dragged it out onto the gallery surrounding the lantern. When the relief crew were finally able to land after several months, they found Griffith's corpse and discovered that Howell had been driven to total madness. The tragedy changed the way lighthouses were crewed, and thereafter three keepers were always appointed to lighthouse teams.

Back on dry land I met up with Neil Hargreaves, a former lighthouse keeper who had been stationed at Smalls himself. I wondered if the lighthouse was jinxed in some way, because during his tour of duty he had got on so badly with his principal keeper that he had written to Trinity House demanding an immediate transfer, otherwise he 'would not be responsible for his actions'!

Conditions on the rock tower were apparently very basic. Personal hygiene involved a strip wash at the kitchen sink when you were off duty, and there was no lavatory, so calls of nature required the 'bucket and chuck it' approach, being very careful to check the direction of the wind before emptying the bucket out of the window.

Heading back to shore, we made a detour to South Bishop, a tall, rocky outcrop just under five miles south-west of St Davids. It has a lighthouse perched right on top of the rock, designed by James Walker and first lit in 1839. Its role was to guide vessels along the Pembrokeshire coastline and to assist their navigation around the Bishops and Clerks rocks. It has a white-painted brick tower, with lantern and gallery. Its white light flashes every five seconds, with a range of nineteen miles. It was converted to solar power and fully automated in 1983.

Since 1971 there has been a helipad next to the lighthouse complex, enabling helicopters to deliver relief crews and supplies. But before then, keepers and maintenance crews had to climb up to the lighthouse using steps cut into the sheer rock face. These are still clearly visible, and my legs weakened just looking at them.

South Bishop.

Returning to St Justinians, I spent a while in quiet reflection, grateful for what I had just experienced. This was week nine, I had travelled about 1,600 miles, and I was yet to miss a single lighthouse. Failing to reach Smalls had been a real possibility, and although getting there had required abandoning my bike 60 miles up the coast, I could now cross it off my list. If I could make it out to Smalls, then surely no lighthouse would be beyond my reach?

Day 58

I returned to Aberaeron along the same bus route. Along the way, news bulletins warned of an imminent heatwave, with temperatures expected to rise to levels more commonly witnessed in southern Europe. Warnings were issued about travelling only if it was absolutely essential, so I wasn't exactly ecstatic at the prospect of getting back on the bike.

I pushed on just eighteen miles to Aberystwyth, with a mental promise to make better progress the next day. As it turned out, the rising temperature meant that I descended into Aberystwyth ready to drop.

Aberystwyth was once one of the busiest ports in Wales, having served transatlantic shipping, as well as local shipping to Ireland and Liverpool. The Cardiganshire lead mines also exported from here. Today, the main marine traffic is for leisure, following the construction of a new marina in the 1990s.

During gales in 1859 a number of ships were lost off the coast of Aberystwyth, and during the inquiry that followed, the harbour master was accused of neglect by not switching on the harbour lights to warn passing shipping. The need for a permanent and continuous light was also discussed and, while little is recorded about what was decided following the inquiry, a stone lighthouse is depicted in a painting of ships entering the harbour at Aberystwyth, dated 1864.

The current lighthouse, on the end of the south breakwater, dates from the mid-1990s, when the harbour was remodelled to accommodate a new multi-million-pound marina. It's a tall, cylindrical, concrete tower, painted in white-and-green bands, with a polycarbonate lamp mounted on top. It flashes twice, every ten seconds, either white or green depending on direction.

I cycled along the seafront and then through the town. I had come here once before, in the early 2000s, when I interviewed a coastguard for a children's book I was working on about water safety. I met him at the modern university campus a mile or so out of town, and never saw the town centre itself.

It's a much more attractive place than I had envisaged. I was upset to see the original, grand university building on the seafront closed and boarded up, the move to the modern-day campus now complete. However, I discovered that the buildings were originally designed and built as a railway hotel in the 1860s, and that plans were underway to transform them once again, this time into a vibrant centre for learning, culture and enterprise.

Finding a comfortable budget hotel on the seafront, I requested a 'full English' when the owner asked what I wanted for breakfast. He told me pointedly that my *Welsh* breakfast would be ready at 8.30am.

Day 59

If there was a single day of this expedition that I could erase from my memory, it would be this one. It started off well enough, in bright sunshine, with clear skies and breathtaking views in every direction.

It was a hot day, though, and while it had been quite bearable when I was following the coast road, with a hint of a sea breeze to savour, now that I was ascending more than 1,000 feet alongside Cadair Idris in Snowdonia, there seemed to be no air to breathe at all.

It was the steepest climb of the journey so far, and every few yards I needed to mop the sweat from my face, remove the steam from my glasses and wait for my panting to calm down. Progress was painfully slow, and each moment I stopped moving, a cloud of storm flies collected around me, so close that I swallowed hundreds with each intake of breath.

When the track finally levelled off at the peak, I made an extremely worrying discovery. The cold storage pack containing all my supplies of MS medication was missing from my pannier. Twenty pre-filled hypodermic syringes, representing my next three weeks' supply, had vanished. I called the hotel in Aberystwyth, but nothing had been found in my room. That could only mean that they had fallen out somewhere along the roadside over a distance of twenty miles.

I could have returned to Aberystwyth, in the hope that I might find them on the roadside. However, this was medication that needs to stay cool to be effective, and with the temperature close to 30°C, it was likely that even if found, it would be beyond use. More worrying still, it is medication that needs to be taken every day *without fail*. For nearly 60 days, I had managed to nurse my supplies, transferring them from hotel fridge to cold pack each day, with a fresh supply delivered back at Penzance. Until today I had been proud to demonstrate that even with MS, travel and adventure was still entirely possible. Right now, it looked as though my message was misguided.

I put faith in Teva, the manufacturer and distributor of my medicine, and gave them a call. I explained what I was doing and what had happened. I didn't expect a helicopter dispatch right away, but I did expect at least a little sympathy. How wrong could I have been? The Teva operator told me that they would arrange for a new prescription to be sent out to me, but that it could only be delivered to my home address. As for what I should do in the meantime, given that I needed to inject myself daily, if I was at all worried, I should go to a hospital. 'Would they be able to give me a dose for today or tomorrow?' I asked. 'Very unlikely' was the reply.

With the company refusing to deliver to a hotel, or indeed anywhere other than my home address in Kent, it looked like my adventure was over. My health was more important than seeing the remaining lighthouses. As for my message of hope and encouragement for people who feel trapped by their MS, well, the world is your oyster ... just so long as you can get home to sign for a delivery from Teva.

I phoned home. I'm not sure why, or what I thought Emily might be able to do. I phoned George Pepper, the founder of Shift.ms and the friend who had inspired me to make this journey. I phoned my MS nurse at the hospital in Canterbury. I phoned my GP. I started to feel angry, manic even.

Between the five of us, a plan evolved that served to prove the power and value of social media. There was no time to push on and find somewhere sheltered from the sun, so I sat on boggy marsh grass at the side of the track and got to work. With just one bar of 3G data, I got on to the Companies House website, made a list of directors of Teva Pharmaceuticals, then googled them one by one to track down their Twitter feeds. Meanwhile, the Shift.ms team got in touch with their own contacts, requesting help and advice. I started to tweet about my journey having to end prematurely, thanks to Teva's unwillingness to compromise on their home-delivery policy. I made sure that my tweets were tolerably polite, but was secretly delighted when James Sharp, a fellow MS sufferer from New Orleans who had followed me avidly from day one, started tweeting a series of increasingly aggressive messages saying things like, 'Shame on you Teva Healthcare!'

I am not sure which of our combined efforts caused a change of heart, but an hour or so later, while sheltering from a rainstorm under a pub umbrella in an alleyway in Dolgellau, a member of Teva's UK executive office called me to say that they could deliver a fresh batch of medicine to Barmouth, my next stop, as long as I was there to sign for it in person. I took pleasure in calling Shift.ms with the good news, and getting in touch with James Sharp to ask him to call off the dogs and tweet his appreciation.

The rainstorm stopped as quickly as it had started. Even the trail ahead of me, the final ten-mile stretch to Barmouth, rapidly flattened. I followed the Mawddach Trail cycle route, winding along the disused railway track on the southern edge of the spectacular Mawddach Estuary. There were stunning views in all directions, across to Diffwys and the Rhinogs, and up the estuary to Y Garn and the Arans beyond Dolgellau. The railway once ran from Ruabon, south of Wrexham, all the way to Barmouth on the west coast. With the railway a victim of the Beeching cuts in the 1960s, this cycle path provides a beautiful and lasting legacy.

At the mouth of the estuary, the iconic railway bridge crosses into Barmouth. Despite being hot, dehydrated and tired, both emotionally and physically, it was impossible not to appreciate the scene. The view of the town opposite, and the viaduct itself, can't have changed much since it was constructed for the Aberystwyth and Welsh Coast Railway on its line between Aberystwyth and Pwllheli in the 1860s.

I checked into a charming hotel on the promenade and spent the evening rehydrating myself in the hotel bar before calling it a day.

Days 60 and 61

Teva were true to their word, and clearly keen to prove themselves the saviours of my expedition. I was still eating breakfast (which I remembered to call a 'full Welsh' this time) when a motorbike pulled up in front of the hotel and a courier handed me a fresh box of syringes wrapped in ice packs. I took close-up pictures of the box and tweeted them with gushing thanks to the people who had helped to make it happen.

Still needing to address my state of mind, I decided to rest up for the day and spend a second night in Barmouth. I sobbed down the telephone line for fifteen minutes to my GP, who promptly faxed a prescription for a course of antidepressants to a chemists in the town. My front pannier was now acting as a serviceable pharmacy, with enough medication for all my various ailments to see me through to the end of the journey.

Setting off early on Friday morning, there was a chance I could reach Aberdaron, a small fishing village on the south-west tip of the Llyn Peninsular, by nightfall. I passed a sign to Portmeirion and regretted that my revised schedule meant I couldn't justify the detour. It's somewhere I have always wanted to visit, having first come across it when it served as the location of 'The Village' in the 1960s television show *The Prisoner*. It's an extraordinary place, designed and built by Sir Clough Williams-Ellis between 1925 and 1975 in the style of an Italian village. The architecture is positively Mediterranean, and it has more than a passing resemblance to the village of Portofino, on the Italian Riviera.

Outside Porthmadog, roadworks had reduced the main road to a single carriageway for almost two miles. To make certain that no car was able to share the lane with another coming in the opposite direction, a bright yellow truck followed behind the final car for each phase of the traffic lights. The lights only changed once the truck had passed the waiting queue.

This may have been an ideal system for managing cars, but it was bloody awful for a sluggish cyclist like me. At best, two flat miles had been taking me a little under ten minutes. This stretch, slightly uphill, was going to take more like fifteen. The driver of the yellow truck decided to try to force my pace by remaining within ten feet of my rear wheel the whole way. Whenever I slowed a little to take breath, closer still. When I finally reached the traffic lights at the other end, I was met by a line of irritated drivers and overtaken by the yellow truck's driver, who looked hugely amused. It was clearly his favourite part of the job.

In Abersoch, I got lost in a one-way system looking for a sign to a village with an unpronounceable name, close to where I could get a great view of the lighthouse at St Tudwal's. Abersoch is tiny, yet each time I tried to get out of the village I passed the same pub, with the same people sitting outside it. The third time, it became embarrassing.

For very practical reasons, I couldn't stop and ask for directions. After all, where would you start with a place name like Bwlchtocyn? Eventually, I followed a sign to a golf course, and made my way towards a caravan park that I hoped would be close to the Wales Coast Path. I followed a stone wall heading straight for the cliff edge, where I found myself almost exactly opposite the pair of islands at St Tudwal's.

About half a mile off the south-east coast of the Llyn Peninsula, the islands are reputedly named after the saint who lived here in the 6th century. There are the remains of an 11th-century priory on the island, as well as a holiday home owned by the adventurer Bear Grylls.

This was a popular route for shipping cargo and slate from the local quarries, and the lighthouse was needed because the one nearby at Bardsey was obscured to ships from certain directions.

The lighthouse, on St Tudwal's West, was designed by James Douglass and built by Trinity House in 1877. It has a squat, cylindrical stone tower, with lantern and gallery, as well as single-story keepers' accommodation behind. Today, it shows a white flashing light every fifteen seconds, visible for fourteen miles. It also shows a red flashing light, also every fifteen seconds, visible for ten miles.

In 1922 the light was converted to acetylene and was operated by means of a sun valve, a mechanism invented by Swedish lighthouse engineer Gustaf Dalén. It allowed the lighthouse to be automated, and the keepers' dwellings to be sold in 1935. The lighthouse was modernised and converted to solar power in 1995.

Aberdaron was a final twelve-mile slog south, largely uphill. When I finally descended down to the harbour front, I asked for directions to the B&B I had booked.

'About a mile back up the hill,' came the unwelcome reply.

St Tudwal's.

Day 62

I was up and out early, following the Wales Coast Path to a slipway about a mile beyond the village. There was a boat trip bound for Bardsey Island scheduled for 9am, and I had the last ticket. As well as a splendid lighthouse, Bardsey is a popular destination for day trips and for tranquil getaways in one of a range of historical and traditional buildings. You can take a mobile phone, but you might only be able to pick up a signal from the Irish coast.

Reaching the cove where I was told to meet, all was quiet. I had a number to call for last-minute information about weather cancellations, but no signal to reach it. I was almost back in the village before a voicemail message advised that the boat trip was off and unlikely to run again before Tuesday, so shocking was the forecast over the next few days.

Back at the guesthouse, a series of communication channels were opened. My B&B host, Jan, phoned her husband, Steve, who worked at the village shop. Steve, in turn, phoned Colin, the boat's skipper. He established that although all day trips were off, Colin planned to make a crossing this afternoon to collect several families returning from a week's holiday on the island. There wouldn't be time to explore the island and the crossing would be rough, but he'd be happy for me to tag along at my own risk.

It was clearly the best offer on the table, and one that I wasn't going to turn down. Back at the cove for a second time, I met a couple from Denmark, brother and sister, who were off to Bardsey to meet up with their cousin, who had worked on the island for more than a year. I also met Colin himself, who was clearly delighted to meet three people so excited to be bound for an island that he obviously adored.

The approach is from the south, where a steep rock dominates the skyline and obscures the view of the lighthouse. But as we sought shelter in its shadow and rounded the island in calmer waters, the tower came gloriously into view. When we reached the quay, the plan was to turn passengers and baggage around in less than ten minutes. The forecast was for even choppier seas, and Colin wasn't keen to hang about.

The Bardsey workforce, I discovered, is a family affair, and while bags were being loaded Colin introduced me to Ernest, his father. They had both been wardens of the lighthouse for a while, and Ernest in particular seemed delighted that I was taking such an interest in it. After a brief chat with his son, he told me to jump into his Land Rover, and insisted on giving me a quick lighthouse tour, as long as I promised to return to Bardsey for a proper visit one day.

Ernest seemed sad, almost apologetic, that the lighthouse was in need of a bit of maintenance and a few coats of paint. But he assured me that Trinity House were scheduled for a maintenance visit before the end of the summer, and that it would be looking its best by the autumn.

The lighthouse was built for Trinity House in 1821 by Joseph Nelson, and was designed to guide vessels passing through St George's Channel and the Irish Sea. It stands on the flat southern tip of the island, and is notable for being the tallest square-tower lighthouse in the UK.

The tower itself is nearly 100-feet tall, and painted in broad red-and-white horizontal stripes. Originally, it gave a white light in a cluster of five flashes every fifteen seconds, visible for up to 26 miles. In 2014 a red LED lantern replaced the existing rotating optic, and its flashes are visible for eighteen miles. The lighthouse was converted to solar power at the same time. It has been automated since 1987.

Back at the quay I promised to return, although I discovered later that the island has no electricity and the cottages are without bathrooms. It's a wild, remote and very beautiful place to stay, no doubt, but I'd rate a mobile phone signal, a charging point and a flushing lavatory fairly high up on my list of holiday requirements.

I returned to the guesthouse exhausted, but I couldn't help but feel a certain trepidation at the prospect of a long evening in solitary contemplation. I had started taking the antidepressants that my doctor prescribed, but it can take two or three weeks for the effects to be felt. For a while longer, I would need to keep myself occupied and spend as little time alone as I could.

Bardsey Island.

I was fortunate to bump into Ruth, a fit, plucky pensioner and the only other guest at the B&B. She was visiting from County Durham for the annual festival celebrating the poetry of R.S. Thomas and the art of his wife, M.E. Eldridge. R.S. Thomas was the vicar of St Hywyn's Church in the village between 1967 and 78.

I'm ashamed to admit that I knew nothing about either Thomas' poetry or Eldridge's paintings, murals and book illustrations. But I was happy to spend the evening with Ruth as she filled in the gaps in my education, and I marvelled at how two evidently respected and talented artists gave her such a profound sense of purpose and enduring font of joy. I could do with some of that.

Day 63

As I left Aberdaron after breakfast, the weather forecast suggested that the light rain would clear shortly, and the rest of the day would be overcast but dry. In fact, it poured solidly for all of the 35 miles along the north coast of the Llyn Peninsula to Caernarfon.

Caernarfon is home to Wales' most famous castle and is a UNESCO World Heritage Site. It was built by Edward I in the 13th century as a royal palace and military fortress, and formed the core of a medieval walled town. Behind the castle, the town has a network of attractive narrow back streets, where I hoped to track down a quaint coffee shop and dry out for an hour. I found several, but none were open on a Sunday morning.

I paused at a bus shelter and, with no one about to take offence, changed into a fresh, dry set of clothes. It helped me to push on – I reckoned I was good for another fifteen or twenty miles. A quick search online revealed a large, slightly old-fashioned hotel in Beaumaris that looked ideal. Just my sort of place. I phoned ahead to make sure they'd be happy to hide my bike somewhere safe, and then made my way slowly north.

Getting on to Anglesey involved crossing the wonderful Menai Suspension Bridge, designed by Thomas Telford and opened in 1826. It's one of a pair of famous bridges over the Menai Straits, and was the world's first iron suspension bridge.

Beaumaris, I discovered, is a beautiful seaside town. The architecture is a mix of medieval, Georgian, Victorian and Edwardian buildings, and most of the cottages lining the residential streets are painted in soft pastel colours. It's the greenest seaside town I've visited – not in the ecological sense, but literally. The promenade and seafront walkways are edged with wide expanses of freshly mown lawn. Even the seafront car parks are all grass-lined.

The Bulkeley Hotel was everything I had hoped it would be, a vast and elegant Victorian seafront hotel that somehow manages to cater for rich and poor alike. I passed through an elegant drawing room, where afternoon tea was served on silver cake stands and platters, on tables with starched white tablecloths. In the next room, a much more down-to-earth bar and bistro looked ideal for the under-dressed long-distance cyclist on a budget.

My room was vast, but with the slightly faded decor that inevitably comes with buildings whose maintenance costs have outpaced the purses of the people who stay there. I loved it. The plumbing in my bedroom and bathroom was also Victorian, with a radiator quite a bit larger than my bath. The various runs of hot-water piping provided an instant and welcome washing line, and I hung out every item of wet clothing to dry.

I felt glad to be in Beaumaris and positive, perhaps even buoyant, in anticipation of the exploration of the Anglesey lighthouses that awaited me over the coming days. It was a little soon for my 'happy' medication to have kicked in, but my mood was certainly lifting.

WEEK 10

Day 64

If I could have stretched my daily budget, I would gladly have stayed at the Bulkeley Hotel for the rest of the summer. Judging by the number of elderly ladies looking settled at breakfast, many had clearly decided to do just that. However, I needed to slow my spending down considerably, effective immediately. My starting point was to explore the Anglesey lighthouses from Bangor, where I had managed to book three nights' bed and breakfast in the university's halls for a total of £50.

Right now, though, I was keen to savour the last hour or so of splendour in Beaumaris. However convenient the university would be, my bet was that the refectory would not serve up a breakfast like the one at the Bulkeley.

I guess if I'd really wanted to, I could just about have circled the Anglesey coastline in a single day, conquering another eight lighthouses. For the first time in nearly a month, however, I awoke without the fog of my dark mood and inner anxiety, and concluded that I was in no particular hurry. It's possible that nature was taking its course or, more likely, the effects of my medication were starting to bite. I didn't mind either way.

There's a lighthouse just off the east coast of Anglesey, beyond the village of Penmon, which has been photographed a thousand times for calendars, posters, place mats and jigsaw puzzles. You might well have seen it. It's painted in black-and-white stripes, looks a bit like the rook in a set of chess pieces, and has the words 'NO PASSAGE LANDWARD' painted in large black letters on the side pointing to the shore.

Although often referred to as Penmon Lighthouse, its real name is Trwyn Du, and it's a gentle four-mile cycle from Beaumaris alongside the Menai Straits, with dramatic views of Snowdonia on the other side of the water.

There's not a lot to Penmon village itself, but what there is, is very attractive. There is an ancient well, whose water is said to have healing powers. The stone walls nearby are reputed to have formed part of Seiriol's Church in the 6th century, which would make it the oldest remaining Christian building in Wales. A dovecote near the church, largely intact, dates from the 16th century. The highlight for me, however, was the Pilot House Cafe at Penmon Point, where, on learning that my cycle ride was raising funds for an MS charity, its owner filled my saddle bags with homemade cakes and biscuits for my onward journey.

Walking down to the shingle beach, the tide was out, and I could have reached the lighthouse by clambering over a stretch of rocks covered in seaweed. But I was more than happy to sit cross-legged on the shingle and just take in the view. The water was as calm as any pond, although there are many accounts online of waves high enough to crash over the lantern at the top of the tower. The most beautiful thing about this lighthouse, however, is its fog signal, which comes from an electronic mechanism that strikes a large bell every 30 seconds. It's a beautiful, haunting sound, like a church bell at sea. Today, with the water barely showing a ripple, it was the only sound in an otherwise silent landscape. I was lucky to have no particular goal or destination in mind for the day, and was glad to remain by the shore, gazing at Trwyn Du for a couple of hours.

In 1831 the steamer *Rothsay Castle* struck a sandbank off Penmon, with the loss of 130 of the 150 passengers on board. After this, Trinity House identified a reef between the mainland and Puffin Island as the optimum site for a new lighthouse.

It was designed by James Walker, later responsible for a series of successful rock lighthouses such as Smalls, the Needles and Wolf Rock. First lit in 1838, it has a circular and stepped stone tower, with castellated gallery and a lantern with a conical roof and

Trwyn Du.

weathervane. The tower is painted in broad black-and-white bands. These days, the gallery is decked with solar panels, and a halogen lamp that emits a flashing white light, every five seconds, which is visible for twelve miles. It was the first Trinity House lighthouse to be automated when it was converted to acetylene operation in 1922.

Half a mile further offshore, Puffin Island is clearly visible. It is not open to the public, but regular birdwatching boat trips from Beaumaris circle the island. It's a designated Site of Special Scientific Interest (SSSI), renowned for razorbills, shag, guillemots, kittiwakes, fulmars, herring gulls, lesser black-backed gulls and great black-backed gulls.

Between Trwyn Du and Puffin Island is a smaller rocky outcrop known as Perch Rock, on which is mounted a cone-shaped stone beacon, its top half painted red with a small white lantern on top.

Without warning, the calm sea and skies turned dark, accompanied by a torrential downpour. Fearing that Bangor University's halls of residence were unlikely to offer the extensive lengths of Victorian pipework that I had used to dry my soaked clothes at the Bulkeley Hotel, I packed up quickly to seek shelter.

I reached Bangor University by 3pm, where I was assigned a room that was tiny but cosy, comfortable and spotlessly clean.

Day 65

Crossing the Menai Suspension Bridge for a second time, I made for Amlwch, on the north coast, where there is a harbour lighthouse. My first impressions of the town were not especially promising, but the closer I got to the harbour, the more attractive it became. It's the most northerly town in Wales, and in the 18th and early-19th centuries was a booming mining town that became the centre of a vast global trade in copper ore. Once copper production declined, the port developed a shipbuilding and repair trade, but this too declined early in the 20th century.

The port was altered and extended a few times in the 18th and 19th centuries, and various navigation lights were built. The current lighthouse dates to 1853, a square, slightly tapered stone tower with a brick lantern room attached to a stone building. It's unusual in that its light was displayed through a window that is only visible from the seaward side, and so from the harbour wall it is not instantly recognisable as a lighthouse. The light was visible for six miles. It was decommissioned in 1972, when it was replaced by a fixed navigation light, mounted on a white metal column, positioned right at the harbour entrance.

From Amlwch, I headed for the lighthouse at Point Lynas, on a short promontory just a couple of miles east. For walkers, the coast path hugs the cliff edge all the way and on clear days offers uninterrupted views across the water to the Isle of Man. Cyclists must take a brief detour inland, but the scenery was still stunning as I followed a single-track lane lined with low stone walls, bracken, heather and, inexplicably, a group of well-tended palm trees. The final approach along the headland to the lighthouse was spectacular, offering me the views that the coast path walkers would have enjoyed all the way.

Point Lynas Lighthouse is at the highest point on the headland, and has an imposing castellated gateway, giving the entire complex the feeling of a wealthy landowner's castle. Originally, it was designed to serve as a lookout post for the Liverpool Pilotage Services.

The original tower was constructed in around 1780, with a pair of oil lamps showing lights in two directions. At the same time, a building to provide accommodation for the pilots was built, which also provided the location for the current lighthouse, built in 1835 after the original pair of lamps were declared inadequate.

The current lighthouse was built as a two-storey extension to the seaward side of the accommodation building, with a ground floor semi-circular lamp room. Originally argon powered, it was converted to oil in 1901, then to electricity in 1957. Following electrification, the occulting light was visible for twenty miles. Trinity House assumed responsibility for Point Lynas Lighthouse in 1973, and the lighthouse was automated in 1989.

Llanddwyn Island, where my next pair of lights were, was a relatively straight twenty-mile ride, almost exactly due south. The hills and cliff tops of the northern coast contrast markedly with Anglesey's south coast, where broad sandy beaches meet the dense and silent forestry of the Newborough National Nature Reserve.

There are more than ten miles of footpaths and bridleways within the nature reserve, and I tried several before finding one heading for the seafront and island. Llanddwyn is a tidal island, a peninsula at all times other than at high tide, and it's astonishingly beautiful. There is plenty of evidence of early settlements and habitation, including the remains of a medieval stone church and a Celtic cross that served to point out my

Point Lynas.

path to the south-eastern and south-western extremities of the peninsula, where the two lighthouses are located.

It is not recorded exactly when the two towers were built, but Ordnance Survey maps from the early-19th century show them both and suggest that they served as unlit daymarks or beacons initially.

Records show that the larger of the two was altered in 1845, when a lantern room was installed at ground level, with the keepers' accommodation housed within the tower. The current optic and Fresnel lenses, which were lit by six Argand lamps with reflectors, date to 1861. Its light was visible for seven miles. The lighthouse was decommissioned in the mid-1970s, when a navigation light was fitted to the smaller tower close by.

The smaller tower, known as Twr Bach, was constructed from rubble stone in the early-19th century. It served as a daymark only until 1975, when Trinity House installed a solar-powered flashing navigation light to replace the Twr Mawr Light.

I had read several times that Llanddwyn is a peninsula except at high tide. Somehow the implications of this hadn't sunk in. I had sat cross-legged, with my back leaning against Twr Bach, for half an hour or so, soaking up the view out to sea. I could make out the Llyn Peninsula, and I knew that on a clear day I stood a chance of seeing the Irish coast. By the time I emerged from my reverie it was early evening, and the tide was enveloping the island rapidly.

Below the Celtic cross, where the path meets the sandy beach, the sea was both to my left and right, but there was still a narrowing strip of sand back to the forest footpaths. What I hadn't bargained for was that even though the tide still left me with safe passage, the sand itself was becoming saturated with water, making my feet sink a little with each step. It was fine for me, but not for the bike I was pushing. It was far too heavy, and the wheels were creating ever-deeper ruts in the sand as I made precious little progress back to dry land.

With considerable effort I made it to the safety of the trees on the shoreline, but it was touch and go at several points. I berated myself for failing to notice that every other walker had left some time before me, and I lay down on the sand, exhausted, wondering how I would summon the energy for the ride back to Bangor.

Day 66

A number of Anglesey operators offer RIB rides and scheduled boat trips out to the various islands off the Anglesey coast, and I had hoped to book one that ventured out to the Skerries, a small group of islets around seven miles from Holyhead. The weather was not on my side, however, and there wasn't a single boat trip likely to run for the next few days.

My best alternative was to see the Skerries Lighthouse from the shore, and it looked as though a footpath at Carmel Head represented my best shot. I crossed the Menai Bridge for the third successive day and followed NCN Route 8 towards Holyhead. Short of the port itself, I diverted north-east and discovered a landscape of narrow tracks, bracken, heather and bright-yellow gorse bushes that reminded me of sections of the North Devon coast. At various points I caught glimpses of the Skerries, but it was clear that if I wanted the best view I'd need to jettison the bike. Hiding it behind the stone wall that lined one of the narrower lanes, I struck out towards the coast. When eventually I reached the coast path, alongside a deserted shingle beach, the lighthouse on the Skerries appeared directly ahead, and seemed only a few-hundred metres away. The sun was shining, and I felt irritated that the boat trip might have been cancelled unnecessarily, but when a wave crashed over the rocks on the beach and drenched me, I acknowledged that I was safer here than on a boat.

The first lighthouse on the Skerries was a coal-fired light, built at the highest point on the islands in 1717. The tower was rebuilt in 1759, and an iron balcony and oil-burning lantern and lantern room were added in 1840. At the time, it was the only private lighthouse operating in the British Isles.

A year later, in 1841, Trinity House purchased the remaining lease, and the lighthouse was extensively remodelled by engineer James Walker a few years later. A keepers' cottage was added, the gallery rebuilt in castellated stone, and a new cast-iron lantern installed. The tower is painted white, with a broad red band.

In 1903 a second circular tower was constructed to carry a sectional light at ground level. Converted to electricity in 1927, it flashes a white light, twice every ten seconds, which is visible for 22 miles. The lighthouse was fully automated in 1987, at which time a helicopter landing pad was added.

Holyhead is a substantial port, handling freight and passenger traffic bound for Ireland. The main harbour construction began in 1821, and a lighthouse was built on the Admiralty Pier by renowned civil engineer John Rennie in 1821. It has a tapered stone tower, with lantern and gallery on top.

When work on the outer harbour and breakwater were completed in 1873, the new breakwater light became the principal lighthouse at Holyhead. The breakwater is, at 1.87 miles, the longest in the United Kingdom, and construction took nearly

Skerries.

30 years, consuming 7 million tons of Anglesey limestone and employing 1,300 workers.

The lighthouse was the last building to be constructed on the breakwater and is thought to be the work of Victorian civil engineer John Hawkshaw. It's a handsome three-storey square tower, painted white with a broad black band. It has a circular lantern mounted on the wide, square gallery, which displays a group of white flashing lights every fifteen seconds, visible for fourteen miles. It was automated in 1961.

My Anglesey adventure was almost complete, but I had arguably the most beautiful lighthouse on the island still to see. It's at South Stack, a tiny rocky islet set apart from Holy Island on the north-west coast of Anglesey. Barely three miles north-west of Holyhead, the whole area is a nature reserve, popular with walkers, bird watchers and countryside lovers alike.

All but the final mile are relatively flat, and I reached the nature reserve quickly. It was incredibly busy, and the car park, RSPB building and cafe were all full. Taking in the clifftop scenery from one of any number of vantage points, it wasn't hard to see why.

I queued up for a mug of coffee, found one of the slightly quieter patches of rock to sit on, and looked down onto the rocks below me.

The stretch of coastline north-west of Holyhead is made of large granite cliffs rising sheer from the sea, and the islet at South Stack poses a particular danger to shipping. The lighthouse was built in 1809, designed by Trinity House surveyor Daniel Alexander, and built by Joseph Nelson.

Before construction could begin, Trinity House engineers had to cut 400 steps into the cliff face before they could reach rock level, and then build a rope bridge and cable for the gap between the mainland and the islet itself. The rope bridge was replaced by an iron suspension bridge in 1828.

The lighthouse has a white-painted stone tower and flashes a white light, every ten seconds, visible for 24 miles. It was

South Stack.

originally fitted with Argand oil lamps and reflectors, but these were replaced with paraffin lamps in the mid-1870s. An early form of incandescent light was installed in 1909, which itself was modernised in 1927. The lighthouse was electrified in 1938 and automated in 1984.

It was evening by the time I made it back to Bangor, where I had arranged to meet for dinner with Paul and Marian, another longstanding pair of friends from my days in educational publishing. Although he was in the process of consolidating his business, Paul was commuting regularly between a warehouse in Cheshire and home in Bristol. Today he had timed his journey home to meet me here.

I had first met Paul more than a decade earlier, when he undertook some market research and consultancy for Letts, the publisher I worked for at the time. We hit it off straight away, and I was slightly in awe of how calmly and carefully he seemed able to navigate through whatever challenges, obstacles or disputes came our way. We've devised various businesses and initiatives that have brought us closer together over the years, but sadly nothing has quite stuck.

We caught up on half a decade's news over the course of the evening, and I was so grateful for Paul and Marian's company that I forgot they still had another 200 miles to drive home. Typically upbeat and entertaining, neither gave me the impression that they were keen to get going. It was midnight by the time I finally let them leave, but I still managed to feel at a low ebb when I was back in my room, alone once more.

Day 67

Overnight I had acquired a new sponsor! During dinner with Paul and Marian, I had mentioned that money was looking a bit tight, and that I needed to rein in my spending to be sure of making it back home without interruption. Before breakfast, a text from my bank confirmed that a sizeable deposit had been made. It came with strict instructions from Paul that its sole purpose was to keep the expedition going to the end. An extraordinary and typically generous gesture.

Twenty miles beyond Bangor on the North Wales coast lies Llandudno, often referred to as the 'Queen of Welsh Resorts'. It's a little quaint, and seems to have remained largely unchanged for more than a century. The elegant Victorian promenade is lined with pastel-coloured hotels, and the town boasts the longest pier in Wales.

It's a friendly place for cyclists, too, largely because it is relatively flat, just as the twenty-odd miles from Bangor had been. However, Llandudno stands in the shadow of the Great Orme, a massive limestone headland that rises more than 200 metres out of the sea. I was heading for the northernmost point of the Orme, where there is an interesting castellated former lighthouse.

A single-track road, four miles long, stretches right up to the top and around the Great Orme headland. There are a number of blind corners and several sheer drops on the seaward side, so all but half a mile of the road is one-way. Unfortunately, I pushed up the first mile-and-a-half before realising that I had started from the wrong end. It was too late now, so I hugged the safer side of the lane as closely as I could each time a car passed.

At the top is the Rest and Be Thankful cafe, from whose boundary wall I could make out the Isle of Man ahead of me, the Lake District to the north-east, and back to Anglesey to the west. Just a few-hundred yards beyond the cafe, I found the lighthouse. It's now a guesthouse, whose owner said that I was welcome to take the side gate leading to the lantern room to take some photographs.

The lighthouse on the Great Orme was built in 1862 by the Mersey Docks and Harbour Company to guide shipping heading to and from the Dee and Mersey ports. It was designed by engineer-in-chief George Lister, who later worked on the alterations to the lighthouse at Port Lynas in 1871.

At 325 feet above sea level, the lighthouse on the Great Orme is the highest in Wales. The square, castellated two-storey building is dressed with limestone, and the lantern room is at ground level, with the signal and telegraph room above.

Originally it showed a white flashing light, visible for 24 miles, powered by paraffin burners. The lighthouse was electrified in 1965, and responsibility was handed to Trinity House in 1973. It remained

Great Orme.

in continuous use until 1985, when it was decommissioned. The lighthouse's original lantern optics are on permanent display at the Great Orme Summit Complex visitors' centre.

I free-wheeled the two miles back down into Llandudno, mindful of travelling in the wrong direction down what was a one-way street. It would have been a delight to pick one of any number of the town's seafront hotels to stay at this evening, but it was still early afternoon. Besides, it didn't feel appropriate to blow my daily budget on the very day Paul and Marian had boosted my finances. My research secured a cheap room in a small guesthouse at Rhyl, sixteen miles along the coast.

I followed the seafront the entire way, some of the fastest but warmest miles I had covered in Wales. For the first time for a long while, I felt a small glow of happiness that I hoped was a sign that the antidepressants were starting to do their work. But about two miles short of Rhyl, I suffered the third puncture of my journey, and my attempts to sort it out were nothing short of shambolic. I managed to remove the tyre from the rim easily enough, but when I fitted a replacement inner tube, I forgot to identify what had caused the puncture in the first place. As I was pumping up the tyre, I heard a loud hissing noise and realised that I had managed to puncture the new inner tube as well.

Fortunately, I carried two spare inner tubes, but my second attempt was even less successful. This time, I found and removed the sharp piece of grit embedded in the tyre that had caused both punctures. I fitted my single remaining inner tube, but I failed to seat the tyre properly back into its rim. As I pumped it up, a worrying-looking bulge appeared on one side of the tyre. Before I could do anything about it, the inner tube forced its way into the gap between tyre and rim, and then promptly exploded.

Any sense that my low moods were behind me vanished in an instant. With no shade and the temperature close to 30°C, I was down to my last drop of water and the makeshift cool box containing my MS medication was starting to warm up.

With my reserves of energy all but depleted, I set about with a puncture-repair kit to fix one of the two punctured inner tubes. Old school. At least I had the last ten overs of the second day of the first Test match against Australia for company. We were in good shape, having posted more than 400 runs in the first innings, and then pinning the Australians back with five wickets.

I reached Rhyl at 7pm, tired and with filthy black hands to show for my efforts. Rhyl was not looking at its best, with the entire seafront promenade cut off from the rest of the town by seven-foot-high metal riot fencing. Madness were coming to town for a concert on Saturday, and this improvised venue was being constructed in their honour.

The Pier Hotel was newly opened, and it was the perfect tonic for my efforts at bicycle DIY. The young gay couple who ran it were the most delightfully positive and optimistic hosts, and hugely entertaining company. It wasn't long before the puncture fiasco was a distant memory, my medication was cooling in their wine fridge, and the spark of happiness returned. I mentioned that one of them reminded me of Andy Bell from Erasure, or the celebrity physic Derek Acorah. He seemed delighted to be compared to

Erasure's lead singer, but grossly offended by the comparison to Derek Acorah. As I decided to call it a night, he tried to come up with a damning comparison of his own. Somewhat the worse for drink, and studying my beard carefully, the best he could offer was: 'Goodnight … Father Christmas!'

Day 68

I awoke in Rhyl with the headache I deserved from the previous evening's indulgence in the bar, but grateful that at breakfast there was no evidence I had caused lasting offence from comparing my host to Derek Acorah.

I left the town a day ahead of the Madness concert, and headed towards the headland beyond Talacre, where Point of Ayr Lighthouse was my last in Wales. The first ten miles were a delight, with NCN Route Network 5 hugging the seafront along tarmacked tracks the whole way, the coast road and its tourist traffic far inland.

I passed in front of the Pontins Holiday Park in Prestatyn, and was immediately reminded of Philip Larkin's poem 'Sunny Prestatyn'. I saw no hotel with palms, but no tuberous cock and balls either. I felt a little disappointed, because it was all rather nondescript and there seemed to be little that made the town noteworthy at all.

Looking at the map, I had imagined that the route into Talacre would be a single-track settlement with a handful of houses. Instead, it is a city of bungalows, mobile homes and static caravans, punctuated every few-hundred yards by food stores and ice-cream parlours.

I could no longer see the sea, because of the banks of elevated sand dunes lining the paths to my left. So I had to estimate when to dismount and climb up onto the dune to get the best view of the Point of Ayr Lighthouse. I miscalculated on my first attempt, when the lighthouse was still some distance away. But on my second attempt, I looked straight down onto the beach with the lighthouse in front of me. The tide was out, and the tower itself was still some distance away. Despite being sorely in need of several coats of paint, it was still a beautiful and stirring sight.

The lighthouse was built in 1777 to mark the entrance to the River Dee, at a time when Chester was an important port. It was built by local architect and builder Henry Turner, modelled on the existing Liverpool Docks Board light at Hoylake. Its tower was originally painted in red-and-white stripes, with a red-painted lantern. It showed a fixed white light, seaward, as well as a lower fixed red light towards the Dee Estuary. Both were visible for nine miles.

Responsibility for the lighthouse passed to Trinity House in 1819, after which the lighthouse was renovated, with a new

Point of Ayr.

lantern fitted. Several sources suggest that the lighthouse was decommissioned in 1883, when the Dee lightship was called into service. But one of my guidebooks suggests that the light was discontinued when another screw-pile lighthouse, designed by James Walker, was built in 1844. No trace of the 1844 lighthouse exists today.

The lighthouse at Point of Ayr was sold privately in 2012 for around £90,000. The tower has been repainted and maintained since, although it appears not to have been converted into a dwelling, and the tower is not accessible to the public. It is said to be haunted, with many walkers reporting sightings of a man dressed in uniform standing in the lantern at the top of the tower, staring out to sea.

Having conquered the last lighthouse in Wales, I reached another significant milestone, crossing the River Dee back into England once more. The Chester Millennium Greenway follows an old railway line around the outskirts of the city, and then a series of paths, cycle tracks and bridleways close to the Shropshire Union Canal. The lighthouse I was making for, Whitby Lighthouse at Ellesmere Port, is part of a dock complex on the south side of the River Mersey. It's easy to find, because these days it is part of the National Waterways Museum, and there are signs to it at every road intersection.

The docks at Whitby were built by Thomas Telford in 1796, at the junction between the Shropshire Union Canal and the River Mersey. The lighthouse, constructed from red brick, came much later, in 1880, and was designed to guide ships into the Shropshire Union Canal's dock complex from the River Mersey.

It is a tall, red-brick octagonal tower, with an unusual bell-shaped roof. Its light was visible for nineteen miles. When the Manchester Ship Canal opened in 1894, ships entered the docks from a new canal entrance at Eastham Locks, three miles downstream. As a result, the lighthouse at Ellesmere Port became redundant.

I still needed to get to Birkenhead to see the lighthouse at the Woodside Ferry Terminal. It's where the stone jetty was built for the Liverpool–Birkenhead ferry, the crossing made famous in the Gerry Marsden song 'Ferry Cross the Mersey'. There is an excellent dedicated cycle lane the whole way, and I reached the terminal in around 40 minutes.

When the jetty was built in around 1840, a white lantern, mounted on a short, white-painted conical stone tower was installed. The terminal and jetty were modified not long afterwards, so the light was only active for about fifteen years.

The tower survived, without its lantern, right up to the mid-1980s, when it was refurbished and moved to the newly built landing stage. The original lantern, which during the intervening years had been mounted on a metal lattice bell tower on the river's edge, was reunited with the tower and painted an attractive dark red. The current tower never re-entered service as a lighthouse, although it is comforting to know that it was considered a sufficiently important landmark to be restored.

With the Birkenhead light conquered, my day was done. For only the second time, however, I found myself double-booked. Through the Association of Lighthouse Keepers, I had received two generous offers of accommodation for my time on the Wirral, and without realising how close together they were, I had accepted both. I felt awful having to choose one and let the other down, all the more so because both had been in touch to say how much they were looking forward to meeting me.

I contacted both and arranged to stay with Stephen and Mandy in Bidston, and to drop by on John and Diane in Wallasey for morning coffee the following day. I don't think the arrangement left either party feeling offended, both recognising that it was simply down to my own incompetence. It meant that I had a treat ahead of me, or at least a treat for a lover of lighthouses. Stephen and Mandy owned the lighthouse on Bidston Hill, and tonight I would be staying in one wing of the keepers' accommodation.

Stephen and Mandy were the most genial of hosts. They had bought the tower and principal cottage in 2011, and had spent considerable time and money on a careful and sympathetic restoration. A few months before my arrival they had managed to purchase the remaining cottage, with a plan to reunify the entire complex over time to create one substantial home.

It was easy to warm to Stephen and Mandy. They were my sort of people, refreshingly down to earth, clearly as excited to be renovating their lighthouse as I was to be staying in it. They had invited their friends, Steve and Jackie, to join us, and before supper they gave me the grand tour.

The first lighthouse on Bidston Hill was built in 1771 and was designed to work in conjunction with the Mockbeggar Light at Leasowe, forming a pair of leading lights that guided ships around the sandbanks in Liverpool Bay. The lighthouse itself is unusual, in that it is two miles inland. In fact, it is the furthest inland of any lighthouse around the UK coast.

Following a fire in 1865, the lighthouse was demolished and replaced in 1873 with the current stone tower, with adjacent cottages that provided ample accommodation for three keepers. It also housed a signal station, and its prominent position high up enabled semaphore signals to be used to relay information about the movement of shipping in Liverpool Bay to the merchants of Liverpool. It was a kind of forerunner to the electric telegraph, and it is said that messages could be sent between Holyhead and

Bidston Hill.

Liverpool in less than eight minutes, with the signal station on Bidston Hill playing a pivotal role.

As the sandbanks gradually shifted, silt from the Mersey and Dee estuaries altered the safe passages into and around Liverpool Bay. As a result, the leading lights at Bidston and Leasowe no longer provided a useful leading line. Leasowe's light was decommissioned in 1908, and Bidston's five years later, in 1913.

This was not my first example, nor would it be my last, of a lighthouse made redundant because of shifting sands and tides. Leading lights, where a pair of lights, one above the other, indicate the safe passage when aligned, are especially vulnerable. They are often replaced with navigational buoys and lightships, which can be moved, when required, to indicate the altered safe route.

For nearly 100 years, Bidston Hill Lighthouse was council owned, before it was sold to the Natural Environment Research Council (NERC) in 1981. Stephen and Mandy bought the lighthouse in 2010, and then set about restoring the various buildings to their original configuration. Shortly after my visit, Bidston Lighthouse CIC was formed, a not-for-profit community-interest company dedicated to preserving the lighthouse and celebrating its important role in the development of telecommunications, lighthouse optics and the Port of Liverpool.

It is evident that the lighthouse is in very safe hands, and its heritage status is assured.

Day 69

It was a wrench to leave in the morning, but I had five lighthouses I wanted to reach that day, as well as my coffee meeting with John and Diane. So with a heavy heart, I left the comforts of Bidston Hill after breakfast and reached Wallasey before eleven.

John and Diane were as generous with their hospitality as Stephen and Mandy had been – I think it's in the blood in these parts – and we spent an hour or more discussing our shared obsession with all things lighthouse related. Together, they have written a fascinating history of the *Lighthouses of Liverpool Bay*, and I struggled to conceal how superficial my own knowledge was compared with theirs.

John was concerned that I had given myself too much to do today, especially getting across to Hilbre Island, which can only be reached at low tide by walking across the sands from West Kirby. He didn't rate my chances of wheeling my bike across the sand, nor of having a bike to come back to if I chained it somewhere locally. Instead, he offered to meet me at West Kirby later in the day, where he and Diane would guard my bike while I sprinted across the sand to see the light.

Between them, they devised a route to make my way round the remaining Wirral lighthouses. I would cycle to New Brighton first, at the eastern Wirral shoreline, then follow the seafront promenade to Leasowe and Hoylake, before meeting them both after lunch at West Kirby. I have a watercolour of the lighthouse at New Brighton in my hallway at home, so I knew exactly what I was looking for. Leaving Wallasey, I found the broad seafront promenade and the lighthouse within minutes.

Close to the mouth of the River Mersey at Liverpool Bay, there is a dangerous rocky outcrop known locally as Perch Rock because of the perch timber tripod, onto which a simple navigation light was mounted as early as 1683. As Liverpool's importance as a port grew throughout the 19th century, the beacon was deemed inadequate, and construction of a new tower began in 1827. It was designed by John Foster, Liverpool Corporation's surveyor, broadly copying the design and construction techniques employed by Smeaton's Eddystone Lighthouse 70 years earlier.

The result was an elegant, white-painted, conical tower with a red iron lantern. First lit in 1830, it became known as the Perch Rock Lighthouse. It displayed a flashing light, with a repeated pattern of two white flashes followed by a red flash every minute. The light was visible for fourteen miles.

William Williams Mortimer's 1847 *History of the Hundred of Wirral* describes the newly constructed lighthouse:

At New Brighton on a ledge of rocks which project into the sea, is an admirable Lighthouse which rises 90 feet. It is built with remarkably hard stone. Every stone is dovetailed to the next; each course of masonry united to the previous by iron braces.

Perch Rock, New Brighton.

The lighthouse was automated in 1925 and was in continuous use until decommissioned in 1973, when modern navigational technology made it redundant. It is a much-loved, well-preserved local landmark. Since 2015, thanks to a grant from the Coastal Revival and New Brighton Coastal Community Team (NBCCT), a lantern employing LEDs and solar panels has displayed a light that replicates the original light pattern, although it can only be seen from the land so as not to confuse maritime traffic.

A broad, paved promenade runs almost uninterrupted between New Brighton and Hoylake, along the seven miles of the Wirral seafront. It narrows briefly as it circumvents a golf course, but apart from having to line up behind several groups of 5K runners, my progress to Leasowe was rapid.

Originally, there were two lighthouses built at Leasowe in 1763, forming a pair of range lights, which together marked the safe passage into the Rock Channel and on to the Liverpool docks. The original low light was destroyed by storms just six years later, in 1769. Rather than attempt another offshore light, the light on Bidston Hill was built, acting as a new rear or high light to Leasowe's remaining front or low light.

The surviving lighthouse at Leasowe is a white-painted brick tower, the oldest lighthouse built from bricks in the United Kingdom. Originally coal fired, it was converted to oil in 1772 and showed a fixed white light visible for fifteen miles.

When the Harbour Board introduced a system of flashing buoys to mark the safe passage into the Mersey, the lighthouse became redundant and it was decommissioned in 1908. For a while it was derelict, but it was refurbished in the 1990s by the Friends of Leasowe Lighthouse and is now a visitor centre offering guided tours.

From Leasowe, Hoylake is another three miles along the seafront path. It's an affluent area, with substantial early-Victorian detached homes on one side of the road and expensive-looking modern apartment developments on the other.

The lighthouse tower stands behind an attractive Victorian house, and I rang the doorbell a couple of times, hoping for a tour. Finding no one at home I withdrew to the driveway entrance, which proved to be the ideal location for photographs that took in both tower and house.

Like at Leasowe, there were originally a pair of lighthouses at Hoylake, which together aligned to mark the safe passage into the Hoyle Lake, where ships regularly moored before sailing up the rivers Dee and Mersey to offload their cargo. The original front light was destroyed by the sea in 1771, and a replacement brick structure was constructed alongside the lifeboat station. This light was active until being decommissioned in 1908. It was demolished in 1922.

Leasowe.

The original rear or high light was built inland, on Valentia Road, and was in service until the 1860s, when it was replaced with the current lighthouse. It has an octagonal brick tower with substantial accommodation attached on four floors. Its light was visible for nine miles, and remained in operation until May 1886,

Hoylake.

when the lighthouse was decommissioned. It is now a substantial and elegant private home.

I had one other piece of business to conduct in Hoylake. I had found a number of references online to another lighthouse in the town, as well as photographs of a substantial tower. Further research revealed that this is a faux lighthouse, reputedly built in the 1990s for Warrior from the TV show *Gladiators*.

Unlike more illustrious lights along this stretch of coast, this one wasn't the work of an engineer or architect of the stature of

James Walker, Daniel Alexander or Joseph Nelson. According to internet gossip, it was built by a local brickie known as 'Dave the Crane' Evans, who sometimes went by the moniker 'Mad Dave the Brickie'.

At first sight, however, the tower itself looks quite convincing, albeit attached to a grand though slightly vulgar modern dwelling. I noticed that it was currently on the rental market. Complete with swimming pool, DJ booth, observation tower, sauna and party room, it could be yours for a cool £4,000 a month.

There is very little separation between Hoylake and West Kirby. I found John and Diane waiting for me on South Parade with sandwiches, bananas and cans of beer at the ready. Wirral people seem to have an unfailing knack of producing food and drink at exactly the right moment.

They found a bench where they could sit and look after my bike, while I set off for Hilbre Island, about an hour's walk across the sand. It's a strange experience, because every day hundreds of walkers make this same journey, following exactly the same route, despite the lack of any discernible path, which is washed away with each tide. Evidently this is some sort of pilgrimage. Many come to see the birdlife, others just for the sake of it, but I was one in a long line of walkers of all ages and nationalities, winding my way towards the island in the semi-distance.

Hilbre Island is one of three islands at the mouth of the estuary of the River Dee. These days the island is uninhabited, although there is evidence of occupation as long ago as the Stone Age. It is renowned as an important stopping-off point for the twice-yearly migration of birds along the west coast of Britain.

The current light is really no more than an LED lantern mounted on a white-painted, steel box tower. It displays a flashing red light, visible for five miles, which guides shipping through a channel between Hoylake sands and the entrance to the River Dee.

I was slightly underwhelmed. However, it was a light that my lighthouse-fanatic friend John Best had admitted to me that he had never seen. The thought of bagging a lighthouse ahead of John, however modest a structure, amused me enormously.

Retracing my steps across the sand, I was conscious that John and Diane had been sitting on their bench, guarding my bike, for at least an hour and a half. Because I had been marching to the island and back, I hadn't really noticed the drop in temperature, or that the wind had begun to pick up. When I climbed up the steps back at West Kirby, I found them hugging each other tightly, entirely wrapped in a couple of thick blankets. They looked like a couple of refugees. I wanted this trip to be memorable for any number of reasons, but certainly not for giving my hosts hypothermia.

As I retraced my path back across the Wirral to the Woodside Ferry Terminal, I reflected on the kindness and goodwill I had experienced over the last few days, and wondered whether they would experience the same peerless hospitality if they visited London or the Home Counties. Sadly, I concluded that they would not.

I took the famous ferry across the Mersey, wondering why the scheduled crossing time was 45 minutes when I could see the terminal on the opposite bank quite clearly with the naked eye. The answer, I discovered, was that this was an *experience*, not a *crossing*, which paused frequently to point out local landmarks, taking in great sweeping arcs of the river to create plenty of time for Gerry Marsden's classic song to play several times. Don't get me wrong, it's an unforgettable experience, and the view of the Royal Liver Building and city skyline from the river is as dramatic as any you'll see. And there's no denying it, the lyrics claiming Liverpool people will never turn you away, which I was now hearing for the seventh time, accurately summed up the Merseyside kindness I had experienced. But it was now late afternoon, and I still had a twelve-mile ride south to the lighthouse at Hale Head, followed by a final thirteen-mile sprint north to a hotel I had found in Knowsley. I was itching to get moving.

Within minutes of leaving Liverpool's Pier Head, I cycled through the Albert Docks, where the former lightship *Planet* is moored. It has had a varied history, having started life in 1959 anchored at the Mersey Bar, fifteen miles from Liverpool's Pier Head. It was sold to Trinity House (and became LV23) in 1972, and served at the Kentish Knock, Varne and Channel stations, before being sold again to shipbreakers in 1991. Having been saved from the breakers, the lightship was relocated to Liverpool, partly restored, and has since served as an exhibition centre, a radio station and now a cafe and bar.

With the exception of a mile or so circling John Lennon Airport, there is a cycle path right along the riverfront the whole way to Hale. The village of Hale is pretty, with wide grass verges and trees lined along the high street, and trimmed box hedges fronting many of the houses. The headland seems wild and remote by comparison, and there is a stillness and quiet that is intoxicating. A gravel track meanders the final half mile to the river and the lighthouse I had come to see. The modern bungalow attached to the lighthouse tower is the only sign of habitation for miles around, and I wondered who lived here, and why. However splendid the tower, the somewhat unimaginative 1970s bungalow, together with the high brick wall in front of it to prevent tidal erosion, left me feeling that its significance lies in what it once represented, rather than what it is today.

The lighthouse lies on a dangerous bend in the River Mersey between the city and Runcorn. The current lighthouse was built in 1906, with a slightly tapered, circular brick tower, which displayed a fixed white light that was visible for seven miles. With the gradual loss of trade after the war the lighthouse was deemed unnecessary and was eventually decommissioned in 1958.

Much of the last dozen or so miles to Knowsley were on NCN Route 62, following sections of the disused Liverpool Loop railway line. Despite travelling through a largely urban and industrial landscape, these were some of the quietest and most peaceful miles since leaving Wales.

For the first time in several weeks I realised I was ensnared by the subtle details that had eluded my senses for so long. The immaculately uniform brickwork of a railway tunnel, the evening light dappled though the trees, even the earthy, pungent aroma of cow parsley lining the railway cuttings.

I dared to believe that my darkest feelings were behind me now, and I certainly felt happier, stronger and more positive than I had for several weeks.

Day 70

There were once lighthouses at Formby, Bootle and Crosby, although all have been demolished and no traces remain of any of them. I had an altogether different motive for making a detour to Crosby.

Since driving past the *Angel of the North*, Antony Gormley's contemporary sculpture near Gateshead, I have acquired a love of his work. The beach at Crosby is now the permanent home of *Another Place*, an installation of 100 life-size cast-iron figures spread out along the foreshore, stretching about half a mile out to sea. All point in the same direction, staring at the horizon in silent expectation.

I reached Crosby with the tide far enough out that some of the figures were partially submerged, while others stood firmly on the sand. They have been here since 2005, and I sat down next to one that had barnacles and limpets clinging to its legs up to its knees.

Speaking in 2005, Antony Gormley said the installation was the poetic response to the individual and universal sentiments associated with emigration – sadness at leaving, but the hope of a new future in *Another Place*. I have no experience of emigration, but I found being able to walk and sit within the installation profoundly moving. I couldn't help but stare out to sea myself, spending an hour or so in quiet, even cleansing contemplation, and for a while I felt as routed as the figures themselves. There is something otherworldly about sharing the beach with 100 identical stone figures, but I found the experience positive and uplifting. I couldn't gauge the extent to which my medication was influencing the way I felt, but in that moment on Crosby beach I felt invincible and I would probably conclude that this was the single happiest moment of my adventure.

Afterwards, I headed north towards Preston. I had arranged to meet up and stay with Simon, an ex-soldier and fellow MS sufferer who had seen the article about my journey in the *Telegraph* and got in touch to offer me a place to stay. Lytham was 45 miles distant, involving a substantial detour inland to Preston to cross the River Ribble. My route took me along a network of narrow canal towpaths, and my sense of balance, already impaired by MS, made the slippery paths through the regular short tunnels a formidable challenge.

There have been a number of lighthouses marking the entry to the River Ribble at Lytham over the years, although none exist today. The remains of the most recent, a 1906 pile light, were washed away as recently as 1985. There is a 'Trinity House approved light' on the tower of the Fairhaven United Reformed Church in the town, a vast, white stone building, almost Byzantine in design, known locally simply as the 'White Church'. I failed to see the light, either spiritually or from a navigational point of view.

I met Simon at a beautifully restored windmill at Lytham Green, right on the waterfront. I watched him arrive and limp from his car towards me. It was evident that his MS was more severe and had progressed further than my own. I suggested a pint at a pub of his choice, but he said that he preferred to drink at home. His army training came to the fore when he offered that he didn't often go out drinking because he liked 'to know where a threat is coming from'.

Simon is a fighter, one of those people who has tried every career from frontline soldier to distributor of alternative health and vitamin pills. Yet despite being determined to give everything a try, he seemed somehow a bit lost. We discussed various business ideas he planned to pursue, each of which had merit, but I wasn't sure how committed he was to any of them. He was clearly finding life a bit tough.

The whole family arrived for a pot of tea, and Simon's mother had baked me a fabulous cake and homemade flapjacks for my journey. I got the impression that she thought that by meeting me, Simon might spring into action and set off on a jaunt of his own. I liked Simon a lot and desperately wanted to help him, but I wasn't certain he either needed or wanted it. MS affects people in a myriad of different ways, and it's very hard to determine the impact it can have on a person's physical and mental health. Personally, I am struck down from time to time with the darkest of thoughts and crippling low moods. They are capable of making me shrink away or withdraw from my family completely. I've rarely been able to accept help from other people, so I genuinely didn't know what help or support I could offer someone else. Simon and his partner Claire were excellent company, though, and I felt very glad that he had got in touch.

WEEK 11

Day 71

The thirteen or so miles to Fleetwood the following morning were among the wettest of my journey so far. Other than weaving a path alongside a golf course before Blackpool, I followed the seafront the whole way.

I had been looking forward to cycling the length of Blackpool's Golden Mile, the stretch of promenade between the town's north and south piers. But the combination of the rain, which misted up my glasses, and heavy fog, which reduced my visibility to just the few metres ahead of me, meant that I saw very little. Despite hugging the promenade, I couldn't see the sea at all. Even the famous Blackpool Tower, which on a clear day can be seen from as far away as Wales and the Lake District, only came in to view as I cycled virtually underneath it.

Reaching Fleetwood, I was conscious that the rain had won the battle with my waterproofs and cycling kit. I was soaked through, cold as well as wet. The town was completely deserted, no one as daft as me tempted to test the streets. My *AA Book of the Seaside* from the 1970s lists among the town's attractions trampolines, outdoor band concerts and popular bathing-beauty contests, but none were in evidence today.

I made for the lighthouse on the seafront, where the covered seating provided ample shelter for me to strip, towel down and start afresh with clean, dry clothes. The shelter the lighthouse provided made me warm towards it, and I instantly ranked it among my favourites. It's an elaborate building, with gothic columns and an octagonal lantern. A statement for Fleetwood's Victorian visitors that this was a prosperous town.

It was built in 1840, with a square tower, on top of which is an iron balcony and octagonal stone lantern with a domed roof. It shows a green flashing light, visible for nine miles, through a lantern window.

Fleetwood Low Light.

When the rain let up a little, I walked with the bike into town to track down Fleetwood's second lighthouse. Modelled on the Ancient lighthouse Pharos of Alexandria, its elegant proportions make the beachfront lighthouse seem almost pedestrian.

The Pharos Lighthouse, built in 1840, is a red sandstone circular tower, set back from the sea in a residential part of the town. It has a stone gallery and shows a green flashing light, visible for thirteen miles, through a narrow vertical window. When the lights from the two lighthouses are lined up, with the Pharos Light above and the Beach Light below, they guide shipping through the dangerous sandbanks of the Wyre Estuary.

The town had already offered up two gems, but Fleetwood has a third important light. Offshore, there is a screw-pile lighthouse, known as the Wyre Light. It dates to 1840, reputedly making it the first of its kind anywhere in the world. Despite the thick fog I finally caught sight of it, and was sad to observe that only the pile framework remained intact. It seems that Fleetwood's third lighthouse might soon be lost for ever.

It was designed by Alexander Mitchell, an Irish engineer who developed the concept of screw-pile structures. Seven cast-iron legs were screwed into the sandbank, supporting a platform on which a wood and corrugated iron accommodation building stood. The lantern room was built on the roof of this building, displaying a fixed white light that was visible for ten miles.

The lighthouse was almost completely destroyed by fire in 1948, after which a simple, automatic navigation light was mounted on what was left of the structure. This lasted until 1979, when the light was replaced with a navigation buoy positioned nearby.

At certain low tides it is possible to walk out to the structure, although since my visit the lighthouse has partially collapsed into the sea, and very little remains beyond a few sections of the cast-iron framework.

Crossing the River Wyre involves either a fourteen-mile round trip to the bridge near Hambleton or a ten-minute, half-mile passenger ferry across the water to Knott End, directly opposite Fleetwood. It barely needs recording that I opted for the ferry.

Our captain, Tony, was a warm and jovial fellow. The Wyre Estuary Ferry clearly served as his stage, and he was a confident performer. This might have been a damp and foggy Monday afternoon, but Tony had a quip for each of his regulars and was only too happy to share his somewhat reactionary views on a broad range of topics, whether requested or not. It was, thankfully, just a ten-minute crossing, and I managed to avoid entering the debate.

I was making for an interesting light close to Cockersand Abbey, once one of a pair of lighthouses here. A wooden-framed lighthouse, and a steel tower that replaced it, served as the rear range. Both are long gone. But the front range, known as Plover Scar, has marked the entrance to the River Lune since 1847. The little lane leading to the shore close to Plover Scar is barely wide enough for two bikes to pass, let alone two cars, which made the solitary and delightfully quirky cottage at the end of it all the more appealing.

Together with the lighthouse at Cockersand, Plover Scar guided shipping into the estuary bound for Glasson Dock and the Port of Lancaster. It has a white conical stone tower, with a black lantern and twin galleries, built on a rocky outcrop at the edge of the deep-water channel into the estuary. It displays a flashing white light, every two seconds, that is visible for six miles.

Three miles further north, on the south bank of the River Lune, the small town of Glasson is rather charming. Although there is evidence of modern industry here, with an active dock, it feels like more of a sleepy backwater. Even the docks share the waterfront with a village green, recreation ground and outdoor seating area for the Lantern O'er Lune cafe. It's hard to believe that this was once one of the country's busiest ports.

A white-painted sandstone watch house with slate roof was built at the dock entrance in 1836. At one end of the roof, a small octagonal lantern was fitted, which displayed a fixed white light that was visible for two miles.

When a deep-water channel was dredged as part of the construction of the Glasson branch of the Lancaster Canal, the light became disused. Glasson's importance as a port declined

The Beacon Bike

during the 20th century, although it has witnessed a revival as a marina for pleasure craft. These days a series of electric navigation lamps are displayed from a red-painted metal tower alongside the former lighthouse.

There was once a small passenger ferry service that crossed the river between Glasson and Overton, but today the cyclist must follow the south bank of the river as far as Lancaster before being able to cross. Although it added ten miles or so to my journey, the route followed the course of part of the Lancaster Canal and then a section of disused railway branch line, so it was no great hardship.

Nevertheless, the mist persisted even into Lancaster itself. It is said that from one turret of the castle you can see the peaks of the Isle of Man. Today, I could only really make out the peak of the roof of Sainsbury's, 50 or so yards below me.

There are two lighthouses in Heysham, about five miles south-west of Lancaster. It's a largely industrial town, which expanded throughout the last century such that there is now little distinction between where Heysham ends and the more genteel resort of Morecambe begins. The harbour and dock area at Heysham is workmanlike and a little forbidding, and neither light was particularly interesting.

The lighthouse on the South Pier was built in 1904 and has a red cylindrical cast-iron tower, with a white lantern and gallery. It has an unusual light pattern, showing an occulting green light, six seconds on, followed by one-and-a-half seconds off.

A second lighthouse was built in the same year, to guide shipping safely past a dangerous set of rocks known as Near Naze. This light, appropriately called the Near Naze Light, is just outside the harbour entrance. It has a circular stone tower, 30-feet tall, with gallery on top. It was only active for a few years, before being replaced by a cast-iron tower built only a few feet further seaward, no sign of which remains.

From Heysham, the lighthouse at the jetty in Morecambe is just a three-mile ride along the seafront. I was overjoyed to pass the bronze statue of Eric Morecambe by Graham Ibbeson on the promenade, which, like *Another Place* in Crosby, I had long wanted to see. What I hadn't realised was that alongside Eric himself, the steps and pavement are inscribed with many of the catchphrases and jokes from *The Morecambe & Wise Show*. It's hard not to smile when at your feet are the words:

What do you think of the show so far?
Rubbish!

The Stone Jetty in Morecambe is all that remains of the former harbour, built by the North Western Railway in 1853 as a wharf and rail terminal for both passenger and cargo transport. The sandstone building on the jetty was once a railway station terminus, where passengers could travel onwards by steamer to Peel on the Isle of Man or to the north of Ireland. Adjoining the seaward end of the station building is an octagonal sandstone tower and gallery with white-painted lantern, which displayed a white flashing light, visible for three miles.

The railway closed in 1932, and the importance of Morecambe as a port and harbour declined thereafter. However, the jetty underwent a major refurbishment programme in the 1990s, and since then the lighthouse has displayed a fixed light.

I hadn't planned on stopping in Morecambe, but this was clearly the budget traveller's Mecca. A clean and welcoming seafront hotel, close to the lighthouse, charged £30 for dinner, bed and breakfast. I must have been the only resident neither claiming a pension nor taking part in the evening bingo in the hotel's slightly soulless ballroom. I was certainly the first guest not to arrive by coach for many months, and the presence of my bike proved problematic for a while. But this was my cheapest night since Newquay, and nothing was going to spoil it.

Day 72

An hour or so beyond Morecambe, I realised that I'd had it pretty easy since my final day in Wales. Any suggestion that my increasing daily mileage was down to improved fitness was soon dismissed the moment I left the shore surrounding Morecambe Bay near Heversham and began to climb. The stretch between Mill Side and High Newton was particularly punishing, and while I managed the first few-hundred yards, I was off the bike and pushing for most of the climb.

At Newby Bridge I was so relieved that the roads were flattening out again that I failed to appreciate that I was less than a mile from the southern shores of Lake Windermere. I crossed the River Leven twice, following an enchanting former railway line that meanders through fields and woodland. When it petered out, a delightful narrow lane took me all the way to Ulverston.

Ulverston is a lovely market town with a labyrinth of cobbled streets and side alleys, and many of the old buildings are colourfully rendered in pastel shades. It is a town of some renown, too. In the latter half of the 17th century, it was a centre of religious activity when George Fox, the founder of the Quaker movement, lived here. It is also the birthplace of Stan Laurel and home to the world's only Laurel and Hardy Museum.

My interest was in Sir John Barrow, a founding member of the Royal Geographical Society and an intrepid explorer, who was born in the town. In his honour, a prominent memorial was built on Hoad Hill in 1850, which is very similar in appearance to the third Eddystone Lighthouse designed by John Smeaton.

It has a lantern room, which was originally open to the elements but is now glazed. However, it has never been a functioning lighthouse, although Trinity House contributed £100 towards the monument's construction cost, on the condition that it had the capability to be used as a real lighthouse if deemed necessary at some future time.

Its official name is the Sir John Barrow Monument, but almost everyone calls it the Hoad Monument. Whether you choose to count it as a lighthouse or not, it's worth the steep climb up the hill, because the views of Morecambe Bay and across the Lake District fells will take your breath away.

Pressing on towards Barrow, I hoped to see the lights along the Walney Channel before the end of the day. In the late-19th century Barrow-in-Furness had the largest steelworks in the world, and the port here was the main route used to transport the steel produced in the town. With the abundance of steel, Barrow established a thriving trade in shipbuilding, and has played a vital role in global ship and submarine construction for 150 years.

Entrance to the port at Barrow is via the Walney Channel, a narrow body of water running between the mainland and

Walney Island. My route took me first to the Rampside Leading Light, also known as 'the Needle'. There were once thirteen such range lights, built between 1850 and 1870, that together guided vessels into the port. Today this is the only one of the original lights that has survived.

Built in 1875, it has a tall, slender square tower constructed from red and yellow bricks. The top of the tower is shaped like a pyramid, with a window near the top. A white light is displayed through the window, which is visible for six miles.

Beyond the Rampside Light I continued towards Roa Island, where the road ended at the water's edge alongside Barrow's lifeboat station. From the road, a shingle bank leads onto the Foulney Island Nature Reserve, where there is a futuristic-looking white tower known as the Foulney Island Light.

Although the Rampside Light is the only one of the 19th-century lights remaining, there are several pairs of modern range lights, mainly pile structures, at strategic points on the mainland alongside the Walney Channel. I found them all, and in marked contrast to the two days along the rivers Avon and Severn, I felt no need to question whether they counted or if I should bother to track each one down.

Coasting into Barrow itself, I had a moment of clarity: I had covered close to 2,500 miles and had now seen more than 200 lighthouses. For the first time, I felt certain that I would finish what I set out to do.

Day 73

Barrow-in-Furness may only be separated from Walney Island by the narrowest of channels, but it's hard to think of two places less alike. I'm not suggesting that Barrow is an unattractive town, just that it is a working, industrial and noisy port. By contrast, the single road leading to Biggar on Walney Island seemed silent and desolate, and where cranes and buildings compete for space along the Barrow side of the water, tall trees line the opposite bank.

Walney Island's lighthouse is at the southern end, within one of the island's two nature reserves. Despite the well-maintained track running the length of the reserve, no vehicles or cycles are permitted, so I propped up my bike behind one of the warden's huts.

The lighthouse is still a working light, although the former keepers' cottages and outbuildings are now in private ownership. After the first lighthouse on Walney Island was destroyed by fire in 1803, the current lighthouse and attached cottages were constructed from local stone, shipped across Morecambe Bay from Overton. It has a tall octagonal tower, with a lantern that shows a white flashing light every fifteen seconds, which is visible for eighteen miles.

When the lighthouse was automated in 2003 it was the last manned lighthouse in England. Today the lighthouse is owned and operated by the Lancaster Port Commission.

Another pair of modern pile lights at Haws Point, similar to those I had seen on the mainland, stood between me and my return to Barrow. Ahead of me lay 25 miles of main roads surrounding the Duddon Estuary, although after Foxfield I found a five-mile track that followed a railway line to Millom and saw no one at all along its length.

At Haverigg I found the outer wall, or breakwater, that once enclosed the Hodbarrow iron mine. It's all part of a nature reserve nowadays, and the breakwater encloses a substantial lake on one side and the water of Duddon Sands on the other. With water

Walney Island.

on all sides, cycling the length of the breakwater is an adventure in itself, with the sweet little lighthouse almost exactly halfway. The earlier, disused light is just a few-hundred yards further on.

Hodbarrow was once home to one of the largest and best known of the West Cumbrian iron mines. It was in operation between 1848 and 1968, and over that period it produced about 25 million tons of hematite ore.

In 1866 the Hodbarrow Mining Company built a lighthouse at the edge of the mine to guide ships into dock so they could load up with iron ore. Known as Hodbarrow Beacon, it was built in stone and included a circular tower on a stepped stone plinth. It has a circular window on the west side of the tower, through which its light was displayed, with a cast-iron balcony just below window level.

In 1905 the Hodbarrow Mining Company completed construction on a new, outer breakwater, at which point Hodbarrow Beacon was decommissioned and replaced by Haverigg Lighthouse. Built of cast iron, it is 30-feet tall and has a gallery and dome-roofed lantern. Powered by paraffin throughout its life, it displayed a white occulting light that was visible for ten miles.

The mine itself closed in 1949, after which the lighthouse was decommissioned. The mine shafts were allowed to flood, enabling the RSPB to create a nature reserve from the coastal lagoon and grasslands that resulted. Today this tranquil landscape bears little resemblance to its industrial past, and now supports breeding terns, ringed plovers, redshanks and oystercatchers. There have also been sightings of great crested grebes, a protected species once hunted almost to extinction in the UK.

At Kirksanton, I found an unpromising-looking and empty pub which represented my only option for an evening meal. I stopped for a drink at 6pm and assumed that the landlord was joking when he said that if I wanted dinner I should eat now, or else he couldn't guarantee he would have room for me. Yet within 30 minutes every table was taken and it was standing room only. Not bad for a Wednesday evening. If anyone ever tells you that rural pubs are no longer viable, send them to the King William IV in Kirksanton.

Day 74

The cyclist is poorly served heading north from Kirksanton, with the busy, unyielding A595 offering the only viable route. Beyond the wonderfully tranquil coastal village and harbour at Ravenglass, however, everything changes. The rest of the ride to St Bees weaved through sixteen miles of minor roads, bridleways and dedicated cycle paths, roughly following the dramatic route of the Cumbrian Coast railway line.

Seascale has a quaint and delightfully unspoiled seafront, seemingly at odds with its close neighbour, the Sellafield nuclear processing plant, formerly the first nuclear power station to generate electricity on a commercial scale. Braystones, with its period beachfront bungalows, chalets and huts, is equally untouched, although it narrowly avoided selection as the site of a new nuclear facility a few years ago.

St Bees village is extraordinary, with the dunes and rough grassland of the Cumbrian coast replaced with the perfectly mown lawns and playing fields of St Bees school. The private school was founded in the 16th century, but my arrival coincided with a local war that was being waged between the residents of the village and the trustees and principal stakeholders of the school.

Without any warning, the school governors had announced that due to falling pupil numbers, the school would close at the end of the summer term, just two weeks from now. Placards in windows served to protest against the closure, with local residents calling foul play.

It was all rather undignified. I have no particular fondness for the private education system, but the thought that these lawns, playing fields and campus would be uprooted, developed and built upon was ghastly to contemplate.

Beyond the village itself, the lanes and footpaths climb to St Bees Head and follow the top of the red sandstone cliffs. Unlike a couple of days before, today the skies were completely clear, and from the headland I could make out the Isle of Man, 30 miles to the south-west.

A lane leading to the lighthouse beyond a farmhouse was marked private, but I took it anyway. Pausing in front of the lighthouse, looking out towards the Isle of Man, there was nowhere I'd rather have been at that moment.

There was a coal-fired light here from 1718, but winds on the headland often shrouded it in thick smoke. It remained in operation until 1822, when it was destroyed by fire, killing the keeper's wife and five children.

Trinity House built its replacement in the same year, an oil-fired, circular brick tower light, which itself was replaced by the current taller tower in 1866, under the supervision of James Douglass. The light itself is 335 feet above sea level, displaying a white flashing light, which is visible for twenty miles. It was automated in 1987.

The harbour town of Whitehaven is five miles north of the lighthouse at St Bees, and I was able to remain on cycle tracks and minor roads the whole way. Better still, they were almost entirely downhill, and my final descent took me straight to the marina and harbour.

Whitehaven is a lighthouse bagger's dream, and you can tick three lighthouses off your list, on foot, in about a quarter of an hour. It was a relatively modest fishing village until 1630, after which it developed as a port for exporting coal from the Cumbrian

St Bees.

coalfields. Over time, Whitehaven was transformed into the third-largest trading port in the UK, exporting coal, iron ore and chemicals worldwide. It also served a significant shipbuilding industry.

The first quay, the Old Quay, was built in 1633 for the export of salt and coal. At one end, close to what is now the entrance to the marina, there is a tall stone tower that is often mistaken for an early lighthouse. In fact, a plaque alongside it indicates that it was a watchtower, built around 1730, and used for general surveillance of sailing vessels in the harbour.

Whitehaven's oldest lighthouse was built later, in 1742, on a smaller, dogleg pier somewhat confusingly called the Old New Quay. It has a circular stone tower, with a cast-iron gallery and a window through which an oil-fired light was displayed. This lighthouse was converted to gas in 1841, but was decommissioned soon afterwards, when two new outer harbour lights were built following expansion of the port.

As Whitehaven continued to prosper, two outer piers were constructed – the West Pier, in 1838, and the North Pier, in 1841.

On the North Pier, there is a circular, castellated brick tower with gallery and window. It's dated 1841 and painted white, with bands of red at its base and around the gallery. Originally, the tower showed a fixed red light, although now a pair of lights are displayed from a mast mounted on the tower's roof. On the West Pier, there is a taller, tapered brick lighthouse, dating to the same period. It, too, is painted white, and displays a green flashing light, visible for thirteen miles.

My journey up the west coast was coming to an end. I had only the pairs of lighthouses at Maryport and Silloth left to see.

Old New Quay (left), North Pier (centre) and West Pier (right), Whitehaven.

From Silloth, I planned to head to Carlisle, where I would meet up with Allan again and drive to Berwick on the east coast. Ahead of me were several dedicated cycle tracks that follow the Cumbrian Coastal railway.

Maryport is a smaller and more genteel town than I'd imagined, and I was delighted to discover that the hotel I had found online overlooked the harbour and former lighthouse. I wandered down to the harbour, these days better known for its marina sheltering yachts and small fishing boats, and walked to the head of the pier to take a look at both lights.

A Roman fort in Maryport suggests that the region was an important command and supply base for the coastal defences at the western extremity of Hadrian's Wall. As a port, the town thrived from the mid-18th century, when a local landowner, Humphrey Senhouse, began the development of the town and named it Maryport, after his wife Mary.

Both shipbuilding and coal industries prospered, and an oil-fired light was established on the South Pier in around 1796. When the pier was extended in 1846, the light was replaced by an elegant octagonal cast-iron column mounted on a circular stone base, with lantern on top. For many years it was a tidal light, lit only at night when the tide was high enough for boats to enter the harbour. Originally gas powered, it had a range of six miles. In 1858, new optics were installed that doubled its range to twelve miles.

In 1961 responsibility for the light transferred to Trinity House, who replaced it in 1996 with a small aluminium tower at the far end of the pier extension. It displays a white flashing light, visible for six miles.

Looking out to sea, I saw a series of headlands – and two flashing lights that I didn't recognise. I checked a couple of guidebooks to make sure that I hadn't missed out any lighthouses in my plans. The whole shape of the coastline seemed different from my mental picture, and I was sure that even if I could see my final lights at Silloth from this point, they should be much further to the east. It was only when I took out my roadmap that I realised I was, for the first time, looking at Scotland.

Back in the town centre, the Golden Lion Hotel turned out to be an excellent choice, and I was following several esteemed travellers before me. William Wordsworth stayed here in 1829, George Stephenson in 1836, as well as both Wilkie Collins and Charles Dickens in 1857. Tonight, about 160 years later, a lighthouse-bagging adventurer stayed here too.

Day 75

My final stretch of the west coast. It felt strange knowing that, after tomorrow, every mile I cycled would, in theory, take me closer to home. Only the last two lighthouses at Silloth stood in my way. The fifteen miles from Maryport followed the seafront the whole way, and with a strong tailwind I averaged seventeen miles per hour for the first time.

Silloth developed as a port from the 1850s, after the Carlisle & Silloth Bay Railway & Dock Company brought a railway line from Carlisle and started the construction of a pier and harbour. Its aim was to replace Port Carlisle as the deep-water port for Carlisle traffic.

Initially, imports included timber from the Baltic and Canada, as well as flour and grain from Europe. The main export was coal. By 1880, North American wheat was being imported to supply Carr's, the biscuit makers in Carlisle. Once a new, enlarged dock opened in 1885, the Carr's flour mill was built alongside it.

Like Seascale, Silloth seemed to be another unspoilt seaside town on the Solway coast. For a relatively modest town, it is on quite a grand scale, with a vast green separating the Victorian centre from the long promenade along the Solway Firth, and spectacular views across the water to the Scottish coast.

I made first for the west beach, alongside the docks, where the Lees Scar Lighthouse lies a few-hundred metres offshore. Built in 1841, its pile structure once supported a keepers' building and tower room. However, it was almost completely destroyed by fire in 1911, and these days only the pile legs remain, with a simple platform above, on which is mounted an automatic beacon. A solar-powered light was installed in 2000, which flashes a green light, every five seconds.

The East Cote lighthouse was also built in 1841, guiding shipping heading to and from Port Carlisle. Maintained by the

Silloth Port Authority, it originally displayed a red light out across the Solway Firth. Although designed as a fixed light, it was adapted in the 1850s to run along a short track so that the light could be realigned to accurately mark the channel into Silloth Harbour.

The lighthouse was rebuilt as a square, tapering, metal tower in 1913, with an octagonal lantern room, from which it displays a fixed green light, visible for ten miles.

There was once a third light, at the end of the pier, built of timber in 1857. When the pier gradually subsided in the early 1900s, the lighthouse had to be abandoned. Both the lighthouse and pier were demolished in 1956, and no trace remains today.

Silloth's East Cote Lighthouse is officially the most northerly lighthouse on England's west coast. Although this was another significant milestone reached, I didn't feel the sense of euphoria that I thought I would. It wasn't that I felt unhappy to be here, or that Silloth and its lighthouses proved a disappointment. I think I had built up its significance in my mind. For months, the images of Silloth in my lighthouse guidebooks and directories had seemed as though from a fabled, far-off city. Silloth represented my Atlantis, my Timbuktu, my Kashgar. Now that I was here, it was simply a modest, pleasant English seaside town, its relative inaccessibility making it a little less spoiled or developed than most.

I left Silloth quietly, bound for Carlisle, with the reassuring thought that every mile I covered from now on would lead me one step closer to the comfort of home.

Day 76

I had persuaded Allan to meet me in Carlisle and drive me and the bike from west to east coast. He tracked me down to a launderette on the outskirts of the city, where the drier was robbing me of pound coins and failing to honour its side of the deal. I dare say he had imagined a heroic catch-up over a pub lunch somewhere in the Cumbrian countryside. Instead, we shared a bench and two plastic cups of instant coffee in the launderette.

When my kit was finally dry, we found a cafe for a very late breakfast, before setting off along the route of Hadrian's Wall, bound for Berwick. In the car, Allan asked how I thought Emily and the children were coping without me. The concern in his voice made me question whether I was being fed exclusively positive family updates, and that perhaps all was not well at home. He assured me this was not the case, but it was evident that Allan was receiving less *filtered* news from home than I was. It made me miss the family all the more.

We made it by early afternoon and headed straight for the harbour. It's an attractive town, with three handsome bridges crossing the River Tweed, the earliest of which dates to the early-17th century. The oldest centre of the town is surrounded by remarkably well-preserved medieval stone walls.

We parked up on the narrow lane close to the harbour and walked the length of the pier to the lighthouse. It's a sweet little light, designed and built by Joseph Nelson in 1826. It is England's most northerly lighthouse. It has a circular, slightly tapering stone tower with a conical roof. There is a large recessed window opening on the seaward side, above which is a glazed lantern with external gallery. These days, it displays a flashing white light, every five seconds, which is visible for ten miles. It also shows a fixed green light through a window facing landward, visible for one mile.

Ticking the first lighthouse on the east coast off my list actually felt like more of a milestone than ticking off the last on the west coast. I felt like I was now on the 'home straight'.

Our immediate challenge was to find somewhere for us both to stay the night. There wasn't a room to be had in Berwick, Tweedmouth or anywhere within twenty miles, it seemed. The best we could find was a pair of rooms in a guesthouse in Seahouses, about 25 miles south. So, while Allan drove ahead, I set off for my first experience of NCN Route 1, the 1,264 mile route that runs from Dover right up to the Highlands of Scotland.

It seemed a clever route, hugging the coast as often as it could, weaving inland and crossing the A1, but never following it, whenever the terrain demanded. Close to Waren Mill, I turned off towards Bamburgh, where Allan was parked up close to the castle. We walked to the lighthouse at Black Rock Point, a modern light that I knew Allan would disapprove of. When we found the modest building with a lamp on its roof, his only comment was: 'Is that it?'

It's a circular, metal-framed tower, built in 1910, which remained in service until 1975. Thereafter, an electric light was installed on the roof of the adjoining building, which had once stored the acetylene fuel to power the original light. It is a sector light, showing a group occulting white, red and green light, twice every fifteen seconds. The white light is visible for seventeen miles, while the red and green sector lights have a range of thirteen miles.

The guesthouse I had found was just three miles further along the seafront. Allan arrived before me, and checked us both in. But having assessed both rooms, he was too much of a gentleman to unpack, because one of the rooms was considerably grander than the other. Considering he'd just covered the best part of 400 miles in order to drive me from coast to coast, he had earned the better room.

The second room was so small it had clearly once been a cupboard of some sort. It had internal walls on all sides, and both air and light came from a tiny roof window which was opened with the aid of a long pole. Why the room even needed a radiator I couldn't say, but why it was switched on in mid-July was even more of a mystery. I felt like I was standing inside an industrial oven.

Perhaps the most remarkable thing about this bedroom, no bigger than a small ensuite shower room, was that it had ... a small ensuite shower room. The shower itself demanded that I crouch down on all fours, with a pair of glass doors that I couldn't shut with me inside. I imagined the guesthouse owner watching the first couple of Harry Potter films and then deciding he could get another bedroom or two out of the cupboard under the stairs.

Seahouses began as a small fishing village in the 17th century, but developed a flourishing lime trade in the 18th century, supported by the export of locally mined coal. By the early 1900s, both industries were in decline, and Seahouses fell back on the area's traditional industry of fishing. For a time, the village supported a fleet of 50 herring boats, as well as a substantial curing industry and fish market.

In 1900 an unusual, white-painted, octagonal, brick lighthouse was built at the end of the north-west pier. It displays a flashing green light, visible for twelve miles, from a window on its seaward-facing side.

Day 77

If I had shown Allan pictures of the lights I wanted to see around Lindisfarne, I think he would have invented a compelling reason to head back to Oxford. Lindisfarne, or Holy Island, is a low-lying island off the coast around halfway between Berwick and Bamburgh. The first English diocese was founded here in AD 635, and for many years it was second only to Canterbury as the centre of Christianity in England.

The island is reached by a narrow raised causeway that crosses the muddy sands from Beal. For three hours either side of high tide the causeway is submerged, which meant that timing our visit carefully was essential. It looked, today, as though a late-morning arrival would be ideal.

In the early-19th century Lindisfarne developed a busy harbour. An alarming number of ships ran aground, mistaking Emmanuel Head, at the island's north-eastern point, for the deep channel leading to the safety of the harbour.

I met Allan there. He used the time spent waiting for me to queue up for fresh crab sandwiches from a van in the car park. It was about the best welcome I could imagine. The van was doing a brisk trade, with a queue that any beachfront ice-cream van would be envious of.

I'll admit that there are plenty more beautiful sights on the island than the metal framework, with its modern polycarbonate light, at Heugh Hill. And while the pair of daymarks at Guile Point were more interesting architecturally, only one has a fixed light and can legitimately be defined as a lighthouse.

Meeting up back at Seahouses Harbour, we managed to get a pair of tickets for a two-hour catamaran tour of the Farne Islands that I wagered would restore Allan's lighthouse enthusiasm. Promising grey seals, any number of bird species, as well as the occasional dolphin, the trip would also take in the two Farne Island lighthouses, one of which is among the most famous around our shores.

I had lost count of the number of boat trips I had taken to see offshore lighthouses, but other than the RIB ride out of Cardiff Bay with Emily's uncle John, I had experienced them all on my own. So it felt good to be sharing this one with a mate, and I was happy to miss out on seals and puffins, and reminisce instead about the various clients we'd had the misfortune of working with, as well as the projects we were planning to work on together in the future. Only two lighthouses, and the occasional phone notification of the cricket score, interrupted the conversation.

The Farne Islands comprise almost 30 islands, of which Inner Farne is the largest. The island was home to St Cuthbert, who moved here in 676 and lived as a hermit for more than a decade. While on the island, he attracted pilgrims from all over the Kingdom of Northumbria, because of his reputed gift of healing. Today, the island is owned by the National Trust and is renowned as a summer haven for nesting sea birds.

There are records of a number of attempts to build lights on the island, one of the earliest of which was a coal-burning light built by a Captain John Blackett in 1778. Blackett also built a second light at the southern end of Staple Island, and when this proved ill-sited, he replaced it with a crude coal-fired tower on Brownsman Island. By 1809 both of Blackett's working lights were in disrepair, and Trinity House agreed to take them over and establish new lights.

In 1811, Trinity House built the current Inner Farne Lighthouse to a design by Daniel Alexander. It has a circular white tower with lantern and gallery, and keepers' cottages behind. The lantern displays two white-and-red flashes, every fifteen seconds, which are visible for ten miles.

At the same time, a smaller light tower was built on the north-west point of the island, which remained in operation until 1910, after which it was decommissioned and demolished. At the same time, the remaining principal lighthouse on the island was automated. In 1996 the lighthouse was converted to solar power, and LED lights were installed in 2015.

Inner Farne.

In 1810, the same year that the lighthouse at Inner Farne was under construction, Trinity House built a new lighthouse to replace the coal-fired tower on Brownsman Island. It failed to prevent a number of wrecks on the northern Farne Islands, so was decommissioned. In its place, a new lighthouse was built on Longstone Island, originally known as the Outer Farne.

Longstone Lighthouse was designed and built by Joseph Nelson, and is a red-and-white circular tower built of rough stone, with iron railings around the lantern's gallery. It was completed in 1826, employing Argand oil lamps, and was equipped with one of the world's first revolving flashing optics. It displays a white flashing light, every twenty seconds, which these days has a range of eighteen miles.

The Longstone Lighthouse will forever be renowned for the 1838 wreck of the *Forfarshire* and the role of Grace Darling, the lighthouse keeper's daughter, in rescuing survivors. The *Forfarshire*, with 64 passengers and crew on board, broke in two about half a mile from the lighthouse.

William Darling, the keeper, and the fishermen ashore, thought that a rescue attempt was impossible. However, Grace Darling insisted on trying, and took her place in the small lighthouse boat. While 43 sailors perished, nine lives were saved, due almost entirely to her gallant action. The rescue made newspaper

Longstone.

headlines, and Grace Darling became a national heroine. Sadly, she died of tuberculosis just four years later, aged 26.

Longstone Lighthouse underwent substantial alteration in 1952, including the installation of electricity generators, renewed optics, fog signal and radio beacon. It was automated in 1990.

Back in the harbour at Seahouses, I felt a sudden pang of anxiety brought on by the knowledge that Allan was about to head home. He had a 300-mile journey ahead of him, so I had no right to delay him. He promised to be at Dungeness for my homecoming, which at a rough estimate was probably only three weeks away. While he set off in the direction of the A1, I found my way back to NCN Network Route 1 and pushed on another twenty miles to the stunningly beautiful village of Alnmouth.

Ideally, I would have spaced out evenly the meet-ups with friends and family around the coast. However, Alnmouth is home to Jo, one of the first friends I made in a publishing career that began almost 30 years ago. The opportunity to meet up for dinner was too good to miss, so we spent the evening at the Hope & Anchor, the pub where I was staying, catching up on a decade's worth of news and gossip.

WEEK 12

Day 78

I thought the seven miles to the harbour at Amble were going to be tough, as it looked from my map as though NCN Route 1 followed the A1068 the whole way. What the map didn't show, however, was the dedicated cycle superhighway, running parallel with the road and separated from the traffic by a thick hedge. These were some of the fastest and safest miles I cycled.

Amble itself is quite spread out, and I am not sure I ever really found its centre. The harbour was built in 1838 for the export of coal, and formed by a pair of stone breakwaters, one on each bank of the River Coquet. In 1848 a lighthouse was built on each breakwater. On the south side of the river (the Amble side) there is a cast-iron tower, standing on a concrete base enclosed by iron railings. A modern red lamp is mounted onto it that flashes every six seconds, which is visible for five miles. The current light on the north breakwater is a modern green pole light, with a matching light pattern.

These were fairly unremarkable lights, but I needed to wait at the harbour for a one-hour boat trip out to Coquet Island. Dave Gray's Puffin Cruises is a family business that has been operating boat trips out to Coquet Island, sailing from the dock steps at Amble Harbour, for more than 40 years. Puffins, rare terns and kittiwakes are the main draw for visitors, as well as a population of grey seals.

The lighthouse on Coquet Island was designed for Trinity House by James Walker, and has a white, square tower made of sandstone, with walls more than a metre thick, surrounded by a turreted parapet. There are also substantial castellated accommodation buildings attached.

At the top of the tower is a circular lantern room with conical roof, which originally showed a fixed white light, powered by paraffin. In 1854 red sectors were added, to warn ships of Hauxley Point to the south and Boulmer Rocks to the north.

The light was electrified in 1976, automated in 1990 and converted to solar power in 2008. Today, a small revolving optic flashes a white light three times every 30 seconds, visible for nineteen miles. There is also a red sector, visible for sixteen miles.

From Amble, NCN Route 1 retains its dedicated cycle lane separate from the main road, and I covered the twenty miles to my next lights in Blyth in just over an hour.

Blyth developed as a major port in the 18th and 19th centuries, with coal exports and shipbuilding both playing a significant role. The industry has largely vanished, but the port still continues to operate, importing paper and pulp from

Coquet Island.

Scandinavia for the newspaper trade. The town has also seen substantial investment in renewables, with the development of a number of wind farms, both onshore and offshore.

There has been a lighthouse at Blyth since 1730, but the earliest remaining one is the Blyth High Light, about 100 yards inland. Designed by Sir Matthew White Ridley, it was right on the seashore until land was reclaimed to build the South Harbour. It has a white-painted tapering tower, originally about 40-feet tall. It was oil powered, but was converted to gas in 1857 and to electricity in 1932.

After the South Harbour was developed in 1854 the light was obscured, so the tower was raised in height, first in 1858 and again in 1900. It was eventually deactivated in 1985.

In the harbour itself there have been several lighthouses over the years, including a fifteen-foot-tall metal tower on the West Pier, as well as a number of small, hexagonal wooden towers, displaying fixed blue lights, which served as range lights. Most survived until the mid-1980s, when they were almost all replaced with simple pole lights. I found one of the wooden lights remaining, close to the base of a giant wind turbine.

The main harbour light, on the East Pier, is a white, conical, concrete tower, with gallery and lantern. First lit in 1906, it flashes a white light, four times every ten seconds, which is visible for 21 miles.

Just north of Whitley Bay is the tiny St Mary's (or Bait) Island, a small, rocky tidal island linked to the mainland by a short causeway, which is submerged at high tide. I was particularly keen to get up close to the lighthouse on the island, although the rising tide denied me the chance.

St Mary's lighthouse was designed by Sir Thomas Matthews, then engineer-in-chief for Trinity House, and built in 1898 by the John Miller company of Tynemouth. Construction of the tower and adjacent keepers' cottages reportedly required 645 blocks of stone and 750,000 bricks.

It had a similar rotating optic to the one installed at Lundy North, which displayed a white light that flashed twice every twenty seconds, visible for seventeen miles. It was lit by paraffin, and only electrified in 1977. The lighthouse was

St Mary's.

automated in 1982, but was decommissioned just two years later, in 1984.

Navigating from St Mary's was a breeze, because I could see the pair of lights at Tynemouth on the far horizon. During the Industrial Revolution, Newcastle became one of the country's largest ports, due largely to the export of the region's coal. The entrance to the port, at the mouth of the River Tyne, is protected by two substantial breakwaters: the North Pier, below the

Tynemouth Priory ruins, is 900 metres long, and the South Pier, which was built from the seafront at South Shields, is longer at more than 1,500 metres. There is a lighthouse on each pier, and as I descended, gently circling the priory ruins, I arrived at the head of the North Pier first.

The lighthouse on the North Pier was completed in 1908 and is an elegant, circular stone tower, with gallery and white-painted lantern. It flashes a white light, three times every ten seconds, which is visible for 26 miles.

The lighthouse on the South Pier was first lit in 1895. It is similar in design and construction to the lighthouse on the North Pier, although considerably shorter. It displays white, red and green sector lights, which are visible for thirteen, nine and eight miles respectively, showing the safe channel into the harbour.

There are several splendid former lights to see along the Tyne, starting on the bank of the river just a few-hundred yards away in North Shields. A pair of leading lights were first built in North Shields by Trinity House in 1536. The earliest light still standing, however, dates to 1727, and is now an elegant private house, high up on Beacon Street, with a majestic view across the harbour and beyond to South Shields. It has a tall, square tower, four storeys high, with a small lantern at the top. This was once the high light of a pair of leading lights, with the corresponding low light built on the fish quay. They were initially candle powered, but were converted to oil lamps in 1773.

Over time the safe channel into the harbour changed, and by 1807 the leading lights also needed to be realigned. The High Light was decommissioned, and hereafter referred to as the Old High Light. At the same time, a new Low Light was built, just in front of the old Low Light. Designed by John Stokes, it is an even taller, six-storey, square, brick tower, with a small lantern at the top. It displayed a fixed white light, which was visible for thirteen miles. Having been decommissioned, the former Low Light was converted to almshouses in 1830 and is now a heritage centre and museum.

The following year, in 1808, a new High Light was added, which was also designed by John Stokes. It's shorter, and has a white-painted, brick tower, with a small lantern room on its roof. It also showed a fixed white light, which was visible for sixteen miles.

Old High Light (left), High Light (centre) and Low Light (right), North Shields.

The 1727 Old High Light, the original Low Light, and the 1807 and 1808 leading lights are all still standing, although they no longer display lights. They were succeeded by a sector light installed alongside the lighthouse at Herd Groyne on the opposite bank of the Tyne, which in turn guided shipping into Tynemouth and along the river. Their towers, however, continue to serve as daymarks.

In just over an hour I had chalked up seven lighthouses – the four at North Shields, the two at the mouth of the River Tyne and St Mary's. But there were still two more close by that would make this an exceedingly profitable day of lighthouse-bagging.

Eight miles upriver, in the heart of the city of Newcastle, lie three bridges close together. First is the High Level Bridge, a road and railway bridge designed by Robert Stephenson and opened by Queen Victoria in 1849. It is considered to be the most notable historical engineering work in the city. Second, there is the Tyne Bridge, a through arch bridge over the River Tyne that links Newcastle-upon-Tyne and Gateshead. It was opened in October 1928 by King George V and has since become a much-loved and defining symbol of Tyneside.

However, the bridge I had come to see lies between the two. Said to be one of the industrial wonders of the Victorian age, the Swing Bridge connecting Newcastle and Gateshead was designed by the visionary engineer Lord Armstrong to improve navigation and enable larger ships to access the upper reaches of the river. When it opened in 1876, it was the largest swinging bridge in the world. In the middle of the bridge there is a white-painted, octagonal control room, with a circular lantern, painted blue, on its roof. Although the bridge is still in use, its light has been deactivated for many years.

Retracing my route along the north bank, I took the seven-minute crossing on the Shields Ferry, after which I was only a few minutes' ride from the Herd Groyne Lighthouse, the last of the lights on the Tyne.

Inland of the two long breakwaters at the mouth of the Tyne, the Herd Groyne was constructed on the south side of the river between 1861 and 1867, to protect sand from the Littlehaven beach from being swept upriver by the incoming tide. A small, red-painted, iron lighthouse was erected at the end of the groyne by Trinity House, Newcastle, in 1882. It has an unusual hexagonal design and is supported on twelve iron legs. It's also unusual in that it assists maritime traffic heading both into and out of the port. On its seaward-facing side, it displays an occulting white leading light, marking safe entry through the river entrance, which is visible for thirteen miles. There are also red and green sector lights. On its landward-facing side, it shows a single, fixed light to guide ships safely out of the harbour.

By now it was late afternoon, but there was still time to see the lighthouse at Souter, just four miles further south, and possibly even the pair of lights at Roker, in Sunderland.

I could see Souter ahead of me for almost all of the four miles from South Shields. Arriving perilously close to 5pm, a lovely woman in the National Trust tearoom took pity on me and produced a pot of tea and scones. I was too late for the guided tour, but if I'd been forced to choose between tea or tour, I would have chosen tea every time.

Souter Lighthouse was built to guide ships away from the dangerous reefs of Whitburn Steel, between the Tyne and the Wear, which in 1860 alone were the cause of twenty shipwrecks. Trinity House chose Lizard Point for the site of the new lighthouse, having rejected Souter Point about a mile further south. However, they named the lighthouse Souter to avoid confusion with the Lizard Lighthouse on the south Cornish coast.

Souter Lighthouse was designed by Trinity House engineer-in-chief James Douglass, with construction supervised by civil engineer Henry Norris. First lit in 1871, it has a red-and-white painted circular tower, with a red lantern. There are also ancillary buildings laid out within a square courtyard on the landward side.

The lantern displayed a white light that flashed for five seconds at 30-second intervals, which was visible for 26 miles. It was the first lighthouse anywhere in the world to be powered by alternating current generators. It must be almost unique to have been converted from electricity to oil, rather than the other way around, when a larger lantern was installed in 1914.

Decommissioned by Trinity House in 1989, the lighthouse was never automated. As a result, it retains much of its original machinery and working parts. Now managed by the National Trust, it is open to visitors throughout the season.

I just needed to gather some momentum for a final five-mile push south, allowing for a brief detour to see the lights on Roker Pier and in Roker Cliff Park. Feeling emboldened, I stuck to the main road after Souter, but quickly switched to the broad seafront promenade after Seaburn.

The slim, elegant, cast-iron lighthouse in Roker Cliff Park has only been here since 1983, although it is a much earlier construction. It was originally built in 1856 for the South Pier of Sunderland's dock. Designed by Thomas Meik, it has a circular, white-painted tower, with lantern and gallery. It served only until construction of new piers, with lights, between 1885 and

Souter.

1907 rendered its light redundant. When the old South Pier was shortened in 1983, the lighthouse was dismantled and rebuilt in Roker Cliff Park.

Today, there is a rusting metal framework, with red flashing light, at the end of the shortened Old South Pier. There is also a simple pole light at the end of the Old North Pier displaying a green light. The New South Pier has a cylindrical, white-painted metal tower displaying a white flashing light, at ten second intervals, which is visible for ten miles.

Lastly, on the New North Pier, the elegant conical Roker Pier Lighthouse was built in 1903, in alternating bands of natural white and reddish shades of granite. It is said to be the most powerful port light in the country. It has a rotating lamp, which flashes a white light, every five seconds, visible for 23 miles.

Crossing the Wearmouth Bridge into Sunderland's city centre, I realised I had spent more hours in the saddle, covered more miles and seen more lighthouses than on any other day. I felt strong, upbeat – cocky, even. I may still have been hundreds of miles from home, but I felt that the end was in sight.

Day 79

My bike had been safely secured in a sort of underground vault at the Travelodge overnight, but when I retrieved it I discovered that my front tyre was punctured. It wasn't that I was unwilling to fix it myself, especially since I had replenished my supply of spare inner tubes. But a quick online search established that there were two cycle shops within walking distance, so I decided to act the role of the 'idiot who rides an expensive bike but doesn't know how to maintain it' and get it fixed properly. In any case, the chain hadn't felt like it was engaging properly for a while, and that was probably worth attending to at the same time.

I struck lucky at Cycle World. Paul (aka Rocker) and Stephen (Fibes) listened patiently to my sob story about the bike not having felt right for the last two weeks, and how I'd managed to burst two inner tubes in minutes the previous time I'd tried to fix a puncture. Within the hour they had sorted the tyre, tightened the brakes, taken up the slack in the chain and greased or oiled everywhere that needed it. They wouldn't take a penny, having established that I was cycling the coast for charity, and even planned out their recommended route for the way ahead. I salute them.

My *AA Book of the Seaside* didn't have much to say in Seaham's favour, but I rather liked it. Coffee shops, tapas bars and boutiques line the seafront road, and between the beach and shops, palm trees and tropical plants have been neatly planted within broad grass terraces. It's what an estate agent might call 'up and coming'. Seaham has seen a lot of regeneration funding in recent years, although I think it's fair to say that there's some way to go and the funding hasn't yet penetrated much beyond the seafront.

Seaham is another town whose 19th-century growth was due largely to the export of coal. The first harbour here dates to 1828, but it had to be deepened and enlarged substantially before being officially reopened in 1905. From 1835 there was a lighthouse at Red Acre Point, just to the north of the town.

When the harbour was enlarged in 1905 a new lighthouse was built on the end of the new north breakwater, and the light at Red Acre Point was decommissioned. It was demolished in 1940 so as not to assist enemy bombers or invaders.

The lighthouse on the north breakwater has a cylindrical cast-iron tower with lantern above. It is painted in alternate bands of black and white, and displays a flashing green light, which is visible for eleven miles.

I knew very little about Hartlepool before I arrived, and when I hear the town being mentioned, I only every think of Peter Mandelson, the town's MP between 1992 and 2004. There is a story often told about him, untrue as it turned out, that he mistook a Hartlepool chip shop's mushy peas for guacamole dip. It came to symbolise Mandelson's partiality for the London lifestyle. Personally, I have never referred to mushy peas as anything other than guacamole since.

Hartlepool seems to have several distinct identities, and feels a bit like three towns in one. There's the old town, centred around the limestone headland called the Heugh. Then there's the massive, modern Hartlepool Marina complex, which was built on the area that was formerly docklands. And finally there's West Hartlepool, the principal shopping and residential part of town. It's as if the town isn't certain about quite who it is trying to appeal to.

Hartlepool grew as a port throughout the 19th century and became heavily industrialised with an ironworks and numerous shipyards. In fact, by 1913 there were 43 ship-owning companies in the town. Like the other ports in the North East, Hartlepool also had a healthy coal export trade.

Pilots Pier, on the west side of the harbour entrance, has an unusual square pyramidal wooden lighthouse, which is painted white with two narrow red bands. Built in 1899, the lantern has a rotating radar on top of it, and the lighthouse displays a flashing green light every three seconds, with a white sector indicating the deep-water channel into the Old Harbour and docks.

After coal exports dried up, and with the demise of shipbuilding in the town, the docks were closed and filled in. By 1993 they had been transformed into a substantial marina and leisure complex, with berthing capacity for 500 boats. In the heart of the marina there is an interesting circular stone tower mounted on a square stone base. Missing its original lantern, it was once the high light of a pair of leading lights at Seaton Carew, about a mile south of Hartlepool. After the construction of a lighthouse at South Gare, close to Redcar, in 1884, the Seaton Carew lights became obsolete. The low light was demolished, and the high light fell into disrepair. After the new marina in Hartlepool opened in 1993, the old Seaton Carew high light was acquired, dismantled stone by stone, and re-erected here as a war memorial.

Trinity House built a lighthouse on the Heugh in 1847, which had a tall sandstone tower, powered by natural gas. At the beginning of the First World War, its tower obstructed the line of fire of the defensive guns at the Heugh Battery, so it was dismantled in 1915.

It was replaced in 1927 by the current lighthouse, a white-painted cylindrical steel tower. It was designed to be able to be dismantled in the event of war, so as not to encounter the same problem as the original lighthouse here. From the outset its light was powered by mains electricity and fully automated. It displays two white flashes, every ten seconds, which are visible for nineteen miles.

Before Redcar, I noticed a left turn I was confident led to the South Gare breakwater and lighthouse, at the mouth of the Tees. The skyline alongside the road was completely dominated by the Teesside Steelworks, and the air was pungent with the smell of industry. It was tough to breathe at times, and I thought about the effect it must have on the people who work here, day in, day out. I didn't know then that the steelworks would be mothballed barely a month after my visit.

There is nothing really at South Gare other than the breakwater and lighthouse. I passed a chap walking his dog on a long lead, which seemed a little pointless to me, given that he was the first person, or sign of life, I had seen for five miles. The dog, a handsome German shepherd, seemed happy enough.

The lighthouse at South Gare was built in 1884, with a cylindrical, white-painted, cast-iron tower, with small porthole windows on the north and south sides. Originally there were keepers' cottages further back on the breakwater, but these were demolished when the lighthouse was automated in the 1960s.

These days it flashes a white light, every twelve seconds, which is visible for twenty miles. It also displays red sectors to each side. In 2007 it was the first lighthouse in the world to be powered by a water-cooled hydrogen fuel cell, which was deemed more reliable than mains electricity along the exposed breakwater in stormy weather.

Before heading back to Redcar, I spent ages looking for the pair of lights on the opposite bank of the River Tees at Teesport. It's a mass of heavy industry, with factories, power stations and at least one oil refinery sporting towers and chimneys that could be mistaken for a lighthouse. I found it, eventually, as well as a tall metal lattice tower that serves as the rear range. Both display high-intensity fixed red lights.

Back in Redcar, my hotel was a little bleak. The entrance hallway was adorned with an impressive display of certificates and awards, but by the time I had made it up three flights of faded and slightly stained stair carpet to my room, I wondered whether they were in any way connected with the hotel.

Over supper at the Plimsoll Line on the high street, I was alarmed to read about a pair of range lights that weren't listed in any of my guidebooks. I smiled with relief the moment I found them on my walk back to the hotel. The front range is a lamp on a white pole alongside a shipping container, and the rear range is ... wait for it ... a single red lamp mounted onto the front of Marks & Spencer.

I could relax.

Day 80

When planning my route for the day I realised that at some stage yesterday I had crossed the county border into North Yorkshire. I got chatting to a group of women in a cafe on the esplanade, who seemed less convinced. As far as all but two of the group were concerned, they lived in Redcar and Cleveland, and were unhappy when the local authority had added 'on the Yorkshire Coast' to Redcar's town signs. But the two held their ground, arguing that the town's annual 'Yorkshire Day' events were evidence enough that they were all Yorkshire women. I retreated from the debate, keen to avoid offending either camp.

NCN Route 1 stays on higher ground as far as possible, and I looked down on the delightful beach at Saltburn from the grand Victorian Marine Parade. I passed the entrance to the Cliff Tramway, the oldest water-powered funicular tramway in the country, and couldn't resist taking a single journey down and back up again.

Passing Staithes after an hour, I felt another wave of nostalgia overcome me, as I remembered a childhood summer holiday when we rented one of the small cottages on the hillside road above the town's achingly pretty harbour.

In Whitby I made straight for the harbour, where there are no fewer than four lighthouses, one on each of the four piers. Whitby was a significant fishing port for hundreds of years, but its harbour was developed during the 17th and early-18th centuries from shipbuilding and the mining of alum shale, a kind of clay slate. Whitby Harbour is also where Captain Cook set out in HMS *Endeavour* on a voyage that led to the first European landing on modern-day Australia in 1768.

The current lighthouse on the West Pier dates to 1831, and has a fluted Doric column with an octagonal lantern, and an

Left to right: West Pier Extension, West Pier, East Pier and East Pier Extension, Whitby.

octagonal lead domed roof with a weathervane on top. When built, it displayed a flashing green light, but after new lights on a pair of pier extensions were built in 1914, its light was only displayed when a vessel approached the harbour.

The lighthouse on the East Pier is shorter, and dates to 1855. It has a circular stone tower, with hexagonal lantern mounted on top. It displayed a fixed green light, which was visible for eight miles. It, too, was deactivated following the opening of the pier extensions in 1914.

The 1914 pier extensions each have a small lighthouse. Both have circular lanterns mounted on wooden pyramidal supports. The lantern on the West Pier shows a fixed green light, visible for three miles. The one on the East Pier extension shows a fixed red light, also visible for three miles.

High on the headland on the East Cliff, overlooking the town, stand the haunting, imposing ruins of Whitby Abbey. Founded in 657 by St Hilda, it was recently named Britain's most romantic ruin, and is reckoned to be one of England's most important archaeological sites. It also provided inspiration for Bram Stoker, author of *Dracula*.

After I passed the Abbey entrance, the last couple of miles to the Whitby High Lighthouse were almost entirely flat. Whitby Lighthouse (known as Whitby High so as not to cause confusion with the Whitby Harbour lights) was built by Trinity House in 1858, and was originally one of a pair of leading lights marking nearby Whitby Rock.

Designed by consultant engineer James Walker, the two towers were aligned north to south, and showed fixed lights over the hazardous Whitby Rock. The lower of the two lighthouses had an octagonal tower, with lantern and gallery. It was deactivated in 1890, after a more efficient light was installed in the higher lighthouse. It has since been demolished.

The high light has a white-painted, octagonal tower, with octagonal lantern and gallery. Originally fitted with paraffin lamps, the lighthouse was electrified in 1976 and automated in 1992. Nowadays, it displays a flashing white and red isophase light, every five seconds, with the white light visible for eighteen miles and the red light for sixteen miles.

Most of the last twenty miles to Scarborough followed the Cinder Track, a former coastal railway so named because of its cinder track ballast. The line ran between 1885 and 1965. It's a beautiful route, although a review on Tripadvisor had warned that a better name for it would be the 'Puddles, Mud and Stones Track'. It was nothing of the sort.

Scarborough is an elegant town of Georgian and Victorian buildings, with large green parks, a clifftop castle and a sheltered harbour that dates to the 11th century. The harbour was enlarged considerably in the middle of the 18th century with the construction

Whitby High.

Scarborough.

of outer piers. The Vincent Pier had a circular brick lighthouse on it from 1806, which was damaged so badly in 1914, when German gunboats bombarded the town, that it had to be demolished.

Its replacement wasn't built until 1931, another white-painted, circular, brick tower, with an octagonal lantern room with a domed roof. It displays a white isophase light, at five-second intervals, visible for four miles, as well as two fixed green lights pointing seaward.

My original plan was to stay just outside Scarborough with my friend Rita, whom I had first met at a book publishing seminar I ran a decade or so previously. But I had arrived on the only day in July that she was not at home. A few weeks earlier, a missed connection like this would have felt like a huge setback, perhaps prompting a new spell of low mood and depression. After more than a fortnight on antidepressants, however, I wasn't fazed at all, opting instead for a guesthouse in one of the residential streets behind the cricket ground.

At dinner I met George, a cheerful old man in his eighties, who was here for the County Championship match against Worcestershire. He'd had a good day, with Yorkshire winning the game and Jonny Bairstow making a sublime, unbeaten 74. There weren't many things I'd rather have been doing that day than cycling the North Yorkshire coast, but watching Jonny's innings would certainly have been one of them.

Day 81

Having missed Rita yesterday, I had agreed to meet her at Flamborough Head at lunchtime. I've always been envious of Rita because she has a better claim than me to be a fan of Antony Gormley's work. In 2009 she was selected for *One & Other*, a public art project by Gormley in which 2,400 members of the public occupied the usually vacant fourth plinth in Trafalgar Square for an hour each, for 100 days. Rita had chosen to promote the work of WaterAid, by spending her hour on the plinth sitting on a very convincing replica of a public lavatory. You can't get much more public than that.

We walked to see the old Flamborough light tower, and then on to the current lighthouse, where my arrival was anticipated. Back in Fleetwood, I had planned to meet up with lighthouse enthusiast Michelle, who had seen the newspaper article about my journey and suggested that we walk out to the Wyre pile light at low tide. Our paths didn't quite cross in the end, but Michelle had got in touch with other members of her family, who lived near Flamborough. Gareth gives guided tours at the lighthouse, and he and his nephew Ryan were waiting for me.

Rita and I were given the full VIP treatment, with a tour of the lighthouse, tea and cake, and even someone assigned to guard my bike. But I admit that the highlight of the day was when Ryan approached and asked me for my autograph. There's a celebrity future for me yet.

The first lighthouse at Flamborough, built by Sir John Clayton and completed in 1674, is one of the oldest surviving light towers in England. Built from chalk, it has an octagonal tower nearly 80-feet tall. It was never actually lit, however, and served as a daymark only, something it continues to do to this day.

The tower failed to prevent a number of wrecks and losses during the 18th century, which led to the construction of the current lighthouse, first lit in 1806. Designed by Samuel Wyatt, consulting engineer to Trinity House between 1776 and 1807, it has an elegantly proportioned brick tower and originally had a single gallery with oil-powered lantern.

In 1925 the lantern was made taller, to accommodate a new fifteen-foot lens, which also necessitated the construction of a second iron gallery. The light was converted from oil to electricity in 1940, and automated in 1996. The current light displays four white flashes, every fifteen seconds, which are visible for 21 miles.

Reluctantly, I left Rita, her husband Adrian, Gareth and Ryan, my newly discovered fame having gone to my head. Five miles on, in Bridlington, the fun fair was in town. It was busy, noisy and colourful, and served as a reminder that it was now the school holidays, and I should probably be back at home with my own kids. Not having them with me, I realised, had saved me about £25 in fairground rides, so I had that to be thankful for, at least.

Bridlington is a small fishing port, renowned for its shellfish. In fact, it has earned the title of the 'Lobster Capital of Europe',

Flamborough Head.

landing 300 tonnes of them each year. There was a harbour here in medieval times, but the modern harbour dates to the mid-19th century, when the current stone piers were built.

At the end of the North Pier, there is an attractive lighthouse that resembles an elegant Edwardian streetlight. It has a fluted, white-painted, cast-iron column mounted to a black, tapered square base. It's about 30-feet high and displays a white flashing light, which is visible for nine miles.

There is a second, almost identical light on the north side of the harbour, close to the start of the North Pier. It is redundant, however, and seems a bit less ornate standing, as it does, in front of a waffle restaurant and the town's public toilets.

Following lunch and tea at Flamborough, and a couple of ice creams in Bridlington, the twenty miles on to the guesthouse in Aldbrough felt as though I had added an extra pair of panniers to the bike. But I was pleased with my day's work, had enjoyed the company I had kept, and the fact that, in Ryan's eyes at least, I was famous.

Day 82

I left Aldbrough early in the morning, uncertain about what I would find when I got to Spurn Point. Recent storms had swept aside the metalled track leading on to the spit, and I could not establish whether it had been re-laid, or whether it was even possible to reach the lighthouse at the end of the headland on foot. I would just have to take my chances when I got there.

Before then, I made for the town of Withernsea, where there is an attractive inland lighthouse set back a considerable distance from the seafront. Withernsea is mentioned in the Domesday Book as having a population of just fourteen villagers. In fact, the town's significant expansion came as late as the mid-19th century, with the arrival of the Hull and Holderness Railway, which connected the town with the city of Hull and brought Victorian workers and their families here for holidays by the sea.

There was once a pleasure pier here, but it was short-lived, sustaining considerable damage after being struck by a vessel in 1890. I was intrigued to find the former pier entrance still standing, with a pair of castellated towers standing proudly on the promenade.

I found the lighthouse three streets back from the seafront, with housing, shops and roads now built over the sand dunes thought too susceptible to coastal erosion to risk building a lighthouse on.

Withernsea.

The lighthouse was built in 1894 and was designed to steer ships clear of Bridlington Bay and provide safe passage into and out of the Humber Estuary. Out of fear of coastal erosion, it was positioned well back from the sea, although at the time nothing stood between it and the seafront other than sand dunes and shallow wetland. Expansion of the seafront promenade led to housing being built along roads surrounding the lighthouse, and now the lighthouse stands in the middle of the town.

It has a tapering, octagonal brick tower, with lantern and gallery. Originally oil fuelled, it was electrified in 1936. It displayed a white flashing light, every three seconds, which was visible for seventeen miles. It was decommissioned in July 1976 and is now a popular museum.

The Humber Estuary has always proved dangerous to shipping because of sandbanks that constantly change their shape and position with the tides, as well as through coastal erosion. Spurn Head is a narrow peninsula of sand and shingle at the mouth of the estuary, which is exposed to the gales of the North Sea.

I had read reports of recent erosion so severe that Spurn Head would be inaccessible. However, while I found the main track along the peninsular split and scarred in several places, it was passable. I reached the lighthouse to find it covered in sheeting and scaffolding. Fearing that this was another important monument falling into disrepair, I was pleased to find a detailed sign outlining plans to restore the lighthouse completely. The sheeting wrapped around the scaffolding was to minimise the spread of masonry dust while the peeling paintwork was being shot blasted back to brick, ready for a series of fresh coats.

The earliest reference to a lighthouse at Spurn is from 1428, when a tower was reputedly built by a hermit named Richard Reedbarrow. By the 17th century, there are records of a pair of coal-fired leading lights, which served until the mid-18th century, when the shape of the spit had altered significantly and the lights no longer pointed out the safe passage through the channel.

In 1776 a new pair of lighthouses were designed by John Smeaton. These were brick towers, with enclosed lanterns for their coal fires. The brickwork of the high light was found to be cracked in 1892, so work started on its replacement, the current tower. Completed in 1895, it was designed by Thomas Matthews and

Spurn Point.

has a circular brick tower, with lantern and gallery. It is painted in broad black-and-white bands, and displayed a white flashing light, once every twenty seconds, which was visible for seventeen miles. It also had separate sector lights, which marked particular sandbanks, as well as the main channel along the Humber.

Originally oil powered, it was converted to electricity in 1941, and then to acetylene gas in 1957, at which time the operation of the lighthouse was automated. It was decommissioned in 1985.

Down near the water, below the lighthouse, I found the tower of Smeaton's former low light. After Thomas Matthews' 1895 lighthouse was built, the low light was no longer needed. Its lantern was removed and replaced with a strange-looking water tank. It still stands on the beach, close to the current lighthouse.

For completeness, I walked on to the observation platform right at the tip of Spurn Point, where there is a strange little four-legged tower which displays a green flashing light, before retracing my tracks to Kilnsea.

I was happy to have seen the Spurn Lighthouse, in spite of the scaffolding, and happier still to learn that its future seems secure. I thought that the same might not be true for the pair of wrought-iron leading lights at Thorngumbald, where I had read that the sea defences were breached deliberately a few years ago, creating a controlled flood and making the lighthouses inaccessible. In fact, the track leading to the lights from the village of Paull was perfectly accessible, and the two lights stand on dry ground and are still operational.

They were built in 1870 to replace the lighthouse at Paull, after shifting sands meant that it no longer marked the safe channel along the narrow estuary. The high light is constructed of a red-painted, wrought-iron frame, which displays a white occulting light, visible for eight miles, from a window within its white domed lantern.

The low light, about 100 metres downstream, is a white-painted, circular, metal tower with a white domed lantern. It was originally mounted on a trolley so it could be moved to adjust to changes in the shipping channel. It displays a white occulting light through a lantern-room window, which is visible for nine miles. When the two lights are aligned, they indicate the safe passage for vessels leaving the port of Hull.

Returning to Paull, I found the former lighthouse in the heart of the village. It's a lovely old building whose tower has long since been amalgamated into the terraced house alongside it. It hasn't functioned as a lighthouse for 150 years, but its lantern is still in place, and the views from it across the Humber Estuary must be quite splendid.

Upstream from Paull, the flat, prairie-like fields soon give way to industry and the dockyards of Hull. The city has served as a significant port since the 12th century, when the monks of Meaux needed a port to export wool from their estates. By the mid-17th century, Hull had formed trading links with northern Europe, Scandinavia, the Baltics and the Low Countries.

It is still the country's leading softwood timber port today, while the offshore wind sector on the Humber has led to it becoming known as the UK's 'energy estuary'. However, the city itself has changed beyond recognition, having been the second-most bombed British town or city during the war. It is said that 95 per cent of the city's buildings were damaged or destroyed, leading to a large-scale restoration and rebuilding project that continues even today.

Cycling into Hull, the city's maritime heritage is not immediately apparent. But with the original 1871 dock offices now housing the city's maritime museum, and Hull Marina home to the former *Spurn* Lightvessel No.12, there is plenty to interest the maritime enthusiast.

Day 83

I walked down to Hull Marina first thing in the morning to see the *Spurn* Lightvessel. The marina was opened in 1983, creating berths for 270 pleasure boats on the site of the former Humber and Railway Docks. The lightvessel itself was built in 1927, and was stationed offshore, east of Spurn Point, for nearly fifty years.

I had always thought of lightvessels in bright red livery, but this one was painted black, apparently its original colour. It was also substantially larger than I had imagined, and dominated the corner of the marina where it was moored.

Following decommissioning in 1975, it was acquired by Hull City Council in 1983, and has been moored here since 1987.

Halfway between Hull and Goole, the Humber Estuary divides into two rivers, the Trent, which heads south, and the Ouse, which continues on to Goole. There is a modern light at Trent Falls, the confluence of the two rivers, which is quite difficult to reach by bike. There is also a lighthouse on the south bank of the River Ouse, near Whitgift. And lastly, the original light from Trent Falls has been restored and put on display at the Yorkshire Waterways Museum in Goole. Reaching all three would involve following the Ouse and crossing it at Goole, or following the Trent and crossing at Scunthorpe. Goole sounded like the better option, given that I could stop at the Yorkshire Waterways Museum while I was there.

Goole's docks and industrial area seemed a bit run down to me, and felt like an odd place for a museum, even one focused on the town's industrial heritage. I found it closed, which was unfortunate, but the exhibit I had come to see, the former light from Trent Falls, was clearly visible from the roadside. I managed to poke my camera through the wire-mesh fence and take a handful of decent photographs. It looked a little neglected and needed a fresh coat of red paint, something I was pleased to read it was given just a few weeks after my visit.

Of the current lights along the rivers Ouse and Trent, guiding shipping into and out of the ports at Hull and Goole, there is only one that has a traditional lighthouse tower. It is outside the village of Whitgift, and reaching it involved striding across a muddy field of peas. It's a handsome lighthouse, right on the riverbank, and it was in a decent state of repair.

It was built in the late-19th century, and has a five-storey, white-painted, tapering tower mounted on a circular stone base, with a metal domed lantern room on top. It is still active and displays a red light, flashing twice every four seconds, which is visible for five miles.

The modern light at Trent Falls, the one that replaced the light I had seen in Goole, was harder to find. With help from a warden at the RSPB centre at Blacktoft Sands, I set off on foot along a path that pointed in the direction of the river's edge to find it. It's not an object of beauty, just a light on a white pole, but I was pleased to say that I had found it. It displays a simple green flashing light.

On my return to Hull, I hoped I might be able to cross the Trent by ferry. My map showed a jetty, alongside a pub called the Ferry House Inn at Burton Stather, which gave me some hope. But a quick search online confirmed that no ferry had run for decades, and my only viable route back to Hull was the way I had come. Fifty days ago, the lack of a ferry between St Anthony's Head and Falmouth had all but broken me. Today, I just laughed it off and got back on the bike.

Day 84

I had been looking forward to this day for a month or so, not because of the lighthouses on the route, but because it had been earmarked for meeting up with three friends I had worked with at Stanfords 25 years earlier.

David had swapped the international desk at Stanfords for social work and, more recently, lecturing. He'd tried his hand at local politics for a while, but it was soon apparent that he was far too decent a man and cared far too much to make an effective politician. Meanwhile, John swapped the European desk, and city life, for a career in the police force in Huntingdon. He became the perfect family man, and you'd struggle to find a more loyal and dependable friend. Ever the outdoor enthusiast, Paul left the airless basement at Stanfords, where the British maps and books were sold, for a life of climbing, diving, biking, kayaking and just about every other outdoor pursuit you could imagine.

Although we had picked this particular weekend to meet, I wasn't quite sure where I would be. I think David and Paul imagined meeting up at a dramatic clifftop location somewhere on the North Yorkshire coast. None of us thought it would be at the lighthouses at Killingholme, nestled between a power station, an oil refinery and the heavy industrial complex alongside Immingham, Britain's largest port.

In fact, only John managed to find his way to the riverfront lighthouses unaided. He had to send the rest of us his exact location from his phone. As I cycled down the straight, stony track leading to the river, he took the photo of me that I will forever associate with my adventure. Funny how the candid, unplanned photographs often turn out to be the best.

By the time we all met up, John had befriended Gill Harper, who had purchased the former north low light and called it home 21 years earlier. She produced coffee and biscuits, and although embarrassed about the state of her daughter's tower bedroom, she gave us the full tour.

These were sad times for Gill. The port at Immingham was undergoing expansion, and the land all around her was slowly being purchased, tarmacked and built over. The port authority had secured a compulsory purchase order for Gill's lighthouse home, and had been trying to evict her for the last six years. There would be no reprieve for Gill, and the only dispute remaining was over the compensation being offered.

Wishing her luck, we left Gill and walked along the river to the other two Killingholme lights. Both were looking in quite a sorry state, and I don't think I convinced any of my bookselling friends that lighthouse-bagging was the next big thing.

All three lighthouses are a short distance north of the village of Killingholme. Two are active (the high light and the south low light), while the third (the north low light) is disused. At one time all three operated together, guiding shipping along the Humber and clear of the dangerous sandbanks between Killingholme and Spurn.

The current high light was built in 1876 and has a red-painted tapering tower, with gallery and dome-roofed lantern room. Its occulting red light flashes every four seconds and is visible for fourteen miles.

About 150 metres south stands the south low light, built in 1836 with a conical tapering tower, displaying a flashing isophase red light, at one-second intervals, which is visible for eleven miles.

The former north low light is a few-hundred metres further north. Its tower is broadly similar to the south low light, although it was built fifteen years later, in 1851. This lighthouse was decommissioned in 1920, and after serving as a signal station for a period, it was sold as a private dwelling.

The four of us reconvened an hour later at the Black Bull in East Halton. We spent barely ten minutes catching up on what had happened in the 25 years since we had last met, then nearly three hours reminiscing about the Stanfords days. The people we'd worked with, the customers we'd served, the managers we had run rings around.

By the time we parted company, it was early evening. David and Paul each headed north, while John headed south. It suddenly dawned on me that I didn't quite know where I was headed. South, certainly. But how far, or quite where, I wasn't certain.

WEEK 13

Days 85 and 86

With the only remaining Lincolnshire lighthouse 80 miles south, I chose to continue along NCN Route 1, which headed inland, rather than follow the coast. This was, after all, a lighthouse cycle tour rather than a coastal one, so I didn't feel obliged to have the sea in sight at all times.

For a day and a half, I followed quiet lanes, railway lines (some working, others disused) and riverside paths. I stopped at a tired-looking pub close to the river near Tattershall Bridge, where a dried-out, pre-plated portion of fish pie proved to be the wrong choice from the menu.

The pub was empty, apart from the barman, and a couple on a nearby table arguing about cushions. She wanted a lift into Boston to buy some new cushions, but he was unwilling to provide the lift, arguing that they had enough cushions already. Too many, in fact.

Other than to pause in the delightful market square in Boston, I didn't stop again until Holbeach. As I entered the town, I worried that I had booked the Chequers, which seemed to be on its last legs and partly boarded up. But a quick glance at my phone confirmed that I had booked the Horse & Groom, which looked much more promising.

After the ten miles to Sutton Bridge the following morning, the bleak, exposed landscape alongside the River Nene reminded me of home on Romney Marsh, although perhaps there were even fewer trees here, and even flatter fields. The crosswinds felt very familiar, though, and they made the last mile or so to the lighthouse on the west bank of the river slow going. When I reached the lighthouse, I was only a stone's throw from the one on the opposite bank.

It's not an obvious location for a pair of lighthouses, standing on each bank of a straight, tranquil river mouth, with no obvious rocks or hazards in the sea beyond. They were built in 1831, after the river was realigned and straightened to create the Nene Outfall, where the river emerges into the Wash.

The lighthouses each have tapered, circular towers, about 60-feet tall, and octagonal lanterns with circular windows facing the entry to the channel. Some sources suggest that neither lighthouse was ever lit, while others assert that if a high tide occurred after dark, they were lit to guide ships through the sandbanks and into the river.

Both lighthouses are now comfortable private homes. The lighthouse on the east bank is also known as the Sir Peter Scott Lighthouse, named after the naturalist and artist who lived here in the 1930s. He purchased much of the surrounding marshland and established a nature reserve, now known as the Wildfowl & Wetlands Trust.

Leaving Lincolnshire for Norfolk, I wasn't convinced by the AA's description of Hunstanton as a 'sunny and elegant classic seaside resort', but it was partly down to the weather. I arrived in a downpour, and the seafront promenade was laden with miserable anorak-clad families huddled together around the little brick viewpoint shelters that lined the parade.

As I cycled past one family, a boy aged about nine or ten was stamping his feet aggressively, shouting, 'I just want to go home! Now!'

You and me both, I thought, memories of damp and blustery childhood seaside holidays flooding back to me.

Hunstanton had a pair of stone lighthouses as early as 1665. They were referred to as the 'Chapel Lights', perhaps because before they were built, sailors relied on the lights burning in St Edmund's Chapel to guide them.

The lights were said to be in poor repair by 1710, and the rear lighthouse was destroyed by fire in 1776. In 1837, Trinity House commissioned a new lighthouse designed by James Walker, which was first lit in 1840. It has a white-painted, cylindrical, brick tower, which displayed a fixed white light, visible for sixteen miles. A red sector was added in 1844, which indicated the position of the Roaring Middle shoal.

By 1921, the lightvessel at Inner Dowsing, together with other lights around the Wash, made the Hunstanton Lighthouse redundant. A year later it was decommissioned, and in the century since it has served as an observation post for the Royal Observer Corps, as well as a private home. Nowadays, it is available to all as a splendid and luxurious holiday home.

Since automation in the 1990s, a steady stream of lighthouse keepers' cottages and ancillary buildings have been turned into holiday lets. Many are privately owned, the towers purchased following decommissioning. But plenty are at present working lighthouses, retained by Trinity House, and externally at least are little changed from the days when keepers made them their homes.

Day 87

I left Wells-next-the-Sea feeling anxious and apprehensive once more, and I knew perfectly well why. I had planned on cycling just twenty miles today and seeing only the lighthouse at Cromer, so it was hardly likely to be a demanding undertaking. But I was due to meet up in Cromer with Jason, the friend from Kent who had tried to persuade me to change my original plans beyond recognition.

The more I thought about it, the more I realised that I had felt apprehensive in Jason's company for much of the time I had known him. He could be laid-back, funny, well-meaning and generous. But he could also be dark, critical, monosyllabic and moody, and I was nervous about which Jason I would meet in Cromer that evening.

Distraction came in the form of RAF Langham, a former airfield that played a key role in both the Second World War and the Cold War. It is now a museum, and visitors are encouraged to wander around the grounds, even when officially closed, listening to the archive audio files that are dotted around the field.

Access to the lighthouse at Cromer is via the Royal Cromer Golf Club, and I arrived as day three of the England Girls Amateur Under 14 and Under 16 Championships got underway. I felt somewhat underdressed for the occasion. It's a glorious location for a lighthouse, though, with commanding views over both sea and greens. I don't play golf, but if I did, this is certainly where I would want to play.

A lighthouse tower was built here in around 1670, but the projected cost of maintenance exceeded the dues from passing vessels, so it was not lit until 1719. When the lease expired in 1792, the lighthouse was taken over by Trinity House, who replaced the coal-fired light with an Argand oil-powered flashing light. It survived until 1866, when it was destroyed by a landslip.

Cromer.

The current lighthouse, with a white-painted, octagonal tower, was built earlier, in 1833, about half a mile from the cliff edge. It displays a white flashing light, every five seconds, which is visible for 21 miles. The lighthouse was converted to mains electricity in 1958 and then automated in 1990.

I reached the hotel in Cromer an hour or so before Jason. I was pleased to find that he had brought another friend from Kent, Dave, along for the ride. In case you were wondering, it was the benevolent Jason who turned up, and we had an enjoyable evening, involving a curry and several pints of Woodforde's Wherry. He even handed me one of those giant charity cheques, with an absurdly generous donation made out to Shift.ms. It made me question the anxiety I had felt throughout the day.

Day 88

I had been looking forward to reaching the lighthouse at Happisburgh for weeks, because these days it is the only independently operated lighthouse in the country, managed and run by a trust comprising of fellow members of the Association of Lighthouse Keepers.

One of them, Joy, is a longstanding friend whom I had first met at a business meeting more than fifteen years ago. I believe we were meant to be discussing a marketing campaign to schools and colleges, but once we established our mutual interest in lighthouses, the agenda of the meeting went out of the window. We had stayed in touch ever since.

Both Joy and her husband Patrick were waiting at the lighthouse for my arrival. Patrick was multitasking, taking on the role of tour guide and photographer, as well as features writer for the local newspaper. He performed all three admirably and was enormously good company. I hadn't met up with Joy for a decade or more, and was delighted to discover that she hadn't changed a bit.

Two more ALK members joined us, Melanie and Peter, who are part of the team that runs the lighthouse. As we swapped stories over coffee and cake, it occurred to me that this was the largest gathering of well-wishers I had mustered since Dungeness.

This is the oldest working lighthouse in East Anglia, designed by Norwich architect William Wilkins. It was built in 1790, following severe storms the previous winter that claimed 70 vessels and 600 lives. It is about 400 yards from the shore and was originally one of a pair of leading lights that marked safe passage around the hazardous Happisburgh Sands offshore. It has a circular tapering tower, with lantern and gallery above, and originally displayed a fixed light, which, when lined up with the low light, indicated the safe passage.

The low light survived until 1883, when it was decommissioned and demolished following coastal erosion. The surviving light was then painted with three red bands, and its light changed from fixed to an occulting pattern, in order to distinguish it from the lighthouse at Winterton about twelve miles further along the coast.

Originally gas powered, the lighthouse was converted to paraffin in 1904, and to electricity in 1947. It has been automated since 1929, and these days it displays a white flashing light, three times every 30 seconds, which is visible for fourteen miles.

In 1988, Trinity House announced that the lighthouse would be decommissioned, but following lobbying and fundraising, it was officially handed over to the Happisburgh Lighthouse Trust in August 1990.

Before leaving Happisburgh, Joy told me that she had been chronicling the gradual demise of my ALK baseball cap from my daily posts on social media, and she handed me a new one.

The fourteen miles south to Winterton were relatively tame, punctuated only by a couple of pints of Woodforde's Wherry at the Lion in West Somerton. It was proving to be the surprise discovery of my journey, and rapidly becoming my bitter of choice.

In Winterton, an octagonal lighthouse tower built by Sir Edward Turnour was lit between 1687 and 1840, when Trinity House replaced it with a circular brick and masonry tower, with lantern and gallery, and keepers' accommodation attached. This lighthouse must have been substantially altered or rebuilt not long afterwards, because records show that Trinity House engineer-in-chief James Douglass oversaw construction of a new lighthouse here in 1867.

Happisburgh.

By 1921, its light was redundant, following the installation of a number of floating lights, as well as improvements made to the *Cockle* lightvessel. The tower served as a military lookout post in both world wars, and during the Second World War the lantern was replaced with a circular observation room. The lighthouse has been in private hands since 1921 and is currently a luxury holiday let. In 2012 a replica lantern was reinstated to replace the observation deck.

Although officially part of Great Yarmouth, Gorleston seems altogether calmer and quieter. Marine Parade and the seafront promenade are separated by landscaped gardens, grass tennis courts and the occasional palm tree, while the unfussy Edwardian terraced streets boast enviable sea views.

Down by the quay, the picture was not so rosy. I found the lighthouse nestled between a 1970s office block and a former pound shop, which was in the process of being boarded up. The lighthouse itself is attractive and deserves better neighbours and surroundings.

It has a circular, red-brick tower, 70-feet tall, with a lantern and gallery, and red domed roof with a weathervane. It was built in 1878, on the road immediately behind the harbour entrance. These days the lantern displays a fixed red light, visible for six miles. From a much lower, first-floor window, a white occulting leading light is also displayed, visible for ten miles. This secondary light works in conjunction with a white metal pole light on the opposite side of the road, set into the harbour wall.

Gorleston once had a second lighthouse, a wood and cast-iron tower built at the end of the south pier. It was demolished, along with the pier itself, in 1955.

On a roll, I pushed on towards Lowestoft, reckoning on being able to see the main Lowestoft Lighthouse, as well as the pair of lights in the harbour, before the end of the day.

The main lighthouse in Lowestoft is set back just a few yards from the main road leading into the town, and I managed to pass it completely without noticing it. In a way, that suited me quite well, because the view of the lighthouse when heading out of town is much the more attractive one.

There was a pair of leading lights at Lowestoft as long ago as 1609, which together lined up to mark the deepest water in the Stamford Channel. They had to be rebuilt in 1628, and again in 1676, at which time the high light was moved to the cliff top where the current lighthouse is sited.

The shifting sands required the low light to be rebuilt or repositioned several times during the 18th and 19th centuries. By 1923, the Stamford Channel had disappeared, so the light was decommissioned and demolished.

When Trinity House decided to electrify the high light in the 1870s, the existing tower was not considered strong enough to bear the weight of the new arc lamp and other equipment required. In 1872 work began on a new lighthouse, the current one, which was completed in 1874. It has a three-storey, white-painted, cylindrical brick tower, and flashes a white light, every fifteen seconds, visible for 23 miles.

Although designed for electricity, paraffin oil was efficient and in plentiful supply, so the light was paraffin burning until 1936. It was automated in 1975 and modernised in 1997.

The harbour at Lowestoft is complex, with a series of piers and jetties that separate commercial shipping from various marinas offering berths for yachts and other pleasure craft.

By the mid-19th century the railway had reached Lowestoft, and the town's importance as a port grew as a result. Two stone piers, with matching lighthouses, were built in 1847. They have white-painted hexagonal towers, with skirts, or canopies, at their base, which give them the look of a marquee at a village fete. Each has a hexagonal lantern with a domed roof. The light on

Lowestoft.

the North Pier displays a green flashing light, while the one on the South Pier flashes red. They are visible for eight miles.

Catching up with Emily and the children at the end of the day, it struck me that I could be home in less than a fortnight. Having been away for more than three months, it felt like no time at all before I would be back at Dungeness.

I stared at my legs, tanned and sporting muscles for perhaps the first time in my adult life, and marvelled at how far they had pedalled me. They may have buzzed, twitched, burned and cramped throughout, but they hadn't managed to stop me in my tracks. Indeed, I felt thankful that the sort of MS-related sensations that had formerly prompted me to rest up had not worsened as a result of cycling more than 3,000 miles so far.

Day 89

A couple of miles out of Lowestoft is the large Pontins holiday camp at Pakefield. It seemed an unlikely location for a lighthouse, although I learned that when it was built, it stood in the grounds of Pakefield Hall.

I feared that I would need a pass of some sort to enter the camp, to show that I was a genuine Pontins paying guest. Unchallenged, I cycled up and down lines of chalets, continually craning my neck to the left and right in the hope of spotting a tower.

Although the lighthouse eluded me, something else caught my eye. As a keen hill walker when younger, I was taught never to pass by fresh water without taking the opportunity to refill my water bottle. On this expedition, I had learned not to pass up a vacant launderette. Inside I found an empty washing machine that seemed to be preloaded with credit. I decanted everything that I wasn't actually wearing into the tub, borrowed a couple of healthy scoops of powder from a catering-size box hidden behind a pile of freshly laundered towels, and set off once again in search of the lighthouse.

Checking my map, I established that the lighthouse in fact stands *alongside* the holiday complex, rather than inside it, so I returned to the main entrance and found it within minutes.

It was built in 1832 to guide vessels through the Pakefield Gateway, a safe channel into Lowestoft Harbour. It has a white-painted, circular brick tower, with lantern and gallery above.

Originally, the lighthouse displayed a fixed white light, which was visible for nine miles. But in 1835 the light was changed from a fixed white light to red, because some ships had mistaken the white one for the lights shining from the windows of clifftop houses nearby.

Shifting sands required a light at nearby Kessingland to be built in 1850, and in 1864 the lighthouse at Pakefield was decommissioned. These days it is used by the Pakefield Coastwatch group as a coastal reconnaissance station.

Returning to the launderette, I heard a woman screaming at a Pontins employee, complaining that someone had stolen her machine, her money and her washing powder. The honourable thing to do would be to own up, apologise and reimburse the out-of-pocket camper. I contemplated doing this for a while, before hiding behind a tree until they both left to log her complaint, then stuffed my wet washing into a couple of carrier bags and pedalled out of the park as quickly as I could.

About halfway along the ten-mile route to Southwold, I was enticed off the road by a sign at the Five Bells pub declaring itself 'the last pub before Southwold'. This was Adnams country, and with the brewery just four miles away, in Southwold itself, it wasn't going to get any fresher than this. It certainly gave the Woodforde's Wherry from the previous few days a run for its money.

My *AA Book of the Seaside* calls Southwold a 'gracious old seaside town', but I think it's better than that. It's a delightful town, with neat terraces of red-brick and flint cottages, fine colour-washed houses, plenty of green space, charming clifftop paths and a thriving centre of interesting independent shops. And a lighthouse, of course, which clinches the deal for me.

The lighthouse is right in the centre of town, built by Trinity House in 1887 to guide vessels safely into Southwold Harbour. Construction was supervised by Sir James Douglass, and the lighthouse was first lit in September 1890. The lighthouse replaced several local lighthouses that were threatened by severe coastal erosion to the south.

Southwold.

It has a white-painted, circular, brick tower, with a small adjoining service building. Originally powered by an Argand burner, it was converted to an incandescent oil burner in 1906, to a petroleum vapour burner in 1923, and finally electrified in 1938, at which time the lighthouse was automated.

Threatened with closure in 2005, it not only earned a reprieve but was actually upgraded and uprated in 2012, in advance of the decommissioning of Orfordness Lighthouse further south. It currently displays a white flashing light, once every ten seconds, which is visible for 24 miles.

It was still only lunchtime, and I considered cycling on to Orford, catching the boat across the water to Orford Ness and walking out to the lighthouse there before the end of the day. To fortify me for the journey, I stopped at the Sole Bay Inn for another pint of Adnams and a plate of home-baked ham, egg and chips. By the time I was ready to move on it was past 4pm.

Instead, I made towards Aldeburgh, and found a room at the Butcher's Arms in Knodishall, about three miles inland. I got a text from my friend Simon, who had helped me to plan my expedition and introduced me to several key sponsors. He was on his way from Oxford to join me for a couple of days of lighthouse-bagging.

Day 90

Simon is the friend who cycled to every York City football match, home and away, over the course of an entire season. I met him in the pub car park early the next morning. Ever the adventurer, he had arrived the previous evening, slept on the beach, and had endured a night involving a seafront brawl, a missing person, an air ambulance and plenty of police activity. He seemed cheerful, despite the broken sleep, and arrived clutching cups of coffee and egg and bacon rolls.

It felt strange at first to be cycling with a companion. I had pedalled in silence for 89 days, so having someone to talk to felt novel. It felt good, in fact. I envied Simon's calm, laid-back approach to life. Where I was tied up in knots worrying that we would miss the boat across to Orford Ness, or that there wouldn't be any places left on it, he took the view that both scenarios were unlikely and there was always the perfectly satisfactory option of waiting fifteen minutes for the next one.

He was right, of course. We reached Orford village an hour before the first boat of the day, and ours were the first two tickets booked. Why can't I learn to relax more?

Unlike the many other boat trips of my journey, there was no need for safety briefing or life jackets, and our skipper seemed dressed for the country club rather than the water. The briefing from the warden on the Ness, however, was exhaustive, and nearly fifteen minutes long.

Although an internationally important site for nature conservation, Orford Ness was out of bounds for much of the 20th century, home to a Ministry of Defence testing facility. The site was used in the testing and development of radar in the 1930s, and the Atomic Weapons Establishment also had a base on the site in the decades following. Simon and I might have come here to see a lighthouse, but the former defence buildings, containing relics from the Cold War including all but the most lethal parts of an atomic bomb, made compelling, if somewhat shocking viewing.

I knew that I would find the current state of the lighthouse particularly hard to accept. Decommissioned in 2013 as a result of rapid coastal erosion, it had months, possibly a few years of life left before it would fall prey to the tide. As we approached, I noticed the shingle and sandbags piled up in front of the tower, an attempt to shore up the structure following the most recent damage. One of the buildings beyond the tower had already been lost to the sea.

Since the first lights at Orford Ness as early as 1637, there have been a number of attempts to build a lighthouse here during the 18th century. All were eventually either washed away or destroyed by fire.

In 1792, Lord Braybrooke built a new lighthouse, designed by architect William Wilkins. It had a slightly tapering brick tower, painted in red-and-white bands, and for most of its life it displayed a flashing white light that was visible for 25 miles.

When the low light finally succumbed to coastal erosion in 1887, red and green sector lights were added to the 1792 tower, and a new lighthouse built at Southwold to compensate for the loss.

Originally, the lighthouse was nearly 1,500 yards away from the shore. However, by 2013 the coastal erosion had cut the distance down to just 50 yards, and the lighthouse was decommissioned. Various attempts were made to protect the site, or even to move the lighthouse, but it was inevitable that it would eventually be lost to the encroaching sea. It has been demolished since my visit.

Orfordness.

Between Orford and Harwich, there are two rivers to cross, each with its own regular passenger (and bicycle) ferry service. The River Deben ferry between Bawdsey and Felixstowe is tiny, and the crossing takes just a few minutes. But crossing the mouth of the River Stour between Felixstowe and Harwich involves booking tickets and phoning ahead to make sure there is room on board for one of the handful of spaces for bicycles. I'm sure I don't need to say that I found the whole process very stressful, while Simon seemed to take it all in his stride.

Even Simon had to admit that we'd cut it a bit fine. We arrived minutes before the last ferry of the day, and we secured the last two tickets. There were already too many bikes on board, but we were able to stand alongside ours in a gangway at the bow.

Harwich is an odd sort of place. It feels like a sizeable town, with quite an elegant seafront, but it appears to have absolutely no shops whatsoever. There are a couple of pubs, and a hotel or two close to the harbour, but if you want so much as a pint of milk, you have to head over to neighbouring Dovercourt.

Harwich does boast two lighthouses, however. They are both long redundant, but they were once a pair of leading lights marking safe passage into Harwich Harbour. We were due to meet up with my friend (and former lighthouse keeper) Neil Hargreaves at the High Light at the end of the day. So we hugged the waterfront to make our way to the former low light, which is now a maritime museum. It's an elaborate ten-sided brick tower, 45-feet tall, and its construction was supervised in 1818 by the famous English engineer John Rennie, later responsible for London Bridge.

The High Lighthouse is a seven-storey, nine-sided brick tower, 90-feet tall, with lantern room and unusual half gallery. It was designed by architect and engineer Daniel Alexander, and construction was once again supervised by John Rennie. Its light was visible for thirteen miles.

Following shifting sands, the two Harwich lights were decommissioned in 1863 and replaced by a pair of cast-iron leading lights at nearby Dovercourt. Both lighthouses were sold in 1909 and the High Lighthouse was used as a private house until the late 1960s. Its last tenant was a well-known local character known as 'Lighthouse Lil', who was said to have offered sailors services unrelated to maritime navigation.

Neil was waiting for us at the High Light, and seemed genuinely pleased to see me. As well as being a former Trinity House lighthouse keeper, with stints at Smalls, Portland Bill and Inner Dowsing under his belt, he is also the founder of the ALK. Despite it being early evening, he was happy to give us a guided tour. As well as plenty of archive material about the lighthouse itself, the tower is now an art gallery and creative space, with six storeys of hanging wall space.

Harwich High Light.

With Neil as our guide, we wandered down to the pair of Dovercourt lighthouses. Built in 1863, they have cast-iron, screw-pile frameworks, with white-painted wooden lantern rooms above. They were designed to be moveable so that they could be realigned if necessary. The high light is on the beach alongside the Dovercourt promenade, while the low light stands in front of it, about 200 yards out to sea.

They showed fixed white lights, the high light visible for eleven miles and the low light nine. In the early 1900s, when they were converted to gas, they were changed to a flashing light pattern. By 1917, the safe deep-water channel was marked with a series of lighted buoys, making both Dovercourt lighthouses redundant.

I would happily have talked with Neil all evening, but we hadn't booked anywhere to stay, and we needed to press on. Simon had a tent, and he cycled off in search of somewhere to pitch it. Tentless, I found a guesthouse on the seafront.

Day 91

I remember admiring Simon's confidence that 'there was bound to be a campsite on the road leading out of Dovercourt', and he had been proved right. Although the site was closed, he had managed to get in and pitch his tent in the dark.

I met him there, just as he was wedging his tent back into its sleeve. I had passed a cafe on my way, so it was my turn to arrive with bacon rolls and coffee. We were heading for Walton-on-the-Naze, but because of the estuaries and marshland renowned along this part of the Essex coast, the route was largely inland.

Just north of Walton-on-the-Naze is a grassy headland set above low cliffs, known simply as the Naze. In 1720, Trinity House built an octagonal red-brick tower, nearly 90-feet tall, commonly known as the Naze Tower. In conjunction with the nearby Walton Hall Tower, it guided vessels through the Goldmer Gap and on to the harbour at Harwich.

There is much debate about whether or not the tower was ever lit, or if it operated solely as a daymark. If it was ever a genuine lighthouse, then it would probably have had an open coal fire on top of the tower.

Over the years, the Naze Tower has had a number of uses, including a tea house, a lookout (during the Napoleonic Wars and the First World War) and as a radar station (during the Second World War). Following complete restoration in 2004, it is now a popular visitor attraction, with gallery, museum and tea rooms.

There is a former lighthouse at Gunfleet, about six miles offshore, which is visible from the Naze Tower. Getting up close to it required chartering a boat, something I couldn't justify, so I settled for a long-lens photograph.

It once marked the Gunfleet Sands, and the north entry into the River Thames. Built by Trinity House's engineer-in-chief James Walker in 1850, it is a hexagonal screw-pile structure, once equipped with living room, bedroom, kitchen/washroom and storeroom, and a small lantern above. It displayed a rotating white light, which was visible for ten miles.

The light was deactivated in 1921, having been replaced by a lit buoy, although the tower is still used as an automated weather station by the Port of London Authority. It made news headlines in 1974 when it was briefly commandeered by the pirate radio station Radio Atlantis.

South of the Naze Tower, our route followed ten miles of seafront promenade through the resorts of Walton, Frinton and Clacton. On a sunny Saturday morning in late July, the seafront was crowded with families, dogs, buckets and spades, balls and frisbees.

From time to time the promenade narrowed, and cycling was forbidden. When it did, we switched to the clifftop road, or enjoyed the opportunity to dismount and continue on foot. At Colne Point, I paused to secure a perfectly decent long-distance shot of the two modern Blacktail lights that mark the Maplin Sands.

For now, though, we could go no further south without finding a way to cross the Blackwater Estuary, an area of marsh and wetland covering nearly 5,000 hectares surrounding the mouths of the rivers Colne and Blackwater. One option was the Brightlingsea ferry across to Mersea Island, which is connected to the mainland by a road bridge. Another was the Wivenhoe ferry that crosses the River Colne a few miles south of Colchester. Neither turned out to be viable, as we'd missed the last Brightlingsea crossing, and by the time we reached Wivenhoe we discovered that the ferry only runs for a couple of hours either side of high tide.

So we followed the Wivenhoe Trail, a cycle track nestled between the river and the railway line, all the way into Colchester. It was easy going, very pretty and delightfully quiet. It was the right decision from a lighthouse perspective too, because it led us to the TS *Colne* Light, a former Trinity House lightvessel, built in 1953, that is now home to Colchester's Sea Cadets.

Taking a quick rest alongside the river, Simon offered to take charge of finding accommodation for the night. Given his almost perpetual sense of calm and optimism, I thought I would set the bar high. I requested a quintessentially English inn, preferably on a village green, serving Adnams bitter, with a cheap ensuite room for me, a campsite behind the pub garden for Simon, decent food and safe storage for the bikes.

He wandered off with his phone, and returned to the riverbank ten minutes later with a broad grin on his face. Ten miles south of Colchester, we arrived at the Hare and Hounds at Layer Breton, a pub on an attractive village green with ensuite rooms in a separate building by the car park, and an entrance hallway perfect for a pair of bikes. There was a campsite in the field behind. And yes, they served Adnams.

WEEK 14

Day 92

Simon and I set off in opposite directions. Simon was making his way back to his car near Aldeburgh, and knowing his luck he would find a new, traffic-free shortcut that would cut his journey in half. Meanwhile, I decided to head for Shoeburyness, on the edge of Southend-on-Sea, to see if I could get a closer view of the pair of modern lights near Maplin Sands.

By lunchtime, I regretted that decision. First, because the lights themselves were entirely unremarkable. Second, because by coming here I had probably added 40 miles to my journey and had almost nothing to show for it.

The original lighthouse at Maplin Sands was a famous one, having been the world's first screw-pile lighthouse. The sharp-eyed readers among you will remember that this was a claim also made of the Wyre Light, off the coast at Fleetwood. The truth is a little complicated. The Maplin structure's screw piles were the first in place, although the Wyre Light was the first to display a light. Either way, it's an academic argument, since the Maplin light was swept away by the sea in 1932.

There were once a number of other lights along the Thames Estuary, at Chapman Sands, Mucking and Purfleet, but all have long since been demolished and replaced with a series of lit markers and buoys. There are, however, a number of lights of interest further along the River Thames itself, so I planned out a route that would take me along the north bank of the river as far as Trinity Buoy Wharf, near Blackwall, then cross the river using the Woolwich Ferry to follow the south bank until it reached the north Kent coast.

The only part of the plan I didn't like was the first twenty miles out of Southend-on-Sea. Whichever route-planner service I consulted, the only feasible way seemed to involve the main A13 road into London. As soon as I was outside the town, the road became a dual carriageway at regular intervals and the traffic speed doubled as a result. At one point I found myself on the inside lane as another dual carriageway merged into mine. All four lanes were full of fast-moving traffic, and I was suddenly right in the middle of them.

Beyond Tilbury, I left the A13, by now a nervous wreck. I found a hotel, still shaking with fear, and made straight for the bar, where I drank two large glasses of Cognac to calm my nerves.

Day 93

After the trauma of the previous afternoon, I vowed not to cycle along a single main road all day. Cycle tracks and minor roads would be okay, but I would rather walk the Thames Path, pushing my bike, than experience anything remotely similar to the previous afternoon.

Fortunately, the Thames Path is a well-defined, metalled track for much of the route heading along the north bank of the river towards the city. I threaded my way towards the river at Grays, found the path, and then made for the lighthouse at Stone Ness. I was surprised to find a landscape not dissimilar to the tranquil wetlands of the Thames Estuary, albeit with the sight and distant sounds of heavy industry all around me.

Like many of the Thames lights, the lighthouse at Stone Ness has a red-painted, skeletal, metal-framework tower, with a circular lantern room and gallery above. Built in 1885, it displays a flashing green light, which is visible for six miles.

Heading further along the Thames Path, it became clear that it was meant for walkers rather than cyclists. Every pier, jetty or body of water is navigated via a series of narrow steel bridges, with steep flights of steps on either side. Under most circumstances, it would be folly to continue along this particular route with my bike, but I had vowed to stay safely away from roads today, and I planned to stick to that commitment.

The challenge was that the bridges were too narrow to accommodate a bicycle with loaded panniers. In any case, it was far too heavy to carry, fully laden, up each flight of steel steps. So every few-hundred yards I needed to dismount, remove my four panniers, carry the bike over the bridge, return for the panniers, reattach them and then set off again. In one stretch of a mile or so, I did this four times. It was the sort of daft endeavour better suited to *It's a Knockout*, albeit without having to wear a clown's outfit or carry two full buckets of water at the same time.

Rainham Marshes were astonishingly peaceful, and it was hard to believe that I was so close to the centre of London. At a bend in the river at Erith Reach, there is a lighthouse at Coldharbour Point. Like Stone Ness, it was built in 1885 and is another red-painted, metal-lattice tower. It has a small gallery, with lamp mounted on top, access to which is via an external metal staircase. It displays a flashing white light, which is visible for three miles.

Ten miles upstream is Trinity Buoy Wharf, near Blackwall, where there is a splendid 'experimental' lighthouse, as well as a lightvessel permanently moored. Although I had no choice other than to join the road network around London City Airport, I was now in the city, and so enjoyed the luxury of safe, wide and segregated cycle lanes the whole way.

There have been two lighthouses at Trinity Buoy Wharf, although neither were ever used to aid navigation on the Thames. The first was built by James Walker in 1854. Its purpose was to test and develop various forms of illumination for Trinity House's network of lighthouses, lightships and buoys. Michael Faraday worked as a scientific advisor to Trinity House between 1836 and 1865, and his laboratory was based here at Trinity Buoy Wharf.

In 1864 the depot was rebuilt, and a second lighthouse, designed by Sir James Douglass, was built alongside the first. James Walker's light was eventually demolished in the 1920s.

The 1864 lighthouse is still standing, and has a hexagonal brick tower attached to the other depot buildings. It has a gallery and lantern above, whose optics were changed according to the lighting being tested. Trinity House also used the lighthouse for the training of lighthouse keepers and maintenance personnel, a function it performed until 1988.

Today, Trinity Buoy Wharf has been transformed from an empty, derelict site into a dynamic workspace and centre for arts and cultural activities.

I crossed the river on the Woolwich Ferry, something I hadn't done for more than twenty years. As I weaved my way back around the airport complex, I wasn't even certain that the ferry still operated. As it was, it hadn't changed a bit, and of all the ferries, boat trips and crossings I'd made, I would rank this five-minute crossing of the Thames among my favourites.

I was now heading east, following the south bank of the Thames towards a lighthouse at Tripcock Ness. It was a little underwhelming, largely because of its similarity to the light at

Trinity Buoy Wharf.

Coldharbour Point I had already seen. This one was built in 1902, and displays a flashing white light, visible for eight miles. You clearly get a rougher crowd on the south bank of the river, because unlike the Coldharbour light, this one had a forbidding metal fence topped with razor wire to protect it.

On this stretch of the river the Thames Path doubles as a genuine cycle path, and the going was much easier and quicker. Two miles downstream is another, almost identical light at Cross Ness. This one is earlier, built in 1895, but has an identical light pattern to Tripcock Ness, displaying a flashing white light, which is visible for eight miles. It, too, is fenced in securely.

These Thames lights are not inspiring, and I was glad when beyond Erith the riverbank started to feel green and marsh-like once more, albeit alongside the skeletal remains of former industry.

The light at Crayford Ness is displayed from a platform halfway up the smaller of two radar towers. It required all my imagination to recognise the Crayford Ness tower as a lighthouse. To my untrained eye, it looked like an electricity pylon that was missing its cables. Not for the first time, this was starting to feel like a box-ticking exercise rather than a genuine hunt for lighthouses.

After Greenhithe and Swanscombe, the main cycle track turns towards Northfleet, and the last mile or so to the light at Broadness was mainly on foot. Even the footpath avoids the Broadness Salt Marsh, and I have a feeling that I might have been trespassing along this final stretch. It will come as no surprise that the light here has a red-painted metal tower, with a gallery and lamp installed at the top.

In Northfleet, I found the former lower light on India Arms Wharf. At least this has a gallery with a proper lantern on top, with a window through which its light was displayed. It is earlier, as well, dating to 1859, and was a working light until 2001.

The light marked on my map at Bevans Wharf was arguably the most questionable of the whole trip, as its lantern is mounted onto the roof of a modern office block.

With the red metal-lattice towers behind me, I made for Gravesend, where I timed my arrival to enjoy a couple of pints with my friend James, who worked nearby. I booked into the Clarendon Royal Hotel, an elegant and somewhat luxurious hotel right on the river front. It was a treat paid for by Val and

David, my lovely friends from the village we moved to when we first left London. The service was immaculate, but I looked the other way when a porter wheeled my bike across a thick carpet towards a storeroom, leaving muddy tyre tracks behind him.

Day 94

Although I had seen them briefly the previous evening with James, I decided to take a closer look at the two Gravesend piers with lights. These days, the Royal Terrace Pier is owned by the Port of London Authority, and access is prohibited. But it's possible to get a decent enough view of the lighthouse tower from the riverfront. The Town Pier is open and accessible, and as well as a ferry service across to Tilbury, it also houses a bar and restaurant.

The Town Pier is said to be the oldest remaining cast-iron pier in the world. It opened in July 1834 and occupies the same site as the original Town Quay mentioned in the Domesday Book. Before the railways, it was an important passenger terminus, and today it is still the terminal for a passenger ferry crossing the Thames to Tilbury. Between the two pavilions is a cast-iron cylindrical lighthouse, with a light at the top surmounted by a finial. When it operated it displayed a fixed red light.

The Royal Terrace Pier was built in 1844 and earned its royal title when Princess Alexandra of Denmark arrived there in 1863 to marry the Prince of Wales, later King Edward VII. The pier has a tower rising above the single-storey building, with an open, white-painted lantern from which a fixed red light is displayed.

Gravesend marks the start of the Saxon Shore Way, an underrated long-distance footpath that follows the ancient course of the Kent and Sussex coastline to Hastings. Once past the riverfront promenade, the path weaves through a series of industrial backstreets, before heading back to the river and the ruins of Shornemead Fort.

At Denton Wharf, in the industrial outskirts of the town, I found the former light that once stood close to the riverbank at Shorne Marshes. It was replaced with a modern cylindrical tower in 2003, and since then this 1913 metal tower and lantern have lain abandoned, unloved and rusting in one corner of an industrial yard, behind tall security fencing. It deserves a better fate than this.

The replacement Shornemead light flashes white, red and green sector lights, powered by solar panels. It is not an object of great beauty, but there is something striking about it nonetheless. I stopped for a rest among the ruins of Shornemead Fort and discovered that the tower could be framed perfectly within one of the fort's windows.

Shortly after Shornemead, I left the Saxon Shore Way for the Isle of Grain, a flat and featureless landscape with a fifteen-mile straightish road leading to a formidable power station at the far end. There's a modern lattice framework light close by, with a lamp mounted on an open gallery at the top. It is taller than I anticipated, and mounted on a four-legged platform, giving the structure the appearance of an attentive giraffe. Like the Shornemead light, it flashes white, red and green sectors.

As I cycled through Rochester, Chatham and Sittingbourne, all towns that were familiar to me, I argued with Google Maps at frequent intervals, taking short cuts I had known about for years. It got me wondering just how many of the 3,350 miles I had cycled could have been avoided if I had known every coastal town as well as I knew these.

Beyond Faversham, I rejoined the seafront at Seasalter, and then headed straight for Whitstable, a fashionable seaside town known for its quirky independent shops and world-famous oyster trade. My parents were waiting for me there, having booked a couple of rooms in the smartest hotel in town. We sat on their seafront balcony, glass of Champagne in hand, and caught up with their take on the news from home.

They updated me about which of their friends had been in touch to congratulate me, and described how worried they had been at certain times, and how elated at others. Never mind *my* mental health, I had clearly given *them* plenty of anxious moments along the way.

It felt a little awkward being told off and praised by your parents when you're in your forties, and I felt myself squirming at times. But when they told me how proud they were, I felt a glow that I hadn't felt since childhood, the one that comes with a favourable end-of-term school report.

Day 95

It seemed odd that a town like Whitstable, whose trade relied so heavily on the sea, was without a lighthouse. There was once a pair of leading lights in the harbour, with lanterns made from polished copper, but these were demolished when the harbour fell into disuse in the 1960s. These days the only aids to navigation are fixed lamps on metal poles at the end of each quay.

Only a mile or two along the coast are two lighthouses in Herne Bay, one in considerably better condition than the other. Herne Bay once had the longest pier in the UK, at the far end of which is an octagonal tower, mounted on top of a wooden octagonal base. It dates from the mid-19th century, to a time when Herne Bay was a fashionable stopping-off point for excursion steamers.

The pier was deliberately breached by the army during the Second World War to prevent an enemy landing, and was almost totally destroyed by storms in 1978. The pier head and lantern still stand, isolated and half a mile offshore. The quick-flashing light it once gave now comes from a solar-powered lamp mounted on a triangular skeletal mast.

In the 1990s a concrete breakwater, known as Neptune's Arm, was built to prevent the most vulnerable parts of Herne Bay from flooding. At the far end is an octagonal viewing platform, on which a pair of fixed red lamps are mounted on a single metal pole.

All fifteen miles of the north Kent coast between Herne Bay and Margate are a cyclist's dream. The first landmark is Reculver, where the 12th-century towers of the former monastic church dominate the skyline for miles around, and have acted as a navigation marker for shipping throughout the centuries since.

After Reculver, the Viking Coastal Trail continues off-road, following the sea wall almost all the way to Margate, hugging the spectacular chalk cliffs and periodically passing through crowded family beaches one minute, and quiet unspoilt bays the next.

I used to visit Margate frequently as a teenager, queuing up with friends for the Looping Star and the Mary Rose rides at Bembom Brothers amusement park. It has recently been restored, and it looked just as I remember it. I must be getting old, though, because these days it is called a 'vintage theme park'.

The current Margate Lighthouse is at the end of the Harbour Arm, a long stone pier that has been redeveloped in recent years to accommodate a number of cafes, bars, micropubs and restaurants. The lighthouse has a hexagonal stone tower, built in 1954 to replace an earlier, taller lighthouse from 1829, which collapsed into the sea during the famous winter storm at the end of January 1953. It stands on a square base, and has a gallery and hexagonal lantern, from which a fixed red light is displayed, visible for three miles.

Despite the bars and restaurants, this is more of a working pier than a pleasure pier, and even the lighthouse, while not unattractive, seems built for function rather than form.

I had just a handful of lighthouses left to see, at North and South Foreland, Ramsgate, Dover and Folkestone. A reunion of friends and family was planned for my arrival back at Dungeness on Saturday, and at my current pace I'd be home by early Friday afternoon, so for perhaps the first time I needed to slow right down.

Leaving the Harbour Arm behind me, I was grateful that the cycle route out of Margate was off-road, following paths and lanes that were new to me. I looked down on several sandy beaches, all with names that reminded me of children's story books – Joss Bay, Botany Bay, Kingsland Bay. As I climbed towards the lighthouse at North Foreland, it occurred to me that it wouldn't be long before I'd be able to look down over Romney Marsh, and perhaps even see New Romney, my home town. The thought propelled me up the final climb to the lighthouse gates.

There is said to have been a light at North Foreland as early as 1499, but the first lighthouse for which records exist dates to around 1637, when Sir John Meldrum was granted a patent from Charles I to collected dues from foreign vessels passing the North and South Forelands. His was a wooden tower, which survived until 1683, when it was burned to the ground.

Following a number of years with a temporary light, a brick and stone octagonal tower with an open fire basket was built in 1691. For a few years in the early 18th century the light was enclosed within a lantern, but it often sooted-up, so the open light was restored.

The tower was increased in height in 1793, a lantern was installed and the coal fire was replaced with a series of eighteen oil lamps. Trinity House took on responsibility for the lighthouse in 1832, and in 1866 engineer-in-chief James Walker was commissioned to undertake alterations and modernisation.

The lighthouse was electrified in 1920, and in 1998 it was the last Trinity House lighthouse to be automated. It displays a white flashing light, with red sectors, which is visible for nineteen miles.

North Foreland.

Broadstairs is a charming resort, frequented and much loved by Charles Dickens. He worked on several of his best-known novels here during regular stays at Bleak House (then known as Fort House) on the cliffs above the harbour. And he described the town as 'one of the freshest, freest watering places in the world'.

It was also where my first girlfriend went to art college, and I cycled past the spot where a telephone box once stood, which I would phone at the same time each afternoon, timed to coincide with her walk between classes. Judging by the length of the grass covering the square concrete plinth where the telephone box once stood, it would seem it fell into disrepair at about the same time as the relationship.

Ramsgate ought to be a thriving seaside town, but I thought it looked neglected and unloved as I made the final descent into the harbour. As a child, I remember taking the ferry from here to Ostend, in Belgium, and have always preferred the bustling, cosmopolitan feel of the town over Dover or Folkestone. The *AA Book of the Seaside*, published in the 1970s, went as far as describing Ramsgate as like a miniature Monte Carlo. But in 2013 the ferry service was suspended, since when Ramsgate seems to have lost its pride, along with its purpose.

The shops around the harbour no longer seem certain whether they should be selling Buckingham Palace postcards and Big Ben key rings to the Europeans, or buckets and spades for the day trippers from London. There is talk of a new freight ferry service, which, if successful, might lead to a resumption of passenger traffic. Dredging of the silted harbour has begun. But for now, at least, Ramsgate was a rather sad place to be. There is a lighthouse on the West Pier, however, which is why I was here.

The original pier light here was designed by John Smeaton (designer of the third Eddystone Lighthouse), although construction was completed by Samuel Wyatt following Smeaton's death in 1792.

During the first part of the 19th century it became apparent that the lighthouse had been positioned too close to the end of the pier, and yardarms on ships frequently struck it when negotiating the harbour entrance. As a result, it was replaced in 1842 with a new circular stone tower, 38-feet tall, set back from the end of the pier. It has an ornate red-painted lantern, with a weathervane on top.

Originally lit by an oil lamp, the lighthouse was converted to electricity early in the 20th century. When the ferries operated, it displayed a fixed red or green light, depending on the height of the tide at the harbour entrance. These days, however, it displays just a fixed red light, which is visible for four miles.

Approaching Sandwich, the landscape becomes industrial, and I had to leave the seafront to navigate a route around a giant complex of science and technology parks. But this was a small blot on an otherwise faultless landscape, and Sandwich itself is achingly pretty. As a reward for tolerating the industry, NCN Route 1 proceeds along an empty toll road through the famous Sandwich golf course.

As I descended into Deal, I reached into my saddle bag for my radio and discovered that Australia were all out for 60, with England 263 for three in reply, with Root and Bairstow both digging in. At this rate I'd be home before the match ended.

Day 96

Home was just 40 miles away, but timing the journey to meet what I hoped would be a decent crowd at Dungeness the next day meant continuing to slow down, and finding one final night's accommodation.

Setting off in the direction of the White Cliffs, NCN Route 1 follows the seafront past Walmer Castle and on to Kingsdown and St Margaret's at Cliffe. Kingsdown itself was so sheltered by the cliffs to my right, and so exposed to the sea on my left, that my phone forgot where it was for a while, and I inadvertently joined a French mobile network. A text message welcomed me to France and advised me to switch off mobile roaming if I was worried about data charges.

About six miles off the coast at South Foreland lie the Goodwin Sands, a ten-mile long sandbank that has caused more than 2,000 vessels to be wrecked or run aground. A single storm in 1836 caused the loss of 30 vessels alone.

A pair of wood and plaster lighthouses were built here in 1636, and they served until the middle of the 19th century, after Trinity House had taken over responsibility for them. The current high and low lights at South Foreland were built in 1843 and 1846 by Trinity House engineer-in-chief James Walker. Both have octagonal stone towers, with circular lanterns and stone galleries. When vessels lined up the two lights, one above the other, the safe passage through the Goodwin Sands was marked.

South Foreland.

Following movement in the Goodwin Sands, the leading lights no longer indicated the safe passage, and the low light was decommissioned in 1904. The current high light endured and was adapted to a rotating group flashing white light, which was visible for 26 miles. It was eventually decommissioned in 1988 and has been in National Trust hands ever since.

I took the guided tour and was delighted to see how well the optics and other equipment have been preserved. I imagined that the light could be brought back into service tomorrow, if needed. It was a beautifully clear early afternoon, and the Goodwin Sands were visible on the near horizon.

The redundant, decaying low lighthouse was also easy to see from the top of the tower. It is now in private hands, inaccessible and in poor condition, hidden within the walled grounds of a substantial private home only a few feet away from the eroded cliff edge.

Onwards towards Dover, and the views from the cliff top over the English Channel were truly spectacular. The Maritime & Coastguard Agency, whose co-ordination centre I passed, must have the finest sea views in the country.

There was once a pair of Roman octagonal lighthouse towers in Dover. They were built of rubble stone, on either side of the harbour entrance, and were known as the Eastern and Western Pharos. Much of the eastern tower still stands, the most complete standing Roman building in England and one of only three Roman lighthouses to survive. It stands alongside the Church of St Mary in Castro on Castle Hill, within the perimeter wall of the medieval Dover Castle.

About 100 yards in front of it, I reached an English Heritage kiosk, staffed by Georgina, an absurdly posh and unobliging teenager, who delighted in telling me that if I wanted a photograph of the lighthouse I'd need to pay a £20 entrance fee to the whole castle.

I paid up, but also vented my frustration on social media. I was pleased to discover that while I was photographing the lighthouse, my Facebook post was gathering some momentum. As I passed Georgina on my way out, she cheerfully asked if I had found the lighthouse, in a patronising sing-song sort of way. I raised two digits at her to indicate that I had.

Before getting back on my bike, my phone pinged and I received a tweet of apology from English Heritage, along with an offer to refund my money. I declined the offer but couldn't resist returning to the kiosk to share the good news with Georgina herself.

There are four lighthouses on the various piers and breakwaters that make up the harbour at Dover, and they are all fairly close together. Access is restricted because of the cross-channel port at one end of the harbour and the cruise terminal at the other. But the Prince of Wales Pier and Admiralty Pier both allowed public access, so I could get up close to two of the lighthouses, and take decent photographs of the remaining two.

At the end of the Admiralty Pier, a circular, white-painted, cast-iron tower was built in 1908. It displays a white flashing light, which is visible for twenty miles. At the end of the Prince of Wales Pier, which separates the inner and outer harbours, there is a white-painted, circular, stone tower, with a galleried lantern and a weathervane on top. It displays a very quick-flashing green light, which is visible for four miles.

At the west end of the outer breakwater there is a slightly tapering, white-painted, cast-iron tower, which was built in 1909. It displays a red occulting light inside the harbour, as well as a white light outside the harbour, which is visible for eighteen miles.

Lastly, on the breakwater knuckle, there is another circular, white-painted, cast-iron lighthouse, built in 1909. Its light flashes four times every ten seconds, red inside the harbour and white outside, which is visible for thirteen miles.

Leaving Dover behind me, I had probably only one more steep climb beyond Samphire Hoe, and for once I made it to the top without getting off to push. The descent on the other side into Folkestone was a joy.

Construction of the pier and harbour at Folkestone was completed in 1820, but it was only after the harbour was taken over by the South Eastern Railway Company in 1842 that a lighthouse was considered.

When a new breakwater was built in 1860, a tapering stone lighthouse was added, 28-feet tall, with white-painted lantern and gallery. It flashes a white light, twice every ten seconds,

Left to right: Prince of Wales Pier, Admiralty Breakwater and Breakwater
Knuckle Lights, Dover.

increasing to every two seconds in fog. The light is visible for
ten miles.

Since the closure of Folkestone as a cross-channel passenger
port in 2000, the future of the harbour had been uncertain.
However, both the former harbour railway station and lighthouse
have since undergone considerable renovation, with a new
walkway making access to the lighthouse very simple.

From this point onwards I had no need for maps or guidebooks.
I cycled to Sandgate through a recently landscaped seafront
park, which had been a tiny toll road when I was a kid. I made
it to Hythe by 5pm and could have been home within half an
hour. Instead, I found a pub with rooms on the high street and
arranged to meet up with the family for fish and chips on the
seafront. I wanted tomorrow's return to Dungeness to feel like a
true homecoming.

As we sat on the beach eating supper out of the paper, there
were lots of hugs and hand holding and many smiles. But very
few words were needed.

Day 97

I had more than three hours to cycle the ten or so miles to
Dungeness. Generous, even at my pace. Beyond Hythe the route
left the main coast road to follow the Royal Military Canal,
originally built in the first decade of the 19th century as a third
line of defence against Napoleon.

A mile or so along the canal I passed the perimeter fence of Port Lympne Safari Park. I remember, as a young boy, being on a Sunday drive near here, a year or so before the animal park formally opened. We didn't even know it was there at the time. My grandmother was sitting in the back seat, and suddenly declared that she had just seen a rhinoceros. My father humoured her, letting it pass without comment. It was only after she died that the park opened, and we realised that she hadn't lost her marbles that day after all.

Still keen not to reach Dungeness too early, I stopped for coffee at Lathe Barn, the small children's farm that had been such a favourite with Zoe, my eldest daughter. On her first visit she had fallen in love with a rabbit named Fudge, and we were always relieved to find Fudge in his hutch each time we visited, year after year, although he wasn't always the same shade of brown. In fact, one year Fudge wasn't brown at all.

Before the final push I discovered that England had beaten Australia and regained the Ashes as a result. Darren, a friend from my cricket club, tweeted that he had just arrived at Dungeness for a double celebration – the Ashes regained and the Beacon Bike returned!

I got a text from Allan saying that the police were holding up traffic on the M25 because of two horses on the hard shoulder. Ironic, really, because when I asked Allan the previous week whether he would be there for my return, he told me that wild horses wouldn't stop him.

The last five miles from New Romney were a bit of a blur, although I was aware that they seemed a lot easier than when I had covered these same miles back in May. I guess if you cycle 3,500 miles then you should expect to be a bit fitter at the end compared to the beginning.

I passed Derek Jarman's cottage, then Mrs Thomas' fish shack. I saw a decent crowd gathered around the base of the Old Lighthouse up ahead, and dared to believe that they were there because of me.

The first person I recognised was Lottie, my youngest daughter. Only she runs like that. As I drew close, a very British round of applause began, to the bemusement of others around. Allan had made it in time, having fended off the wild horses. My brother, a trustee of Shift.ms, even gave a speech about how the money I had raised might be spent. My lovely friend Sue had driven down from London, as had Douglas, my very first boss from my Stanfords days. Friends from the cricket club, from the village, from the school gates, and from afar all turned out. It was humbling, and I enjoyed wondering what other event or occasion might bring this particular group of people together.

I would love to claim that my return prompted a moment of epiphany, or that it heralded a change in the way I viewed the world or felt about myself. But over a barbecue that evening, dressed in a favourite T-shirt and jeans that I hadn't worn in months, my main reflection was that I had seen an awful lot of lighthouses, and that I had cycled a bloody long way.

POSTSCRIPT

It seems strange to be writing these words now that I am home. I made this journey a few summers ago, and only started writing about it over some fairly lean working months during the pandemic.

Since my return we have lost, or will lose imminently, at least three lighthouses of historical importance. The Wyre Light, the one that vies with Maplin Sands for the title of the world's first screw-pile lighthouse, has almost entirely collapsed following heavy storms in July 2017. The basic metal framework remains, but only a seasoned lighthouse enthusiast would recognise it for what it once was.

In August 2020, the Association of British Ports issued an official warning for mariners to navigate with caution when entering Fleetwood Channel, as the remaining structure is now routinely covered by the sea during the higher tides. As the former lighthouse is now a hazard rather than an aid to navigation, it can only be a matter of time before the remaining framework is removed altogether.

Just off the Sussex coast, Trinity House decommissioned the Royal Sovereign Lighthouse in March 2022. Built with an anticipated working life of 50 years back in 1971, concrete fatigue in the platform on which the tower stands was causing concern. During August and September 2023, both the distinctive red-and-white lantern tower and the platform housing the accommodation and engine rooms were dismantled and removed. The role the lighthouse played will be performed by a combination of lit buoys, as well as by increasing the range of the Beachy Head Lighthouse closer to the shore. I am pleased to say that I am a founding member of a heritage body that has managed to acquire the tower itself, with the goal of rebuilding it on the seafront at Bexhill.

Perhaps saddest of all is the fate of the famous lighthouse at Orford Ness. Following winter storms at the start of 2020, the encroaching tides finally reached the lighthouse compound, and only the tower itself remained undamaged. Any hope of continuing to keep the water at bay was lost, and the lighthouse was demolished in August 2020. The lantern and certain other artefacts were saved, and there is talk of them being exhibited in a lighthouse museum somewhere on the mainland.

These will not be the last lighthouses to be lost. Belle Tout Lighthouse, renowned for being winched seventeen metres back from the eroded cliff edge in 1998, is now close to the cliff edge once more, following cliff falls in August 2021. Its current owners are confident that they can move the building for a second time, rather than allow it to succumb to the elements.

The pair of leading lights at Dovercourt are now in a very poor state of repair, and were recently added to English Heritage's register of buildings at risk. Following a structural survey, the cost of restoration work has been estimated at £400,000. Agreement on where the money will come from is needed before any work begins.

At Hurst Castle, heavy storms in March 2021 undermined the foundations of the castle's east wing, causing a large part of the sea wall to collapse. Although the damage is some distance from both the current lighthouse and the pair of former lighthouses, it is a worrying sign nonetheless.

In October 2023, Storm Babet wreaked havoc in various parts of the country, and the Port of Tyne reported that the top dome of the lighthouse on South Shields pier had 'been forcibly removed by the relentless combination of sea and wind'.

The news does not all focus on decay and the demolishing of lighthouses that are beyond saving, however. As lighthouse enthusiasts, we should be pleased that so many are being maintained properly, and applaud efforts to modernise them so they are fit for the 21st century.

There is good news at Whitehaven, for example, where a funding bid to repair and refurbish the historic harbour lighthouses was given the green light towards the end of 2018, and the work was finally completed in 2022.

Good news, too, at Shornemead, where the former lighthouse, unloved for so many years, has been restored and now stands proudly at the entrance to the Port of London Authority's depot at Denton, on the outskirts of Gravesend.

Inevitably, some of these modernisation efforts will alter the character of the light or building. Like at Trwyn Du Lighthouse, on the Isle of Anglesey, where plans are underway to replace the beautiful and haunting fog signal bell, which has rung every 30 seconds since 1922. A modern electronic foghorn will take its place. The Facebook group 'Save the Trwyn Du Lighthouse bell' has vowed to fight the decision, through the courts if necessary.

At Portland Bill, a modernisation programme has involved the installation of a modern, non-rotating LED light source. The lantern which gave the lighthouse's beam its broad, sweeping motion has been switched off and its optics have been removed.

These modernisation efforts are regrettable, but for the lighthouses this is what progress looks like. I would sooner have a 'non-rotating LED light source' than no light at all. In an age when GPS units can give a vessel's precise location to within a metre, we must be grateful that we retain as many working, maintained lighthouses as we do. Their days must surely be numbered.

On an even more positive note, there are several lights whose prospects have brightened since my journey's end. At Spurn Point, for example, a complete restoration programme has been completed since I was there, and the lighthouse has now reopened as a visitor centre.

The lighthouse at Plover Scar, in Lancashire, might well have been replaced by a simple lit buoy after it was struck by a passing commercial vessel. Instead, the stone tower was rebuilt and the lantern renovated, giving the lighthouse a clean bill of health for another hundred years.

Closer to home, I was honoured to be invited to an extremely moving event at South Foreland in November 2018, where the lantern was brought back into service, for one night only, to mark the centenary of the end of the First World War.

And what of my health? It has been a mixed picture. Successive MRI scans of my brain and spinal column in 2017 and 2018 showed increasing numbers of plaques or lesions, the areas where the protective myelin sheath is stripped away from the nerves. It prompted a change in medication, in the form of a daily pill rather than the invasive injections that became part of my daily cycling-adventure ritual. I don't really understand how it works, but the idea is that it slows or prevents movement of lymphocytes out of lymph nodes, thereby limiting inflammation in the central nervous system. Make of that what you will.

Since the change in medication, I have had few further relapses. Like many people with MS, I do battle with anxiety and depression at regular intervals, and I'm not always good company for Emily and my children. My legs are often unreliable: a flight of stairs can defeat me one week, but a five-mile walk is perfectly manageable the next. What gives?

Perhaps strangest of all, cycling is easier and less painful for me than walking. On two legs, I feel uncertain about whether and when my feet are in contact with the ground, causing me to trip or stumble frequently. On two wheels, my feet stay rooted to the pedals and I can keep moving in relative comfort.

It would be hard, now, to imagine a way of life that didn't involve my bike. It's my main form of exercise, and where some feel guilty if they don't get to the gym each week, I am restless if I don't manage a regular bike ride.

The Beacon Bike – the wonderful Tonka-yellow Thorn Nomad tourer – is still my most prized possession. I refuse to consign it to the garden shed, and between rides it takes up residence in the spare bedroom, much to Emily's irritation. I wheel it into the hallway whenever Helen, Emily's mother comes to stay.

With my MS medication designed to suppress my immune system, I was one of the many required to shield, and live hermit-like, for nearly eighteen months during the pandemic. It was inevitable that rebuilding the rusty, seized-up Dawes

Street Sharp from my London days would become one of many lockdown projects.

I became obsessive about originality, tracking down Dawes parts from owners and enthusiasts whenever I could, and spending hours on YouTube learning how to repair or replace every component down to the last nut and bolt. The final bill far exceeded what the bike could possibly be worth.

So now I have two bikes – one for every day, and one for when it counts. Between them, they keep me mobile and fit, and I would be lost without them. For now, the prognosis for my health is good, although never certain, and my goal is to stay this way until new, or better, medication improves or even reverses my condition.

Perhaps the Scottish lighthouses are still there for the taking. Who knows?

Thank you for following me on my journey.